African
Witchcraft
and Otherness

African
Witchcraft
and Otherness

A Philosophical and Theological
Critique of Intersubjective Relations

Elias Kifon Bongmba

State University of New York Press

Published by
State University of New York Press, Albany

Printed in the United States of America

For information, address State University of New York Press,
90 State Street, Suite 700, Albany, N.Y. 12207

Production by Michael Haggett
Marketing by Patrick Durocher

Library of Congress Cataloging-in-Publication Data

Bongmba, Elias Kifon, 1953–
    African witchcraft and otherness : a philosophical and theological
critique of intersubjective relations / Elias Kifon Bongmba.
        p. cm.
    Includes bibliographical references and index.
    ISBN 0-7914-4989-0 (alk. paper) — ISBN 0-7914-4990-4 (pbk : alk. paper)
    1. Witchcraft—Cameroon—Donga and Mantung. 2. Limbum (African
people)—Religion. 3. Interpersonal relations—Moral and ethical
aspects—Cameroon—Donga and Mantung. 4. Lâvinas, Emmanuel—
Ethics. 5. Donga and Mantung (Cameroon)—Religious life and customs.
I. Title.

BF1584.C17 Z7 2001
133.4'3'096711—dc21   00-067103

10 9 8 7 6 5 4 3 2 1

Dedication

To my parents
Johaness Bongmba and Monica Munkeng
and
My children
Donald Afanyui, Dino Kong, and Douglas Ginyui

African problems are human problems
African witchcraft different from
other witchcraft. Recognize Other as ethical
other. Eschatological finish a myth. Under-
lying concept of all culture, one culture
and it forms. Culture based on meaning
meaning at level of liveability not just
discursive analysis. Not question of meaning,
but meaning of meaning. Disciplines are
culture producing practices.

lewgord @ yahoo.com.

Contents

Acknowledgments

I am grateful to the following for permission to quote from their publications: University of Pennsylvania, to quote from *Beyond Objectivism and Relativism*, 1988; Indiana University Press, for quotations from *The Invention of Africa*, 1988; William B. Eerdmans Publishing Company, for quotations from *God the Mystery of the World*; Oxford University Press, for quotations from *Love, Power and Justice*; and Duquesne University Press, for quotations from *Totality and Infinity* and *Time and the Other.*

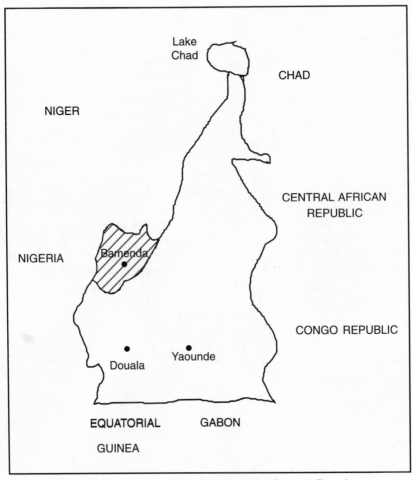

Map of Cameroon Showing the Northwest Province

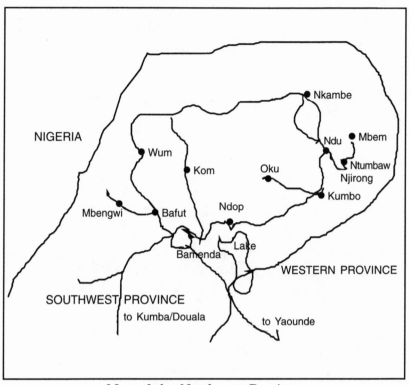

Map of the Northwest Province

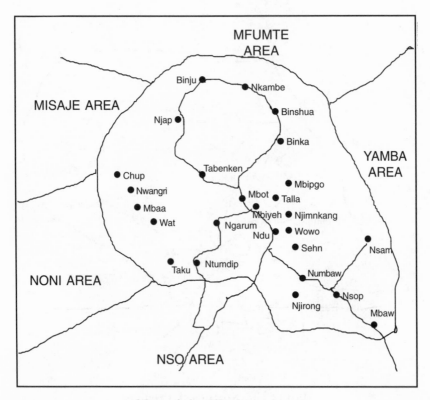

Map of the Wimbum Area

Preface

In this study, I analyze and critique Wimbum *tfu* beliefs. *Tfu* is the Wimbum word that comes close to the English term *witchcraft*, which is used to explain misfortune. In addition to claims that this power can be used for good intentions, its negative uses are a cause for concern, fear, anger, and pain to many families among the Wimbum people. It is alleged that people use *tfu* to cause sickness and death and to consume another's flesh in secret meetings. *Tfu* continues to be a major problem among the Wimbum people. Early in 1999, several people were evicted from their homes and villages. In the town, of Ntumbaw, an alleged victim died in transit from one town to the next. In another town, a woman was forced to take her children, grandchildren, and great grandchildren and return to her home of origin because she was suspected of practicing *tfu*. Concern about *tfu* seems to have been taken to new heights among the Wimbum. Wimbum chiefs met recently and adopted a resolution affirming that they will continue to expel those who practice *tfu*. In addition, some will be asked to pay fines, which may require an accused individual to give a female member of his or her family to the chief as a wife. *Tfu* involves all facets of Wimbum life and can be disruptive in many ways.

I analyze the different conceptions of this occult power and use Levinas's argument of the Other to construct a critique of the negative employment of such powers. I do not claim that his ideas are similar to Wimbum ideas, for Levinas's commitment to Greek thought and the Bible seems to overshadow other perspectives. I contend, however, that his argument can be applied cross-culturally.[1] In drawing from Levinas, a European philosopher, I do not engage in anything new since Africans have been open to ideas that provide insights into critical discourse. This openness that draws from the studies of others is evident in the work of V. Y. Mudimbe (1988), Léopold Sédar Senghor (1970), and Kwame Nkrumah

(1964), to name only a few who have articulated philosophical positions.

There are differences between the thought of Levinas and the ideas of Wimbum.

First, Levinas writes within the tradition of Western philosophical discourse, where the mode of approach privileges a massive philosophical library. Wimbum ethical ideas are not embodied in a text but in thoughts expressed in actions, words, songs, proverbs, rituals, and public discourses, such as a practice called *sa nta*. In this performance, the *fon*'s spokesperson goes to the market to communicate warnings to the entire town from the *fon* and the *nwarong* society. Rituals such as witch cleansing are ethical discourses, because in these rituals people claim that someone has violated their dignity through the use of *tfu*. Some of the rituals affirm and restore community values.

Second, Levinas writes in the Western tradition that stresses individualism, while Wimbum culture emphasizes community. I argue that *tfu* discourses comprise a complex engagement with questions of individuality *and* community. These discourses involve nuclear families, extended families, and even the entire town. Through these engagements, the community confronts those who are accused of negative *tfu* practices because they have violated someone's dignity and brought disease to the community. Such actions highlight a human Other, because the activities call attention to an individual whose dignity has been violated. It is important that I spell out in some detail the importance of Levinas's work in a critique of *tfu*.

First I draw from Levinas to articulate a cross-cultural and interdisciplinary critique to the study of *tfu*. Evans-Pritchard's landmark work, *Witchcraft, Oracles and Magic among the Azande* (1937), launched a multidisciplinary conversation attracting scholarly debates from different fields. My work takes this debate beyond the focus on the rationality of witchcraft beliefs to an engagement in contextual ethics. I find Levinas's formulation of ethics compelling and open to cross-cultural application.

Second I draw from Levinas's work because he unapologetically articulates the question of a human Other, and in doing so, he invites us to focus on a genuine human face and to rethink the false dichotomy between community and individuals. I develop his position in Chapter 4 and Chapter 5 of this book.

Third, Levinas brings together the issues of singularity and justice without anchoring them to some meta-narrative or theory. Singularity in Levinas privileges a human Other and links justice to individuality. Justice is not an abstract concept but a relationship between people, which Levinas describes as a face-to-face encounter, which has implications that cannot be appreciated when reduced to theoretical constructs, even if such constructs are premised on individualism or communalism (Sandel, 1983). The self is found in the face-to-face relationship in the midst of a pluralism that implies society (Levinas 1969, 291).

Furthermore, Levinas departs from constructs such as John Rawls' (Rawls, 1971). In the third section of *Totality and Infinity*, Levinas discusses justice and starts with questions about traditional notions of freedom. He opposes the Western understanding of truth and transcendence with the activity he calls "desire" which does not remain at the level of cognition but finds expression in discourse that presents itself as justice "in the uprightness of the welcome made to the face" (Levinas 1969, 82).[2] Justice for Levinas implies several things.

Justice is the exercise of the privilege of letting the Other speak on his or her behalf in a face-to-face encounter that implies community (Levinas 1969, 298). In the Wimbum community, contesting *tfu* powers often offers an opportunity for victims to speak for themselves or to have senior members of the family speak on their behalf. Together, members of the immediate family and extended family constitute what one could consider, for Levinas, a "third party."

Levinas also argues that justice is a relation. Local Wimbum specialists (diviners, seers, rulers) all analyze relational issues to establish or restore a proper relationship among people so that justice will reign. Justice also is a recognition on one's part that injustice has been done to the Other. "The first consciousness of my immorality is not my submission to facts, but to the infinite Other."[3] The Other as an interlocutor challenges our freedom and our attempts to put him or her to shame.[4] This view of justice has powerful implications for *tfu* where the misapplication of privileged knowledge and power depends on the freedom of the one who allegedly has such powers and could use it to silence the Other.

Justice in Wimbum society is administered by heads of households, the quarter head, who is called *fai*, and the chief, called *nkfu*. Colonial administrators consolidated this practice into what they called "native law and custom." This consolidation did not destroy a sense of justice among Wimbum people. I find in Wimbum beliefs and in the work of Levinas humanistic values that strengthen the view that justice is doing what is right to save an individual, especially when that individual is affected by negative *tfu. Tfu* accusations could provide opportunities for the exercise of justice if they lead to a check on abusive powers. I remember a confrontation that involved teenaged boys who publicly accused Shey Riba[5] for allegedly using *tfu* to give them human flesh and demanded that they repay him with the flesh of their own relatives. For justice to be done in this case, the youths had to address Shey Riba in the presence of a third party, in this case, the elders of the town.

Fourth, Levinas's post-phenomenology opens postmodern paths and makes it possible for one to question the knowledge and power of witchcraft.[6] Levinas has introduced postmodern doubts about meta-narratives with radical implications for understanding intersubjectivity. "The essential problem is: can we speak of an absolute commandment after Auschwitz. Can we speak of morality after the failure of morality?"(Bernasconi and Wood 1988). It is obvious that *tfu* poses different problems than Auschwitz, but when *tfu* powers are used in a negative way, one can talk of Auschwitz on a small scale.

First, Levinas's work is postmodern because he calls into question systematic thought and its resulting ideality and representations of the Other. Like Lyotard (1984), he questions the meta-narratives because these stories have focused on the journey of self-consciousness and remain content with the *Seinsfrage* at the expense of the question of the Other.[6]

Second, Levinas's postmodernist challenge "cuts through institutional and often unnoticed cultural presuppositions without returning to moral intuitionism."[7] Levinas neither calls for chaos nor offers a chaos theory that requires the abandonment of institutions and historical traditions. Rather, the Levinasian strategy of grafting, to which Derrida and Caputo are both indebted, pushes the philosophical tradition beyond its egoistic and theorizing bent.[8]

An epistemological choice for a project such as this leaves out other viable and engaging paths of discussion. First, I have not followed Alasdair MacIntyre's virtue- and tradition-based ethics (MacIntyre 1981, 1988). Beginning in *After Virtue,* MacIntyre offers a narrative of philosophical ethics and highlights not only conceptual "conflict" but the emotive nature of rival ethical visions, obligations, and arguments inherited from the past (MacIntyre 1981, 139). These inherited practices are traditions, which for MacIntyre constitute an ongoing argument that is constantly scrutinized and reconstituted as tradition in a contested atmosphere (MacIntyre 1988, 12).

MacIntyre laments that we have arrived at a new Dark Ages, and he blames the erosion of tradition-based morality on the En-

lightenment project, "which should not have commenced in the
first place" (MacIntyre 1981, 111; 1988, 8).[9] At the end of *After
Virtue,* MacIntyre seems to indicate, through his now-famous rhe-
torical phrase "Nietzsche or Aristotle," that people ought to go back
to the Aristotelian notion of virtues.[10] MacIntyre indicates his preference for the Thomistic and Augustinian Christian tradition in
Whose Justice, but he does not tell us why the justice of *De Civitas
Dei* and the scholastics are superior or if they will settle rival
ethical visions.

MacIntyre's recognition of competing voices is on target, and
his dismissal of the Enlightenment echoes postmodern disenchant-
ment with modernity, but his project departs from postmodern vision
because he calls for a return to what he claims is a coherent story
located in premodern societies and their rationalities. A return to
such a tradition on the subject of *tfu* may simply return to a new
dark age, because MacIntyre's preferred traditions will demonize
tfu and inhibit a fruitful discussion of all of its various aspects.[11]

The other path that I have not followed is a rich discussion of
personhood and individuality in Africanist discourse. My account
does not refute, compete, or seek to improve this rich tradition but
builds on that literature and introduces Levinas's perspective. First,
Riesman points out that there is a rich tradition of reflection on
personhood and individuality in African thought. The stage for this
discussion was set by French anthropology with *La notion de
personne en Afrique noire.* Riesman argues that literature ranging
from the Griaulian school to the ethnophilosophical investigations
of Placide Tempels demonstrates an interest in the person and in
the person's spiritual elements, behavior, and personality (Riesman
1986, 71–74). Social anthropologists since Evans-Pritchard have
paid attention to how people regard their relationships in society
and to how they think of persons (Ibid., 81). Ritual studies also
give us insights into how people think of persons.

Riesman argues that the symbolic analysis of African cultures
gives us different notions of a person as an individual; one who
leaves tracks, relates to others, and derives his or her identity from
them (Riesman 1986, 97). Furthermore, phenomenological and
artistic expressions use stories to give us a much more pronounced
view of a person. "Works that give us a sense, albeit imperfect, of
how life is experienced and lived from within the mind of a person,
however, make us realize that to view culture as acting on a person
is too simplistic. We cannot any longer take for granted that we
know why a person is doing something when his action happens to
coincide with the supposed dictates of his or her culture" (Ibid.,

103). Riesman argues that the Fulbes [Fulbes are found in several
W. African Countries] maintain a body language and joking relationship through which they are able to share the self yet maintain
individuality (Ibid., 56).

Jacobson-Widding argues that in Congolese society, the notion
of shadow underscores the individuality of a person because there
is a strong belief that one's shadow is a reflection of who one is
(Jacobson-Widding 1990, 31ff.). One does not cross a person's
shadow if they see his or her shadow on the ground. People also
express concern when their pictures are taken because the photo-
graphs may end up in the wrong hands and their enemies could
use them to do something evil to them (Ibid., 47). I find the notion
of shadow very suggestive, since the Wimbum talk of *ngho ku*,
which literally means "to scoop someone's foot." This is the belief
that someone can take the soil from where another person has
stepped and use it to harm that person, which stresses individuality.

Being Wimbum, I bring a critical *Einfühlung* to the discussion,
mindful that I am not stricken by "Tempels" and that I claim to
have found *the* key or solution to dealing with all Bantu "witchcraft" problems.[13] I highlight an individual's experience in the life
world and *la chose du texte* I illuminate must be seen "as a fact of
tradition" (Okolo 1991, 201–210). This work is a personal journey
in several ways. The first step of my study was taken when I
studied African religions with Allen Roberts at the University of
Iowa in 1991. It was during that course that I read for the third
time the Evans-Pritchard classic, *Witchcraft, Oracles, and Magic
among the Azande*. Although I was deeply disturbed by the colonial
episteme of Evans-Pritchard, I was nevertheless motivated by his
exposition to reflect on Wimbum *tfu*.

The second significant experience in my journey was reading
Mudimbe's work *The Invention of Africa*. At this time, I was beginning doctoral studies at the University of Denver and the Iliff School
of Theology. Mudimbe's critical exposition of the discourse on Africa
in the postmodern and post-phenomenological tradition was a homecoming experience for me and provided a context in which to address the issues raised by Evans-Pritchard and other writers on
the subject. In deconstructing discourses on Africa, Mudimbe re-
constructs African discourse in a new way and provides a point of
entry into a subject such as *tfu*.

Third, I participated in two doctoral seminars—one on Levinas,
the other on the question of Otherness, both conducted by Professor Jere Surber. Levinas's magnum opus, *Totality and Infinity*,
was a revelation, that opened up the question of Otherness in a

new way. It became clear to me that Mudimbe and Levinas provide the intellectual path needed for such a critical discourse on *tfu*. My studies of witchcraft are not ethnographic in the classic sense of the word. Methodologically, I have chosen to interpret the concept of witchcraft drawing from my knowledge of the discourse on witchcraft and my discussions with parishioners who were involved in witchcraft issues during my tenure as pastor in Wat and Ntumbaw. The professional interest that I bring to my topic is an ethical one.

My engagement with the subject is substantial enough to undertake a study and a critique, so I was surprised when an anonymous reviewer of my work suggested that I rely only on my own anecdotes. Another reviewer questioned my use of Emmanuel Levinas's work, asking, "What has Levinas got to do with it?" I wonder if behind the dismissive views I encountered was a greater agenda, possibly an attempt at the gurufication of witchcraft studies, or turning them into an occult enterprise where a few select ethnographers become licensed practitioners and spokespersons for African communities.[14] I question the anxiety scholars have about any attempt to criticize local African practices. If scholars feel awkward about critical discourse on Africa, then contemporary African scholarship has touched Africa with a "fatal kindness," to borrow a metaphor from Friedrich Schleiermacher.

Several issues at stake here call for reflection. (1) Does one single discipline hold the key to the study of witchcraft? Can it be defined as an ethnographic key? (2) Can those of us who are so-called insiders contribute insightfully to the debate? (3) Is it possible to open the door for a critical approach to witchcraft studies? (4) What resources should be employed in such a critique?

MULTIDISCIPLINARY APPROACHES

My answer to the first question is simply no. There is no doubt that social anthropology has a lot to contribute and will continue to do so through reformulation of the aporias of the ethnographic enterprise. Every critique of the ethnographic enterprise should always be tempered with humility because of the massive library it opens. Anthropology and its scholarly tool the ethnographic imagination have contributed immensely to what has emerged as African studies. It would be folly to ignore this influence (Kuper 1983; More 1985; Goody 1995). I am fascinated by the positive achievements of anthropologists but at the same time disturbed, as is Mudimbe (1988), by stereotypes of Africa that are found in many accounts.

From its Edwardian and Victorian days, anthropologists have carried on an interesting debate about the priorities of the discipline. Evans-Pritchard himself was critical of earlier anthropologists for misrepresenting so-called primitive people (Evans-Pritchard 1965, 4, 15). Recent debates have further raised a number of issues of interest to Africanists.

My interest in witchcraft has led me to familiarize myself with some of the debates about the nature and "mission" of anthropology (Hymes 1969; Diamond 1974; Crapanzano 1977; Ruby 1982; Asad 1983; Fabian 1983, 1991; Comaroff and Comaroff 1985; Clifford and Marcus 1986; Marcus and Fischer 1986). What is fascinating about these debates is the reflexivity that some of the best minds and practitioners of the anthropological craft have brought to their own work (Driessen 1993, 1). But more importantly, as Henk Driessen points out, these scholars grapple with the politics of writing and reading ethnography as part of the postmodern problematic. They have made a case for the use of multiple genres and have restated forcefully the case for relativism (Driessen 1993). Feminist and indigenous voices have been raised in the debate (Caplan 1988; Hammersley and Atkinson 1983; More 1988; Owusu 1976, 1997; Alorki and El-Sohl 1988; Pina-Cabral 1992).[15]

New issues of focus include autobiographical accounts, political issues, moral perspectives, and insiders views (Driessen 1993, 2). According to Driessen (Ibid.), "There is the constructivist position which argues that people constitute their society and culture through their own actions and interpretations." Throughout the debates, scholars affirm that the reality articulated in anthropological monographs combines realism as well as construction.[16] These debates reinforce multivocality, and raise questions about signature, authority, advocacy, narrative strategies, and the voice given to informants.[17] Richard Fardon argues that these debates chastise

"the orthodox and conventions which had previously been seen as hallmarks of professionalism in anthropology, [they] have become susceptible to re-presentation as the terms of a hegemonic power/style: the persona of the fieldworker was twined with that of a writer glimpsed only occasionally in the first person; writing in an assured tone, described and observed [the] field in realist terms; the writer's monopoly of the text denied other voices, the space to represent themselves (Fardon 1990, 8).

My sympathies lie with the postmodernists, and I am appreciative of anthropologists who have opened up past texts to scrutiny (Ricoeur 1981).[18]

It is important to state several things. First, critics of anthropological discourse do not want to destroy ethnography. (Indeed, I do not call for its demise.) They merely attempt to recover what Marcus calls the promise of anthropology, which is:

> To enlighten us about other human possibilities, engendering an awareness that we are merely one pattern among many, to make accessible the normally unexamined assumption by which we operate and through which we encounter members of other cultures. Anthropology is not the mindless collection of the exotic, but the use of cultural richness for self-reflection and self-growth (Marcus 1986, ix–x).

Michael Jackson's recent work, *Minima Ethnographica* (1998) reconfigures the ethnographic project along what he calls "the existential-phenomenological implications of Lévi-Strauss's conception of anthropology as a 'general theory of relationships'" (Ibid., 3). Jackson emphasizes inter-existence and inter-corporeity between people that should probe a life-world (*Lebenswelt*) rather than *Weltanschauung* (Ibid., 5). Methodologically, Jackson takes an intersubjective turn, because he sees intersubjectivity as a mediating position between the universal and the particular as well as a mode of relationality that recognizes subjectivity and alterity (Ibid., 9).[19] I find the recent interest in intersubjectivity refreshing because from graduate school days, I saw intersubjectivity as an important conceptual tool. I emphasize intersubjectivity in witchcraft studies not to kill ethnography but to open issues raised in witchcraft studies for ethical analysis.

Second, I am convinced that the study of witchcraft cannot be done through an ethnographic approach alone. If witchcraft intersects with other issues then it can be studied from different disciplines, and it is a folly to claim that one cannot raise important issues regarding witchcraft from a philosophical perspective.

REPRESENTATION: WHEN IS AN INSIDER'S PERSPECTIVE VALID?

The role of an insider is crucial here. During my tenure at the Berean Baptist Church of Kumba, a well-known member of the

church became ill and eventually died. It was alleged that his father caused his death through witchcraft. As a pastor in Yaounde,
I worked with a family whose son died and his relatives accused
other members of the family of witchcraft. In both of these cases,
I had conversations with some of the people involved as I tried to
understand what had happened.

Some researchers claim that the knowledge insiders bring is
nothing but anecdotes. I suspect the implicit claim is that a researcher who has spent one or two years in the field has a better
grasp of the issues than I do. It is possible that the researcher who
goes to study another culture may be far more prepared to ask and
look for specific information that the insider might take for granted
or overlook.[20] Insiders bring a critical perspective, but they are
sometimes hindered from doing so effectively by outsiders and their
African allies, who continue to insist that they have a better reading of what goes on because they have done the fieldwork.

TOWARD A CRITIQUE OF WITCHCRAFT

Two problems exist in attempting a critique of witchcraft. First,
earlier anthropological studies convey a skeptical attitude toward
witchcraft and dwell on the irrationality of such beliefs. Second,
this attitude forces recent writers to move away from what Peter
Geschiere calls a "moralizing terminology," which he describes as
"an unequivocal opposition between good and evil, even when the
local terminology hardly lends itself to this" (Geschiere 1997, 12).
One cannot simply brush aside the issues that Geschiere raises
about a moralizing trend, especially if the first thing that comes to
mind is to reduce witchcraft to good and evil. However, as a realm
of discourse and practice, one has to reflect on a number of questions. Does the discourse on witchcraft present any ethical problems? Are there any ethical implications from such a discourse in
the daily lives of the people? Put differently, are there times when
occult powers can be employed in a way that raises ethical issues
that cannot be categorized as right and wrong? If this is the case,
are there legitimate ways of addressing the ethical problems without simply reducing them to one's vision of good and evil. Furthermore, when locals talk about these issues, do they use language
that invokes ethical practice? I answer all of these questions in the
affirmative, because it is alleged that people can employ occult
powers negatively so that one can discuss these ethical implications without resorting to their own vision of good and evil.

To support this argument, I highlight some troubling notions that raise ethical questions in Geschiere's overview of the subject matter in the introduction to his book. Geschiere is not doing ethics, and he may find my interpretation of his work on *djambe* among the Maka unacceptable. His excellent presentation, however, certainly invites a meta-ethical probe of the phenomenon he elucidates in that work.

First, Geschiere argues that it is clear that the Maka people believe that others use occult powers to do "evil to people" and hinder development; indeed, some civil servants use these powers in a politically subversive way (Geschiere 1997, 1, 4, 5, 7). Second, in terms of kinship and the wider political context, people use the metaphor "eat the state" because they want to take care of the "jealousy of greedy kin" (Ibid., 11). The conflicts that arise bring out the "dark side of kinship," and in its most extreme form, people believe that *djambe* can be used to kill (Ibid., 11, 13). Third, people believe that occult powers tend to invade and corrupt new power relations. These powers become a leveling force that is perceived by some people as dangerous and by the Maka and other people in Cameroon as a vicious power (Ibid., 15, 16, 18). Fourth, Geschiere points out that although the new accumulation strategies are considered problematic, there are times when communities will "whitewash" it—in other words, will render those wrongful accumulation practices acceptable (Ibid., 19). Finally, speaking about the recent court trials that he and Cyprian Fisiy analyze so well, Geschiere contends that by trying those cases in the courts, the "state ventures deep into the treacherous terrain of *la sorcellierie*" (Ibid., 19).

The problems that Geschiere highlights can be found in some measure among the Wimbum. Given a clear perception among the people that legitimate power and force can be and often is employed in negative ways, there is justifiable reason to raise ethical questions. To walk away from such evidence would be to abandon the quest for the good. One certainly understands the hesitation of a foreign anthropologist who might not wish to take on an advocacy role or to carry on an Aristotelian project of praise and blame, even if studies indicate that certain uses of witchcraft that disrupt the common good are voluntary.[21] The reluctance of ethnographers to be critical of other cultures should not hinder insiders from formulating preliminary questions on the ethics of *tfu*.

It is important that I indicate what I mean by critique. I use critique in both its classic philosophical and Marxist sense. It involves an attempt to understand and present a coherent analysis of an issue or a situation with the goal of offering possible solutions.

Concerning the question of witchcraft, local ideas and perspectives will be mapped out in order to articulate meanings of the occult as participants understand it. In the Marxist sense, my understanding of critique here is similar to the view that Cornel West espouses—that a critique involves "understanding of the internal dynamics of power relations of a society or civilizations. This understanding requires a social theory whose aim is to demystify present ideological distortions or misreadings of society, to bring to light who possesses power and wealth, why they do, how they acquire it, sustain and enlarge it and why the poor have so little" (West 1998, 416–417). The goal of such a critique is to provide possibilities for a new social and "humane order" (Ibid., 417).[22]

At the African Studies Association's annual meeting in Orlando, Florida, in 1995, Emmanuel Eze discussed philosophical reflections on a critique of postcolonial identities by the philosopher Kalanda from the Democratic Republic of Congo. Eze argued that part of the critique of postcolonial society by Africans should assume the responsibility of avoiding the distortion of the life-world.

> It is a zone charged with the energy of myth and utopia. But between the truths that myths in their fictional energy impose at the very depths of our being, and the more objective truths provided by scientific and philosophical analysis, it is the field of the imaginary representations that carries the heaviest weight in the determination of conduct and collective orientation. Thus, when this "zone"—the zone of the social imaginary—is "distorted" or "diseased" and "inflamed," then, our actions and "knowledge" becomes systematically distorted as well. Are we surprised, therefore, that our will to freedom is riddled with inconsistencies that have rendered us enigma—even to ourselves? (Eze 1997, 8)

Witchcraft occupies nearly all areas of the life-world, or what Eze calls "zones" in the lives of the people I know. Although I accept that it can be used in a positive way in healing, governance, the arts, and other areas of life, there is no doubt that when it goes wrong, we are dealing with a "distorted, diseased," and "inflamed social imagery," and something ought to be said about the ethical implications without reducing the conversation to good and evil.

My interest in the critique of witchcraft also includes various shades of critique. It is Kantian in the sense that I do want to touch on the scope and limitations of occult powers. By this, I mean that claims about the positive aspects of witchcraft have to be analyzed and debated. It is only in such a critical engagement that one can begin to see the limitations of the concept. It also is Marxist, in the sense that I argue that once we understand some of the dynamics, we can begin to formulate ethical responses to what remains an intersubjective engagement par excellence. This is only a provisional attempt that at best opens up witchcraft and this very critique to scrutiny from other perspectives.

The argument will proceed in the following manner. In Chapter 1 I present a brief sociohistorical sketch of the Wimbum, a group of patrilocal, exogamous subsistence farmers who inhabit the Donga-Mantung Plateau of the Northwest Province of Cameroon. Although studies of the Wimbum people go back to colonial times (Jeffreys 1962; Mafiamba 1969), recently the Wimbum people have been the subject of more intensive studies, as have other peoples of "The Grassfields" of Cameroon. I analyze these recent studies to articulate the *Weltanschauung* of the Wimbum people (Mbunwe-Samba 1989).

In Chapter 2 I present a hermeneutics of *tfu* by analyzing the terms that are employed by the Wimbum people. I define Wimbum ideas that express the phenomenon commonly called "witchcraft." These ideas have been expanded and transformed as a response to stress on the extended social fabric and horizon of the Wimbum people. Such stress has resulted from increasing urbanization, commercialization, and the mobility it entails. I discuss recent interpretations of "witchcraft" in light of the discourse of postmodernity.

In Chapter 3 I analyze the discussion of the rationality of *tfu* practice, arguing that Mudimbe's historical anthropology and philosophy not only constitute a new insight into the discourse on Africa but also heighten the issues involved in "otherness." Mudimbe's analysis provides a platform for raising the question of the rationality of *tfu* beliefs in the Wimbum context. I argue that Winch's perspective for contextual discourse is still valid. I also draw from Bernstein's contextualism to argue that *tfu* beliefs deal with "meaning-making" activities in the Wimbum context, and that this context should provide the basis for a critique of *tfu*. These terms will be discussed to show how the Wimbum understand the world and the intersubjective relations that give rise to *tfu* practice.

In Chapter 4 I discuss Levinas's articulation of a human Other who challenges "totality" so that I can then carve in bold relief the radical "Other" that he proposes. As an introduction to Levinasian ethics, I argue that there are dimensions of individuality among the Wimbum that justify problematizing the question of an Other, who can be and often is the target of negative practices of *tfu*. To define this dimension of individuality, I analyze the Wimbum expression *fo ni nwe* (pride exists only in a person). Such Wimbum notions echo general humanistic visions, and I radicalize such notions by drawing from Levinas to articulate the ethical problematic in *tfu* practice.

In Chapter 5 I offer proposals for a theological conversation on *tfu*. I assume the validity of theological reflection that speaks to the African experience, so that the "the African Cry" (Wimbum cry) is one that comes out of and expresses the faith of an African.[23] Levinas's "phenomenology of eros" spells a metaphysical desire that could be expressed in a nontotalizing manner toward the Other. I argue that Levinas's notion of desire should be considered in formulating a theological response to *tfu*.

I owe much to many people. First, I thank Jere Surber, who supervised this project as a doctoral thesis, along with my other supportive committee members: Allen Roberts, Carl Raschke, and Alton Templin. Cyprian Fisiy and Diane Ciekawy provided me with references and resources on witchcraft in Cameroon and Kenya. V. Y. Mudimbe, Wyatt McGaffey, and Richard Bernstein read the dissertation and provided critical comments. Edith Wyschogrod, Alphonso Lingis, Emmanuel Eze, Cleo Kearns, Stephen Tyler, George Marcus, Johaness Fabian, Lewis Gordon, and Robert Bernasconi read the manuscript and provided critical comments that helped me sharpen my reading of Levinas and postmodern philosophy. Graduate students Eric Boynton and Stephen Hood read the entire manuscript and provided editorial assistance.

I also express my appreciation to my professors, who introduced me to reading theology and philosophy: David E. Klemm, Charles Marsh, Diana Cates, and James McCue at the University of Iowa and Stanley Grenz, Thomas Johnson, and Randy Maddox at the North American Baptist Seminary and the University of Sioux Falls. My friend Cecile Siewe read and edited the manuscript and gave me very valuable criticism.

Chapter 3 was presented at a session on philosophy organized at the African Studies Association in Orlando, Florida, in November 1995. Chapter 4 was presented at an anthropology colloquium at Rice University in October 1995 devoted to the relevance of Levinas to the anthropology of misfortune. I express my thanks to Professor George Marcus for extending that invitation. Chapter 5 on the phenomenology of eros was presented at a colloquium organized by the Religious Studies Department at Rice University. I extend thanks to my colleagues there for their suggestions. During the period that I was writing the dissertation, I was able to travel to Cameroon to check some of my sources. I thank Abel Bongmba, Augustine Safe, Dr. Anthony Ndi, Hon. Cyprian Awudu, Pa Yerima Ngiri, Pa Samuel Ndzi, the Reverend Peter Nyumloh, General Secretary of the Cameroon Baptist Convention, Dr. Orym Meinerts, Dr. Helen Schmidt, both North American Baptist missionaries to Cameroon, and Dr. Wilfred Fon, president of the Cameroon Baptist Theological Seminary, for their hospitality and assistance. I also thank Heidi Loushbaugh, Mary Joe Brown, and Margueritte Torrey, who graciously read earlier versions of the manuscript and turned my *Limbum* into English. I am thankful to Claudia Logerquist for working with me on the German texts.

My sons, Donald Afanyui Bongmba, Dino Kong Bongmba, and Douglas Ginyui Bongmba, have all been very patient with me, even though it did not make sense to them that I was going over the same "stuff" again. My parents, Johaness Bongmba and Monica Munkeng, also have been supportive of my work. In addition, my sisters and brothers, Alice Ntalah, Caroline Mbagon, Mary Ntoshi, Abel Bongmba and Ndzi Christian Bongmba, have provided much support since I left Cameroon. I express my appreciation to all of them, as well as to my colleagues in the Religious Studies Department at Rice University for nurturing a great intellectual climate in which to plunge into the hazardous field of interdisciplinary scholarship. I also express appreciation to Dean Judith Brown of the School of Humanities and Becky Heye for a faculty grant that enabled me to complete this manuscript. A shorter version of Chapter 2 was published in *African Studies Review,* Vol. 41, No. 3 (December 1998), pp. 165–191. Chapter 3 appeared in *African Philosophy*, Vol. 12, No. 2, (1999), pp. 125–148, and a shorter version of Chapter 5 was published in *The Journal of Theology for Southern Africa,* March 2000. These chapters have been revised. I am grateful to these publications for permission to use the material for this book.

Finally, I thank my editors at State University of New York Press, especially Nancy Ellegate, Fran Keneston, Michael Haggett, Patrick Durocher, copyeditor Michele Lansing and graphic artist Amy Stirnkorb for their patience and professionalism.

Even though I have brought together several voices to this project, the project remains mine in its conception and method of execution, thus I assume responsibility for the material that is presented here.

African
Witchcraft
and Otherness

Chapter 1

The Wimbum People

THE WIMBUM PEOPLE OF
THE DONGA-MANTUNG DIVISION

The Wimbum and other people who also inhabit the Northwest Province have similar institutional structures and beliefs about the extended family. Wimbum views and beliefs about witchcraft are somewhat the same among the people of the Northwest Province, commonly called "The Grassfields." The Wimbum people inhabit the Donga-Mantung Plateau (formerly Nkambe) of the Northwest Province.[1] The name "Wimbum" is descriptive and means the "Mbum people."[2] They speak *Limbum;* the prefix "li" means language, thus *Limbum* means the "language of the Mbum people."[3] The Wimbum language shares certain affinities for other languages of the Northwest Province. For example, both the Wimbum and the Nso people use the title *kibai* to designate a council of elders, also called by the Wimbum *ptala*, the heads of different families.[4] The Northwest Province has polyglot populations that fall under three broad classifications of languages—the Momo, Ring, and the Mbam-Nkam. *Limbum* falls in Mbam-Nkam group as do Adere, Mungaka, Bamoum, Bafut, Mankon, Jo, Fefe, Dschang, and Bangante (Nkwi and Warnier 1982, 35). The Nso language is placed in the Ring group, along with the Babungo, Kom, and We, but it is important to point out that despite multiple permutations, the different peoples of the Northwest Province have 57 percent of their vocabulary in common (Ibid., p. 19). Thus, although *Lamnso* (the language of the Nso people) and *Limbum* are in different language groups, there

1

are similarities in much of their vocabulary. Many words in both languages sound similar and have similar meanings.[5] There are three clans in the Wimbum community (the Wiya, Witang, and Wiwarr). The clan heads are not paramount chiefs, but rather each Wimbum village has its own village head called *nkfu,* otherwise called *fon* by other ethnic groups of the Northwest Province.[6] The *fons* govern their villages with the assistance of a council of elders. The villages are generally divided into quarters, and each quarter is ruled by a sub-chief called *fai.* Members of a quarter constitute an extended family and practice exogamy.

The Wimbum consider themselves one people. In his well-known essay on the Wiya people, Dr. Jeffreys, a social anthropologist and colonial district officer of the area, referred to the Wiya as a "tribe" (Jeffreys 1962, 83ff). This designation is misleading, because it implies that the Wiya people belong to a different group from the other groups of the Wimbum people. Perhaps Jeffreys did this because of the migration theory, which holds that the Wiya are part of the Tikar people who migrated into the Northwest Province from Kimi.

THE PEOPLING OF THE WIMBUM AREA

The peopling of the Donga-Mantung Plateau, in general, and the Wimbum area, in particular, is a complex subject, and no single theory can account for this process. Earlier studies that addressed the settling of the Wimbum on the present site include those by Nkwi and Warnier, Dr. P. Mafiamba, and Jones Mangoh (Mafiamba 1969; Mangoh 1986). Mafiamba argues that the Wimbum people who are related to the Tikar group of the Northwest Province arrived on the plateau from Kimi. According to Mafiamba's reconstruction, the Warr, who were the first people on the plateau, settled at Mbirbaw, the present Mbot (Mafiamba 1969, 64). Mangoh argues that the Warr were the aborigines of the area and were later joined by the Wiya and Witang (Mangoh 1986, 28).[7]

Some members of the Warr people moved to different locations on the plateau and formed the different towns that make up the different Warr people; indeed the name "Warr" itself means "scatter." According to Mangoh, the first Warr to move away from Mbirbaw was Ntumbaw, followed by Sop and Chup. By the seventeenth century, other towns of the present Warr people were founded at sites including Nkambe, Kungi, Binshua, Saah, Njap, Mbaa, and Wat (Mangoh 1986, 32). At first, these towns, which were known in *Limbum* as *mlaa* (meaning "compounds"), did not establish the same kind of authority structure they left behind at Mbot. Later they developed a similar structure by establishing the institution of the *fon* when they crowned their leaders as *nkfu*. The *nkfu* of Mbirbaw was still regarded as their leader, but he had no direct control over the affairs of the newly established realms. In this structure, a *fon* or *nkfu* ruled the town and was assisted by several leaders known as *kibai*, *tar nte*, or *tallanwe*. These leaders were in charge of family groups within a specific town ruled by *nkfu*.

The other two groups of the Wimbum, the Wiya and the Witang, are believed to have migrated to the area as part of the Tikar wave of immigration provoked by Borno and Hausa expansionism and slave raiding (Mangoh 1986, 37). The Wiyah people migrated to the present area, where they now live, from Kimi, under their leader, Nyankimji. Part of the group settled at Mbiriqua under the leadership of Nyankimji's brother. The rest proceeded to the present site, making brief stops at Konchep and Fuh. When the Wiya settled on the plateau, the first dispute with the Warr people started when the Wiyah leader and his people refused to offer a buffalo they had caught as homage to the *nkfu* of Mbirbaw. As a result of this dispute, the Wiyah people moved to Mbandfung.

The Witang first moved to Nguu when they left Kimi. They settled briefly at Mbajeng but moved because the Wiya people claimed that Mbajeng was their territory. Some of the Witang went to Mbasong, others to Mbam and Nseh, but both are now part of the Bui Division. The group that remained on the Nkambe Plateau formed the present Tang clan, out of which came the towns of Sinna, Talla, Ngarum, Taku, Kup, Tabenken, and Bi (Mangoh 1986, 41). The groups that arrived later, such as the Ngang, Sehn, Njilah, and Ngulu were either part of the Wiyah or Tang group. The leader of the Ngulu (a Wiyah group, which settled near Ntumbaw) enjoyed more autonomy than other Wiyah leaders. Both Mangoh and Mafiamba have pointed out that the Luh were an autochthonous people originally driven out of Nso, who settled at the present site and joined the Wiyah group (Ibid., p. 42).[8] When these two groups, the Wiyah and Witang, settled on the plateau, they adopted the settlement patterns set by the Warr people and settled where they thought they could sustain themselves while still maintaining their identity.

THE WIMBUM COMMUNITY

The integration of the Wimbum people into a highly structured society was the result of a slow, complex process that will not be addressed in this book. Other writers suggest that at the center of this society is the *nkfu* of each town. This is partly true because the *nkfu* exerts much influence, but I would argue that the center of the Wimbum society is the family and the extended family system. The configuration of the Wimbum society is family oriented, because the *nkfu* rules the town as head of the royal family. The *ptala* who rule the different extended families that make up the town have control over all of the members of the particular extended family who are descendants of one ancestor. In addition to these political arrangements, economic and social affairs are structured around the family and the family head who also acts as the religious leader. Furthermore, the leader of each family group, along with his advisors, acts as the authority in adjudicating conflicts and is called upon from time to time to settle disputes and even to take actions to ward off threats to the family.

THE STRUCTURE OF WIMBUM SOCIETY: THE WARR PEOPLE

The people of the Warr clan are believed to be the autochthonous residents of the area. They trace their beginnings to Mbirbaw, where their leader, Bomsa, ruled. His four sons later separated, and these individuals formed the nucleus of the present towns of Ntumbaw, Sop, Chup, and Mbot (Mafiamba 1969, 104). Although, the *nkfu,* the town's *fon*, plays an important role in the lives of the people in the town, the families and extended family control the day-to-day activities of the society. Each family lives together on a piece of property that they claim as their own. These families are exogamous and patrilineal. The main leader is called by several names, including *Tallanwe, Kibai*, and *Tar nte*, but generally these leaders are called *fai*. Occasionally people refer to them as "big man." The *fai,* as head of the extended family, is responsible for almost all of the business and affairs of the extended family. For instance, he speaks to the *nkfu* on behalf of the family, he makes sure that the family land and resources are well guarded, and he decides where members will build and cultivate. The *fai* thus controls economic production and distribution. This is not to suggest that the individual members of the extended family have no voice and cannot take any initiative; there is freedom within this structure that recognizes individuality and personhood.

THE ROLE OF THE *FAI* IN THE FAMILY

The *fai* is responsible for the spiritual well-being of his people and is generally the one who will be consulted in case of any difficult problems such as witchcraft accusations. Thus if there is a death, the death celebration will be held in his quarters. All of the women will gather in the house of his senior wife, and all of the men will gather in the court where he receives people. In Ntumbaw, *Fai* Ngafansi has a large room where he receives his guests. This same room is used for other ceremonies, such as death celebrations, and the weekly *ngwa*, a financial association. It is the *fai*'s responsibility to lead or delegate powers to someone who will carry out investigations of "witchcraft." The *fai* also must ensure that the right diviners are consulted when there is a problem (Probst 1992, 148). The *fai* and his elders, and in some cases, the elders of the entire town, including the *fon*, determine the penalties for crimes as well as the rituals that will be done to cleanse and purify the community.

Perhaps nothing demonstrates the *fai*'s authority as much as the marriage transaction. He coordinates all marriage arrangements within the family, choosing the men and women from his own family who will go to the home of the new in-laws when anyone in the family has become engaged to a woman in or out of the town. In some cases, he may make the trip himself. He pays the bride wealth from the family's resources. He would have received this wealth in the past as the bride wealth from others who have married women out of his family. He cannot spend this money for his own personal affairs; rather, he will use it to pay the bride wealth demanded by other families when members of his extended family marry. This structure does not prevent individuals from coming up with their own bride wealth if they can afford it.

I further illustrate the structure and role of the *fai* by looking at *Fai* Ngafansi, who carries out his functions in consultation with several elders who represent different families within *Fai* Ngafansi's extended family. *Fai* Ngafansi's extended family is made up of five households headed by family heads who work with *Fai* Ngafansi to govern the family. These include *Ndap Fai*, the immediate household of the *Fai* himself, *Ndap* Ndzi, *Ndap* Ngwang, *Ndap* Gwei, and *Ndap* Yongka.[9] *Fai* Ngafansi works together with the head of these families to make decisions on behalf of the extended family. Those who head these individual families owe their authority to seniority. For instance, the head of *Ndap* Ngwang today is Samuel

Ndzi, a man who has a good reputation not only in the family of
Fai Ngafansi but also in the entire town of Ntumbaw. When Samuel
Ndzi can no longer exercise his functions as head of the Ngwang
family, that role will not necessarily be taken by any of his sons but
will go to the most senior member of that family—perhaps one of
his brothers, or anyone else in the Ngwang family who is the most
senior member. This arrangement has been challenged recently in
the neighboring town by Moses Tansi, who has argued that his
uncle, Usumanu Nfor, has no right over the Tansi family because
he, Moses, is the rightful successor of his father.[10] Moses has lost
the case in every court that has tried it, both within the Wimbum
community and in the magistrate courts of the Donga-Mantung
Division.

Although a *fai* shares the governing of his *rla* "extended family" with heads of individual families, the heads of these families
cannot succeed him when he dies. Only members of a *fai*'s family
can succeed him in that role—his children or his brothers. His
successor is usually decided on by the leaders of the families in
consultation with the other *fais* of the town and the *nkfu*, who has
the ultimate responsibility in seeing that the transition is smooth.
When a *fai* dies, at the time his successor is crowned a female
member of the family also is installed as *mankfu*. She assists in
ruling the extended family. She cannot marry, but she can take on
lovers who live in the compound and have children with her, but
these children belong to the *fai*'s family.

The role of the *fai*, along with other Wimbum institutions, is
facing challenges posed by the introduction of Western education,
Christianity, and capitalism. In the past, those who occupied this
office worked less than those today. In his illuminating discussion
of some of these changes in the context of witchcraft, power, and
medicine, Probst has noted that in the past, the *fai*, like the *nkfu*,
was supposed to exercise his function by refraining from certain
public activities. The needs of a market economy, however, have
changed all of this and now a *fai* is frequently obliged to participate in economic activities such as commercial agriculture and
normal day-to-day business dealings such as trade in the market
(Probst 1992, 149).[11] Elites are now taking the positions of *fai*
among the Wimbum. They do not have to be restricted and se-
cluded; instead, they are urged to use their offices and power to
foster the growth of the community, provide fees for education, and
encourage participation in the activities of the extended family
(Ibid., 150).

Carrying out these responsibilities has become complicated because *fais* not only have to depend on the heads of families but now have to contend with the "modern elite," who are expected, and who themselves want, to be involved in the running of their towns of origin, even though they may live in urban areas of Cameroon. In addition to going back and forth between their urban area and their hometowns, the modern elite have structured their involvement by the formation of associations and development committees that carry out different projects in their areas.[12]

WIMBUM WORLDVIEW AND RELIGION

The Wimbum worldview is the interplay of social, religious, and political roles, working together to ensure the well-being of the people. Within the Wimbum world, no neat compartmentalization of the sacred and secular exists. The Wimbum believe in the pervasive role of divinity. Religion, culture, and social life come together, making it difficult to isolate purely secular or religious activities. Missionary George Dunger has observed that religion and life among the Cameroonians are one (Dunger 1946, 19).[13] Dunger notes that some Cameroonians see natural phenomena as a representation of the powers of the spirit. However, Dunger's claim that "native" religion cannot contribute to practical ethics is problematic because the preoccupation among the people of the Northwest Province with ethical violations is predicated on a certain ethical code (Ibid., 21, 22). The pervasive religiosity of the Wimbum bears some resemblance to what has been noted in other parts of Africa.[14] In the Geertzian sense, religion and life among the Wimbum are part of a cultural system (Geertz 1973b, 87ff).

THE PROBLEMATIC CONCEPT OF A "HIGH GOD"

Although it is difficult to locate a single word in *Limbum* that describes the concept of religion, the Wimbum people do have a word for god, *Nyu* (the plural form is *Mnyu*). The Wimbum people refer to several divinities called *Nyu ngon*, "the god of the world,"[15] *Nyu lah* "the god of the compound," *Nyu roh*, "the god of water," *Nyu kop*, "the god of the forest," and *Nyu mmkfu*, "the god of the farm." Apart from these many divine beings, there also is a strong temptation to speak of a supreme being similar to a Christian God.

The attempt to search for a supreme God among the Wimbum cannot be solved by dismissing the notion of a personalistic god. By interpreting the religious experience of the Wimbum people as an activity that deals with "ultimate concerns," one need not accept or deny that there is such a thing as a personal god. Pool dismisses the notion of a personalistic High God among the Wimbum, arguing instead that, "Witches are ultimately responsible for the activities which are attributed to the *Mnyu*" (Pool 1994, 251). It is not immediately clear whether Pool specifically rejects the Christian notion of a High God imposed on the Wimbum and other African communities, or personalism in religion *en toto*. If it is a rejection of any notion of personalism in religion among the Wimbum, it seems to me that such a conclusion does not take into consideration the personal references that abound in Wimbum conceptions of God.

Pool's position, and that of his informants, is understandable if one realizes that conversations on illness tend to focus on who is doing what to whom. In such conversations, witches are at the center of the alleged activity, but to attribute all that happens in Wimbum society to witches and to deny that they may have a personal God take the evidence too far.[16]

The notion of a High God among the Africans is a very popular theme. For example, missionary and anthropologist Paul Gebauer writes that among the Yamba of the Nwa Sub-Division, "Beliefs about *Nwie* came nearest to the idea of a high god" (Gebauer 1964, 26). The nearness to a High God that Gebauer describes refers to attributes the Yamba people give to their God *Nwei,* including invisibility, being present everywhere, the ability to change one's abode, one who sees and knows all things, and the creator of the earth and the sky (Ibid.).

The Nigerian scholar Bolaji Idowu argues that there is both a High God and divinities (Idowu 1973, 140). In his attempt to demarcate a different understanding of God in Africa, Idowu has introduced the concept of "diffused monotheism" (Ibid., 135). He argues that there is a monotheistic belief in Africa, making African religions similar to other monotheistic faiths. Attempts to define divinity as a "High God" based on the influence of Christianity are not very helpful, however, because African conceptions of divinity do not necessarily correspond to Christian categories of God. Although the Wimbum people talk of God, gods, and spirits that inhabit the world, they do not raise any questions regarding a supreme deity and the relationship of that deity to other divinities such as *Nyu Ngon* and *Nyu Ro*. I have found Benjamin Ray's polymethodic and multidimensional approach to religion helpful (Ray 1976).[17]

This approach stresses symbols such as deities, ancestors, sacred actions, and images, which all converge to present different elements of society. His approach also encompasses ritual activities that bring together the imaginary and lived worlds. Mythical symbols and rituals are community based and enacted for the good of the people (Ray 1976, 17). During the colonial struggle, community-based activities that employed rites that appealed to a divine power were undertaken in some parts of Africa. From other parts of Africa, we know that indigenous religions have played an essential role in political movements. Both David Lan (1985) and Matthew Schoffeleers (1992) present good examples of how indigenous religions have been part of the colonial protest.

THE WIMBUM PEOPLE AND THE BELIEF IN THE EXISTENCE OF SPIRITS

The Wimbum also recognize the existence of several intermediaries such as spirits and ancestors who interact with humans. The Wimbum speak of good spirits and bad spirits, a designation different from the Christian conception. Among the Wimbum is a spirit called *nyir*, believed to be the spirit of someone who has died but come back to bother people. When people become aware of such a presence, community leaders offer sacrifices to appease these spirits. Pool's informants suggested that ancestors, or *bkfubsi*, as they are called in *Limbum*, do not do all of the things that people say they do. This view certainly calls for further probing, because it is possible that Pool's informers want to dissociate ancestors from negative activities. Ancestors cannot and should not always be associated with negative activities in the community. Jean-Marc Ela argues that ancestors should not always be seen as harmful powers needing to be appeased through rites (Ela 1988, 19). The Wimbum people have a strong belief in the reality of ancestors and their interaction with the community. Whether or not *bkfubsi* cause the difficulties that some attribute to them is a subject for further investigation, but there is no doubt that the Wimbum people believe in their existence and their participation in the lives and activities of the people.

COMMUNITY AND RELIGIOUS LIFE
REINFORCED WITH RITUALS

The Wimbum people carry out many rites in the practice of their religious beliefs. Rituals involve the life cycle of an individual and are meant to ensure the prosperity and well-being of the people. They sometimes call this practice *mshep*.[18] The practice of *mshep* as a ritual may involve preparing medicines for members of the family when the family needs cleansing. On such an occasion, it is customary for a fowl to be offered either to the gods or ancestors. Wimbum people refer to this as "fixing," or *kupse mshep*. This activity can be undertaken as a precaution against illness, a perceived or an apparent danger, or to appease the gods so that treatment for a particular illness can be effective. Since twins are considered very powerful, it is important to give them medicines in a ritual, which is called *nusi* (Ngala, 2000). In a family where twins have been born, a specialist prepares medicines and performs rituals because it is believed that twins become people who can see and do things that other people cannot. The person designated to do this usually mixes local raffia or palm wine with herbs and other medicines, giving it to the twins to drink so that their power will be tamed and channeled into positive actions. It is believed that if the twins are not treated this way, they can eventually hurt their parents. No one associates twins with witches and evil actions; rather, the belief is that twins are special children who have special powers, in a different category than witches.

The most important religious ritual among the Wimbum is an offering called *tangsi*. The Wimbum people perform *tangsi* in several ways. If it is a family *tangsi*, the head of the family, or someone designated by the head, can perform it at the family shrine. If it involves the entire town, the religious leaders of the town, under the supervision of the *fon,* will enact it. *Tangsi* is undertaken for almost everything imaginable. If the people are preparing to go hunting, they can hold a special *tangsi*.[19] *Tangsi* can be undertaken before the planting or weeding season, or to purify the land. When they do *tangsi* to purify the land, it is different from the protective measures taken by the closed society called *Nsingong,* responsible for placing medicines on the borders and all of the strategic points of Njirong and Ntumbaw to prevent evil doers and witches from bringing misfortune into the towns.

At Ntumbaw, for instance, a *tangsi* can be enacted at one of three places. The first is the *Ndap Ngong*, the sacred spot where most of the religious rituals that pertain to the entire town are performed. At Ntumbaw, only a select few enter *Ndap Ngong*. The second place where the *tangsi* can be performed is in a shrine centrally located at the entrance to the palace. The third place is known as *tseri*, a site about 200 meters from the palace. The *tseri* itself refers to a tall boulder that has a round shape. The stone is planted in the ground and rises about six or seven feet. This *tseri* has been allowed to fall down and is now broken into pieces. It is not clear whether this was caused by vandalism or if the people simply neglected it. At all of these places, a ritual performance may include the sacrifice of a fowl. If this particular *tangsi* is offered for hunting or during farming season, the blood from the fowl is spread on the hoes or spears. During these ceremonies, special palm wine is blessed. Participants drink the wine and eat the fowl that was sacrificed. They also offer prayers to *Nyu* and call on ancestors to bless the land and to bring prosperity (Nkwi and Warnier 1982, 164).[20]

These religious activities usually are combined with different types of divination, which remains an important means of forecasting the future or determining the cause of an illness or a death. In pidgin English, divination is known as *ngambe* and is practiced by many of the peoples of the Northwest Province. The Wimbum typically refer to divination as *seng*; the person who performs divination is called *Nwe Seng*. In most Wimbum towns, there are people who specialize in different forms of divination. These people use various objects to assist them in deciphering the problems that their clients bring. If there is a dispute, the people consult another diviner. In the past, if a problem was not resolved after proper divination procedures were followed in Ntumbaw, people went to a town in the Nwa Sub-District area to consult with the diviner known as Tonga, who was highly reputable.

The classic work on divination in the Northwest Province is Paul Gebauer's *Spider Divination in the Cameroons* (Gebauer, 1964). Gebauer writes about the Yamba people who are neighbors to the Wimbum, and he indicates that the *ngam* divination is the predominant method employed among the Yamba people. Gebauer, however, gives it a wider context.

> It is used for any practice of any oracular nature, but it is also the name for the gods or ancestors who speak through a diviner or his instruments. Variations of this term appear among neighboring grassland tribes, such as *nga* in *Limbuni*, *ngamb* in *Bikom*, *ngamo* in Kwang (Gebauer 1964, 35).

Gebauer describes the process of *ngam* divination as an activity that involves the interpretation of a message from a set of leaf cards held in the hands of the diviner. After initial descriptions of the problems, the diviner proceeds to determine the voice of the powers he is consulting.

> Holding the pack of cards between his two hands he blows them repeatedly, then with the set of cards pressed between the thumb and index finger he lowers his hand and rests it on the piece of fur. Still holding the cards securely with the left hand he now brings his right hand behind the cards and with the index finger snaps the center of the pack letting the cards scatter forward along the outstretched fur and across the bar. . . . In a leisurely manner the diviner picks up the cards that have crossed the bar to read their meaning to his client (Gebauer 1964, 38–39).

Gebauer indicates that this process can go on until the diviner is assured that the powers he is consulting have given him a clear picture about the issues involved. Divination among the Wimbum and their neighbors, the Yamba, bears some resemblance to Victor Turner's understanding of the practice of divination as social analysis (Turner 1975). He argues that such social analysis involves ambivalence that comes out in the diviner, characterized by Turner as a marginal individual whose activity reflects the conflicts inherent in the society that has rejected him or her. Turner portrays the resolutions that clients seek as a solution that the diviner brings out in conflictual terms. "Resolution is achieved only at the cost of running total hate, and sometimes of the actual ostracism or physical punishment of the secret plotter, 'the witch'" (Turner 1975, 24–25). However, I do not believe that the ritual process is only the unveiling of the world of marginality. The goal of divination is to attempt to find some resolution that should not be seen only as hate and punishment, since the diviner who undertakes a diagnosis can also tell his or her client to hold a celebration. Divination also can lead to healing, although the diviner who may only serve as a diagnostician may not do the healing. There are indeed times when diviners may demonstrate a certain amount of hallucination, and this does not necessarily imply that there is marginality involved in their background. Some of the diviners tend to be rather organized and operate in a structured environment. The ones Gebauer observed were organized and demonstrated a clear structure.

The role of the diviner—*nganga,* as they are known in the literature—continues to be important. Schoffeleers argues that the *nganga* could, and should, be seen as a paradigm for Christology in Africa (Schoffeleers 1989, 157–183). Schoffeleers demonstrates that the *nganga* performs certain roles such as preparing charms, using herbal medicines, healing, detecting, and eradicating witchcraft. The image of Christ as healer is the parallel Schoffeleers draws from these different roles, though prominent clergy in Africa, such as Milingo, who have had a well publicized healing ministry are reluctant to see themselves as *nganga.* Members of the clergy are sometimes called *nganga* in parts of East Africa. Michael Kirwen's work overturns previous interpretations of the diviner, viewed by missionaries as an enemy and agent of the devil (Kirwen 1987).

In his brilliant, programmatic essay, "Perspectives on Divination in Contemporary Sub-Saharan Africa," Renaat Devisch proposes a praseological approach to the understanding of divination (Devisch 1985, 50–83). Devisch argues that such an approach, while drawing from previous attempts, focuses on the subject, namely, the diviner, his or her congregation, and the "decision-making group constituting itself in the source of the divinatory process." This approach stresses the "purposeful articulation of meaning" and praxis in which "the oracle of the diviner brings out what is problematic by giving it metaphoric form, through rhetoric, or dramatic bridging of physiological, sensitive, cognitive, social, historical and cosmological domains" (Ibid., 77). In my view, what Devisch proposes takes the insights of Turner further by seeing the communication of meaning through the process as an all-encompassing revelatory transaction on which healing and emancipatory projects can be constituted by the community. I would argue that, beyond self-legitimation and generation of the concerns of the individual, a praseological approach to divination opens liberating dimensions. "This performance can bring about insight, mastery of cognitive complexity, transition in the existential or social condition of the individual or of the group. It can bring about a change in the relations of power, mediation between the individual and the group, the old and the new, or can perform other dynamic functions" (Ibid., 77).

THE COMING OF CHRISTIANITY TO WIMBUM

Christianity was first introduced to the Wimbum people in the early part of the twentieth century by Cameroonian evangelists who became Christians while working in the southwest area of

Cameroon. The Baptist church dominates in the Wimbum area, which also has the largest number of professing Baptists in the Cameroon Baptist Convention. This church was started through the initiative of Jamaican Baptists and spread from the coastal areas of Cameroon inland largely through the efforts of Cameroonian evangelists (Gwei 1966; Kwast 1971; Sanneh 1983; Mangoh 1986; Weber 1993). Christianity moved into the Wimbum area via Songka and Fonfuka in the Mentchum Division, where Joseph Mamadu, a Grasslander who became a Christian on the coast, started the first Baptist churches.[21]

Later, missionary Johaness Sieber established a station at Mbirpka in the Mbaw Plains. He was forced to move the station to its present location at Ndu Town in 1932 (Ibid.). In typical mission- ary language, Kwast notes that the station was destroyed by "hos- tile enemies" in 1933. It was rebuilt, and the work spread throughout the area (Ibid.). Since Kwast writes about church growth history, he accounts for the spread of the Baptist church in the area in the pragmatic, programmatic language of the church growth school. The factors of growth were the tenacity of missionaries, the contri- bution of schools, the responsive nature of the Wimbum people, and, to a certain extent, the establishment of a theological school at Ndu.

Mangoh argues that the missionaries succeeded among the Wimbum because they established local headquarters. The Bap- tists also did not have a strong central system, and this seemed to fit well with the Wimbum people, who are organized into clans, though each town is independent and has its own *fon* (Mangoh 1986, 151). I should point out that what is missing from the ac- count given by Kwast and Mangoh is the extent to which the in- digenous religious worldview might have played a role. Given the nature of the religious world of the Wimbum people, it seems that Lamin Sanneh rightly argues that in carrying out the *Missio Dei*, the church has not always been willing to recognize that in places such as Africa, "Divine love and reconciliation . . .was long diffused in the local religious traditions before the missionary came on the scene" (Sanneh 1983, 247).[22]

WIMBUM RELIGION AND SOCIAL TENSIONS: EXAMPLE FROM NTUMBAW

The practice of the Wimbum religion is alive today. The late 1960s and early 1970s were a difficult period for the people of Ntumbaw.

This also was a time when a serious attempt was made to revive popular culture. A major chieftaincy dispute in the town lasted over a decade. In addition, a chieftaincy dispute occurred among the Hausas and the Fulanis who lived in Ntumbaw. Thus, among the Wimbum who claimed to be the original settlers of Ntumbaw, there were two *fons*. One was installed in 1961 but was deposed by the people in 1972 after numerous accusations of witchcraft and moral failures. The people installed a member of the royal family to rule in his place, but the former *fon* did not go away. He received the backing of the divisional administrators, who argued that to depose a *fon* was unlawful. Among the Hausas of Ntumbaw, there were two people, each claiming to be the rightful *Sarki Hausawa*, and among the Fulbe residents of Ntumbaw, there were two individuals, each claiming to be the *Ardo*.[23] In addition to these problems, which made Ntumbaw a fertile ground for bribery, corruption, and all kinds of intimidation from the divisional officers and the ever-present gendarmes, attendance in the Ntumbaw Market declined significantly.[24]

Several reasons have been given for these problems. First, concerning the decline of the market, some members of the Ntumbaw community argued that the chieftaincy disputes in the Wimbum, Hausa, and Fulani communities were a factor. Second, others observed that the economic decline of the town was brought about because the *fon* had allowed the market to be transferred to a new, unsuitable location. Furthermore, they argued that a symbolic tree planted at the site of the market had been cut down. It was a Wimbum practice to concretize the reality of a market and all of the economic transactions that would be undertaken there by placing medicines and charged objects in a hole at a center of the market and planting a fig tree there. The tree that was planted was supposed to grow and stand forever as a symbol of the market. It was argued that since the *fon* of Ntumbaw had ignored customs and had allowed the tree to be cut down, the market also had been destroyed.[25]

Other members of the Ntumbaw community have given a reason for the conflicts in their town. Some have observed that these conflicts developed because no one was concerned about the religious practice of the town. The *fon* had converted to Islam. Many people became devout Muslims in Ntumbaw, which has an important Mosque in the division. The *Fon* became a Moslem because Ahidjo, the president of Cameroon at that time, was a Moslem. In addition to the *fon's* conversion to Islam, many of the *fais* and other leaders of the town became Christians and claimed that they had given up the practice of indigenous religions. Thus, when they faced many difficulties, even while trying to revive indigenous culture, some people argued that the town of Ntumbaw was paying a price for the neglect of religious customs. The elites of Ntumbaw Town worked hard in the late 1970s and most of the 1980s to restore some of these traditions, which some members of the Ntumbaw community believed their chief and others neglected. During this period of crisis, *tfu* accusations and alleged activities of witches and sorcerers forced a return to the practice of some Wimbum religious values that had been neglected. The crisis is far from over, but this rough sketch of aspects of the Wimbum worldview that is intertwined with religious values helps set the stage for my hermeneutics of *tfu,* discussed in the next chapter.

Chapter 2

Toward a Hermeneutics
of Wimbum *Tfu*

In this chapter I undertake a hermeneutics of *tfu* among Wimbum people in the Northwest Province of Cameroon. I use hermeneutics here in the general sense, the interpretation of a phenomenon. The phenomenon in question is commonly called "witchcraft."[1] I have specifically chosen this as an exercise in hermeneutics for several reasons. First, the material on which my work is based was not gathered through fieldwork. Rather, my work engages my own experiences living in the Wimbum society and conducting pastoral work among the Wimbum people at Wanti Baptist Church in Wat and the Ntumbaw Baptist Church, both in the Donga-Mantung Division of the Northwest Province. Given these experiences and my knowledge of Wimbum culture, I have developed an interest in *tfu*. I grew up in the Wimbum culture, except for when I taught school in the Gongola State of Nigeria, took up pastorates at Baptist churches in Kumba, Southwest Province, and Yaounde, the capital city of Cameroon. My interpretation has been furthered by conversations with elders in the Wimbum society and my interaction with members of the different churches where I served as pastor. Training in the philosophy of religion has familiarized me with the traditions of interpretation that aid my ability to formulate and convey what I have learned about *tfu*.

I consider the subject *tfu* an important concept around which many Wimbum people of the Northwest Province of Cameroon organize their lives. Many aspects of Wimbum life depend on understanding the dynamics of *tfu*.[2] The Wimbum people use three different terms—*bfui, bri,* and *tfu*—to differente among various

17

phenomena that are often lumped together under the term *witch-craft* in much of Western literature. The first of these core ideas, *bfui*, refers to a neutral ability to perform tricks and magical activi-ties. The second, *brii*, refers to the performance of malevolent acts through some alleged power, such as causing rain to fall or bring-ing disruption to a gathering. It also can be used in a more light-hearted way, such as accomplishing with ease something that another previously had trouble with. The last term, *tfu*, depending on the use, can be considered positive or negative and thus disrup-tive of interpersonal relationships within the community. This term is used to refer to various activities that may range from the ability of foresight to causing another's illness or death (Pool 1989, 148, 1994).

I analyze these terms and provide a broader analysis of the way in which Wimbum people use and understand these words incommensurate with the assumptions established by the English term *witchcraft* (Crick 1970, 343).[3] Locating the discussion in a particular cultural sphere such as that of the Wimbum makes it possible to appreciate Malcolm Crick's claim that the use of that term in further studies could amount to "semantic nonsense."[4] In addition to the employment of appropriate terminology, Crick ar-gues that human actions should be evaluated and analyzed as a "system of person categories" (Ibid., 347). Put differently, Crick calls for probing the "moral space" of different cultures and for an in-depth analysis of the concept of "person," because real people interact with others through "evaluatory ideas" and "systems of beliefs" within their communities, which he identifies as "moral space." In my discussion of Wimbum discourses on *bfui*, *brii*, and *tfu*, I argue that these enable moral discussion and critique. I set the stage for a discussion of the Wimbum materials with a brief excursus of the study of African witchcraft.

THE STUDY OF AFRICAN "WITCHCRAFT": MULTIPLE PERSPECTIVES

I continue to treat Evans-Pritchard's work as a landmark publica-tion in social anthropology. The critique of this work, having be-come formulaic for some scholars, is now quite familiar and will not be pursued here. But the critiques of Evans-Pritchard's work focusing on his imposition of epistemological superiority on Azande thought are still relevant to the study of African "witchcraft" be-liefs. I address that in Chapters 3 and 4.[5]

Several general observations can be made about the available literature in Africa. First, most of these studies have focused on one particular area or community, since one cannot pretend to present a uniform view of "witchcraft" for the entire continent.[6] One cannot also say that witchcraft is understood and used as an explanation for misfortune in all places in Africa. Forde F. Jacobsen has recently argued that the Beja of Sudan do not conceptualize witchcraft as a malevolent substance employed to harm other people. He points out: "Although the notion is present among Beja people, however, I have never heard about a concrete episode where people applied a specific incidence to a witch" (Jacobsen 1998, 36, 37). This does not mean that "witchcraft" activity in one part cannot shed light on such activity in a different region of Africa or within the same country. For example, an appropriation of new, non-domestic terms for witchcraft in different parts of Cameroon reflects the impact of urbanization and of an industrial, capitalist economy. In the present discussion, I define the indigenous Wimbum terms as well as the ones the Wimbum people have appropriated from different parts of Cameroon.[7] An exploration of the use of terminology is an important development, not only because of local people's adoption of English terms but because the use of both indigenous terms and non-indigenous terms will facilitate a better understanding of the phenomenon (Geschiere 1997; Wilson 1971, 307–313).

Second, other scholars have written about the phenomenon of witchcraft as part of a broad religious question. In this case, witchcraft and divination are seen as "meaning-making" activities and attempts to come to grips with reality. Robert Pool's study, done in Tabenken, a Wimbum town, Eric de Rosny's work in Douala, Cameroon, and Cameroonian theologian Hegba Nlend's research all bring out this dimension because they integrate religious issues with healing, medicine, and divination in a way that shatters the demarcation of religious questions from the totality of human experience (Rosny 1985; Pool 1994).[8]

A third group that includes recent scholars highlights the sociopolitical dimensions of witchcraft. This is not new, but what is different about the recent writings is that such sociopolitical considerations are situated within the discourse of modernity and will increasingly reflect postmodern thought. Hence, the impact of urbanization, political economy, power, and gender issues sheds new light on the organization and comprehension of the discourse.[9] Finally, the philosophical and theological elements of the discussion have received attention both in Cameroon as well as in a broader context. In Cameroon, the work of Tatah Mbuy, Robert

Tanto, and John Mburu has taken up philosophical as well as theological issues surrounding witchcraft.[10]

My work shares with the above an interest in ethical issues and the development of theological discussion on the subject of witchcraft. Through this work, I encourage philosophical and theological conversation that addresses the negative aspects of *tfu* practice among the Wimbum. The particular contribution of this work is to explore and analyze Wimbum *tfu* practice as it concerns the moral terrain of Wimbum thought. My contention is that negative *tfu* practice raises ethical issues within the Wimbum society. Furthermore, these practices can be analyzed from an ethical perspective, and I attempt such an analysis to open further theological discussion. In this chapter, I explore and analyze Wimbum *tfu* practice to provide a bridge from an ethical critique to a theological discourse on *tfu*. Data on witchcraft among Wimbum and other parts of Cameroon, including monographs on the subject by Wimbum priests and intellectuals, is growing and is sufficient for this kind of analysis that will serve as a clearinghouse for philosophical and theological conversation, addressing the negative aspects of *tfu* among the Wimbum.[11] In addition to these studies, anthropological work in Cameroon ranges from what I classify as colonial anthropology, survey essays by Jeffreys, to the more recent studies by Peter Probst, Briggett Bühler, and Robert Pool.[12] I focus on these studies. The difference between the aformentioned work and my study is that, starting with a hermeneutical approach, I call attention to ethical problems and offer proposals for theological reflection and praxis based on a philosophical critique of intersubjectivity.

In the ongoing negotiation of the varied experiences resulting from the interplay of complex and dynamic relationships, *tfu* discourse is employed to account for what some people consider the violation of interpersonal relations within the moral space where too often *tfu* discourses overshadow other ones. My goal is to articulate such a violation as the participants in the discourse see it. I raise moral issues often implied or directly stated in such discourse and the practice of *tfu* within the moral space and conceptual field of the Wimbum people. What I pursue in this chapter is not fantastic tales of witchcraft per se, nor the drama of hunting down witches and cleansing the community of them, but the specific problems perceived among Wimbum when charges and accusations are made by one person against another. In other words, I am interested, as Crick has put it, in "who is causing another to be ill," and how that "other" perceives it. This particularity for me is spelled out and sustained in the interrogation as intersubjectivity—a concept that Michael Jackson (1989, 1998) has developed.

My experiences draw largely from the towns of Ntumbaw, Njirong, and Ndu, each of which holds professional and personal interest for me. I grew up in Ntumbaw, which is adjacent to Njirong, and I attended bible school for six years at Ndu. I was a minister at the Baptist Church in Ntumbaw. I focus on the Wimbum to locate this project in a "moral space," where I find that through the idiom and logic of witchcraft, interpersonal issues are not only articulated but adjudicated as part of the complex web of interactions that hold wide implications for political, economic, gender, and religious *modus vivendi*. The discourse and alleged practice of "witchcraft" is an attempt to make sense of what it means to be human amid the various challenges that confront Wimbum people.

I begin the discussion by defining witchcraft and clarifying the terminology that Wimbum people use when they talk about these phenomena. Then I analyze the dynamics of witchcraft among Wimbum people. Finally, I conclude the chapter with an excursus on the complexity of *tfu* when it is viewed as part of an African discourse of modernity and postmodernity.

BEYOND DEFINITIONS:
A NEED FOR APPROPRIATE TERMINOLOGY

Despite the misunderstanding that comes from using the English term *witchcraft,* any researcher working among the Wimbum soon realizes that these people also have come to employ English terms such as *witchcraft* and *sorcery,* and they use them quite frequently. However, I analyze local terms employed by the Wimbum to provide a wider background and better understanding of the complexity of the subject matter and to make it possible to carve in bold relief the intersubjective dimensions involved. Miriam Goheen notes that among the Nso, who are neighbors to the Wimbum, the concepts that are related to witchcraft such as *sem* are loaded with ambivalence (Goheen 1993, 147; Geschiere 1997). Simon Bockie, writing about this phenomenon in the Democratic Republic of Congo, uses the term *Kindoki* because the local word captures a wide variety of meanings not included in the English term *witchcraft* (Bockie 1993, 41).

The Wimbum people employ three different terms for the phenomenon which, so far, I have been calling "witchcraft" to refer to an overarching conception of local knowledge, power, and interpretation of misfortune. Since there is much ambiguity, my analyses will highlight what the Wimbum consider both positive and negative appropriations of such knowledge and power. I engage in a phenomenology of Wimbum beliefs that seeks to broaden the scope of the conception of local knowledge and power employed in meaning making and the interpretation of misfortune. The emphasis here will be on the view that aspects of this knowledge and power are judged by the people to be positive and highly useful to society. These three terms are not my own; they are employed regularly by the Wimbum people.[13]

Bfiu

The Wimbum use the term *bfiu*[14] to refer to a special skill that a person has that allows him or her to do extraordinary and spectacular things. For instance, Ntumbaw leaders recall past days when such skill was used as they went down from the escarpment to the Mbaw plains during the annual hunting expedition observed to honor the *fon*. They called this expedition *fo nkfu*. *Fo* refers to setting fire to a large section of the forest so that game will be easy to find. Elders claim that they encountered animals such as lions, or even pythons, which required special skill to overcome. In these circumstances, individuals who possessed *bfiu* were called on to kill the game. It was alleged that such persons could hunt strong animals all alone. Furthermore, some members of the community claimed that such individuals were able to escape miraculously if attacked or endangered. Even if injured, persons possessing *bfui* could make a dramatic recovery without medication. This falls in the realm of what Bockie calls good *ndoki* (Bockie 1993, 43).

One such person in Ntumbaw Town is Simon Nfor, widely recognized for having *bfui*.[15] Nfor is a well respected elder in the Ntumbaw community, holds the modest social position of *Ngwang*, one of the offices in the men's society, *Nfu*. Nevertheless, this position has not impeded him from becoming one of the more important elders of the town. For instance, as one of the advisors of *Nkwi* Ntumbaw,[16] he is one of several people who speaks regularly for the *fon*. When the *fon* receives members of the community, he speaks softly while Nfor repeats what the *fon* has said for all to hear. He does not merely repeat the *fon's* words. Sometimes he can turn things around or, if what the *fon* says is not what the council of elders had agreed upon, it is the role of Nfor to convey the "right" message, even though what the *fon* might have said at that particular moment was slightly different. This is a delicate position to hold and demands much knowledge about the dynamics of the politics and spiritual condition of the town. Nfor is well suited for this job. He also has served the municipal authority. He is not what anthropologists now refer to as "modern elite." Rather, his leadership position is grounded in the realm of local knowledge and practice.[17] He officially tastes the wine that is sold locally, including corn beer; he also inspects meat sold in the slaughterhouse. In tandem with the senior sanitary officer, he inspects pit latrines and attends to other issues of sanitation within the town. For instance, many believe that whenever he is involved with any of the lodges in the closed society *nwarong*, the masks that come out during the period of his involvement can outperform others, even flying and jumping to the top of the roof.[18] All of this has enhanced his reputation, but the one thing for which people most respect him is the common assumption that he has *bfui* and is therefore capable of doing many activities that other people cannot. I know of no one in Ntumbaw who calls Simon Nfor a witch, magician, sorcerer, or any other term associated with what we have come to know in the literature as "witchcraft." The people view him as an especially powerful, gifted person who uses his power for the moral well-being of the community. In the 1970s, the women of his quarter used to sing the following about him: "If I could create another brother, I would create Simon Nfor. He shines like a lamp."

Brii

The second word the Wimbum people employ is *brii*. This refers not only to the special ability itself but also to the people who possess such powers. The singular term is *nrii*. It designates a generally malevolent character as well as the person who possesses that character. This word carries a more negative connotation than does *bfiu*. A *nrii* can use his power to cause bad things to happen in the community, such as ruining a celebration by making it rain. In some cases, it is alleged that people who have these powers can incarnate themselves into hyenas and frighten or harm people. The word "*nrii*" is sometimes also used in a lighthearted, joking manner among friends. In this case, they can call someone *nrii* and it would be similar to what people in the West mean when they say that someone is a "computer wiz." However I also must point out that, depending on the context, *brii* in the plural can be used negatively to include not only most of what is called witchcraft or sorcery but also flagrant violations of moral expectations.

Perhaps one way of illustrating this ambiguity is to recall Phyllis Kaberry's discussion of "Witchcraft of the Sun" (Kaberry 1971, 177–197). Writing about the Nso of the Northwest Province of Cameroon, Kaberry discusses the employment of the Nso term *virim*, close in meaning to the Wimbum term *brii*, to describe what the Nso people would consider a serious violation of social mores. In this case, the violation for which the Nso employed the expression "*Virim ve shuivi*" was incest. *Virim* in this context or the Wimbum word *brii* has nothing to do with what we associate with "witchcraft" powers but refers to moral infringements. The expression "*Virim ve shuivi*," which Kaberry translated literally as "witchcraft of the sun," is employed to convey the heinousness of incestuous relations. The implication then is that sexual intercourse with one's relative is akin to practicing in broad daylight "witchcraft," which supposedly is practiced under cover. Both result in harm to other human beings.

Tfu

The third term the Wimbum people use is *tfu*. This is perhaps the most comprehensive term in *Limbum*, the language of the Wimbum people, and it is similar to the English term *witchcraft*. I qualify their relationships because, as will become evident in our discussion, one cannot say that *tfu* is always negative. Some aspects of *tfu* are viewed quite negatively because its practice violates what the Wimbum people perceive as moral. The term *tfu* alone also is used for "night" or "darkness." At nightfall, the Wimbum say *tfu a se*, meaning "night has come." The *Limbum* word for darkness is *tfunji*. One can associate this meaning with the activity of "witchcraft" and claim that *tfu* refers generally to activities carried on at night. The *Limbum* word for black is *se* which also is the same word used for darkness and secrecy. It is reasonable therefore to infer that *tfu* was named such because the Wimbum believed that those harmful activities were carried out at night. Eric de Rosny's work (1981) can be seen as a general description of the experience. The healers with whom he worked did most of their business at night. My discussion of *tfu* will continue to be ambiguous because, among the Wimbum, not all aspects of it are viewed negatively. However, certain aspects of *tfu* do constitute what Wimbum people perceive as harmful to one's individuality and disruptive of intersubjective and community relations. These aspects, I argue,

constitute a violation of Otherness in the sense in which Levinas
has argued. I highlight these other aspects of *tfu* that cause people
to seek an appropriate remedy by using protective medicine or by
persuading the community to discipline the ones alleged to have
used *tfu* powers.

GENERAL CHARACTERISTICS OF *TFU*

It is difficult to come up with one neat sentence that describes
Wimbum *tfu*. Pool, commenting on his interaction with his informants, writes, "Witchcraft is an evil force used for the senseless
destruction of life: jealous brothers strike a man down out of sheer
spite because he has inherited a beautiful wife and his own envious
first wife may attempt to do the same" (Pool 1994, 144). This
identifies from the first *tfu* as an evil force. Pool indicates appropriately that it is difficult to identify the *Limbum* word *tfu* as a
direct translation of the English word witchcraft. John Mburu,
himself a Wimbum, does not define it but describes the person who
is called a witch as one who has "witch-knowledge" (Mburu 1979,
2). This knowledge, according to Mburu, is the ability to interpret
natural phenomena for good or for bad. Peter Probst and Brigitte
Bühler indicate that, "The Wimbum conceptualize *tfu* as a hidden,
non-hereditary, and non-purchasable force both men and women
are born with. So the situation is: either one has *tfu* from the start
or never will" (Probst and Bühler 1990, 449). Mbunwe-Samba (1989)
offers hardly any specific definition of *tfu* in his testimony. Rather,
he describes different activities that people who are engaged in *tfu*
are alleged to carry out: the taking of victims in order to kill them
and consume their flesh, the attendance of meetings at night, or
the carrying out of *tfu* activities at certain places reserved for these
tfu practices.

Although difficult to define, it seems that a central feature in
understanding *tfu* is the idea of secret knowledge. Furthermore, *tfu*
involves "effective knowledge," because it is not only the possession
of knowledge but also the ability to employ that knowledge for
specific purposes. If one were to make broad generalizations, I would
say that, from the way Wimbum people speak of *tfu*, it is an effective secret knowledge that can be intentionally deployed for the
benefit of the practitioner, possibly at the expense of the victim.[19]
Both men and women can have this knowledge. It is non-hereditary,
and for that reason, we can avoid Evan-Pritchard's conclusions
that it seems logical that all people in a given community are

witches. I underscore the idea that among the Wimbum, *tfu* is considered a form of knowledge *and* ability. Although the Wimbum also talk of *nwe rbuv* (*rbuv* meaning the stomach), there is no indication that they consider *tfu* a substance located in the stomach that can be operated on and removed. If that were the case, we could simply argue that biological medicine should take a new turn in surgical practice and amputate the *tfu*. This is hardly the case. In some contexts, *nwe rbuv* may bear some resemblance to the Azande conception of *mangu*. The Azande believe that *mangu* is found in the stomach. That is the reason they conduct a postmortem examination when someone dies.[20]

Some general observations are in order. First, as I have already indicated, the term has some features of the English word witchcraft. Yet such an association does not imply correspondence. For instance, in writing about European witchcraft, Keith Thomas describes it as an innate, involuntary quality. Thomas maintains that European witchcraft also can be a personal trait. Among the Wimbum, *tfu* is not perceived as a personal trait or physiological peculiarity discoverable in an autopsy (Thomas 1971, 463).[21] Second, the working definition I have proposed requires that I clarify the distinction made by Probst and Bühler that *tfu* is "non-purchasable." If by non-purchasable they mean that a person who does not have *tfu* cannot attempt to acquire it, then that is a reasonable claim to make since it takes someone who has the ability to "see" in the *tfu* way to know what he or she wants to purchase. The person who has *tfu* is called *nwe tfu*, while the person who does not have it is called *nwe jaja*. Among the Wimbum, however, there is a clear understanding that a *nwe jaja* could be turned into a *nwe tfu*. Mbunwe-Samba refers to the phenomenon the Wimbum people call the "opening of eyes" (Mbunwe-Samba 1989, 10). This refers to the belief that one who possesses *tfu* can secretly give human flesh to another person to enable that person to possess *tfu*.

The idea here is that when a person has received and consumed human flesh, it will then open his or her eyes and from then on he or she will have *tfu* and all of its powers. Mbunwe-Samba's examples are taken from Binshua where, at one point, even the Catholic Catechist was accused of opening the eyes of certain children. I witnessed a similar discourse in the 1960s when I attended the local primary school at Ntumbaw, which was then a Baptist school. There were all kinds of rumors spreading that during the lunch recess some children were actually selling human flesh in what, to an innocent observer, looked like just a normal exchange of a child's lunch. What the Wimbum people believe is that a *nwe tfu* is capable of giving human flesh to someone by disguising it as regular meat or anything that can be consumed.

In Ntumbaw, a certain Shey Riba was accused of giving human flesh to younger children. The children who allegedly had received the human flesh, *Nya nwe*, made these accusations.[22] In response to the children's complaints, the elders of the town conducted a ritual of cleansing that was supposed to "close their eyes," that is, eliminate their potential ability to participate in *tfu* activities. The ritual to "close their eyes" was undertaken after these victims paid Shey Riba for the human flesh they had consumed. They paid back their debt with a fowl, because by receiving disguised human flesh, they were then indebted to the one who gave them the flesh. Since people believe that the person who gave them the flesh must have killed his or her relative, it was then expected that they pay back this person by killing their own relative and giving him or her the flesh to eat. The cleansing ritual consists of hitting the person accused of selling human flesh with the fowl. Though when not sanctioned by the elders of the town, it is believed that any kind of payment other than human flesh will not work. Similarly, Pool's informants insisted, "You've eaten a man, . . . so you can only pay with another man. They will say: you have eaten my brother, now you have to pay with a man" (Pool 1994, 151).[23] As I have already indicated, if the elders of the town are aware, they can act to cleanse the victims. In this case, they will rule that a fowl should be used to repay the debt. If the dispute remains a private transaction between two individuals, the party that allegedly sold human flesh is going to insist on getting human flesh in return. I now analyze the characteristics of *tfu* that the Wimbum people recognize. These can be roughly grouped into *tfu yibi, tfu yebu,* and *tfu jarr.*[24]

Tfu Yibi

Tfu yibi refers to the aspects of *tfu* in which some allege that others use *tfu* power to eat human flesh. For many people, this is the most feared feature of *tfu* practice. It is believed that a family member who possesses *tfu* can offer his or her consanguinial family members to other practitioners to kill, and the victim's flesh will be distributed among those who practice *tfu yibi.* Although one who has *tfu* could theoretically kill a family member, it is generally believed that people operate as a group and meet together to consume the flesh of the victims who have been killed by their own

relatives who themselves are members of these groups. The Wimbum
term for a *tfu* gathering is the common word *Ngwa*, which normally refers to a meeting constituted by people to contribute money
for various purposes. When used in association with *tfu*, it refers
to the gathering where *tfu* people consume the flesh of someone
contributed to that group by one of its participants. I return to this
idea later when I deal with more recent terms presently employed
among the Wimbum to depict the changing form of *tfu*. In conclusion, *tfu yibi* can be described as that form of *tfu* in which one
person allegedly offers a family member with whom there are
consanguinial ties to an association where the victim is reportedly
killed via *tfu* powers. The victim's flesh is then to be eaten by
members of an association. Marwick indicates that the Cewa believe that sorcerers

> [attack] the victim while he [sic] is asleep; eating him while
> he is still alive, this being the Cewa interpretation of tropi-
> cal ulcers. . . . The belief that sorcerers are necrophagous
> leads to elaborate precautions being taken whenever some-
> one dies, including keeping his death secret until his corpse,
> the grave site and the graveyard have been decorated;
> holding a vigil at the side of the grave for two or three
> nights after burial; and setting a gourdful of magic to en-
> snare any sorcerers who may come when the gravewatchers
> are not there (Marwick, 1967, 107–108).

The essay from which this quotation is taken reflects the functionalist bias that existed among early interpreters by making
the claim that *tfu* people attack persons at night and eat their
souls *as* a Cewa explanation for stomach ulcers. This interpretation seems to deny that *tfu* people eat other people. While I will
not address here the question of whether or not people actually
eat people, I will point out that people may indeed be talking
about physical harm in other forms, which is caused by *tfu* people
through mysterious powers.[25] What this calls for ultimately is a
broader context for analyzing illness, including the complex role
that social problems play in a conceptualization of illness, which
John Janzen observed has been misunderstood by Western observers (Janzen 1978, 9).[26] Janzen points out that there is a relationship between psychosomatic tension, social stress, and disputes
involving illness. These different stress factors, in some cases,
may be what is involved in *tfu yibi*, which then is interpreted as
the main cause of the illness. When a person dies from such an

illness, some people believe that his or her death was caused by
tfu yibi. There is a subtle distinction to be made here—the death
of an individual can be attributed to *tfu yibi*, yet not all of the
victims of *tfu* are necessarily eaten by practitioners of *tfu*. There
are times when the death of a person is attributed to *tfu* activities, but no one is accused of selling the flesh or distributing it in
any *ngwa tfu*. When this happens, the Wimbum believe that the
person has been killed out of jealousy rather than the desire for
human flesh.[27]

Tfu yibi involves many complex conceptualizations and features in accusations brought against people when someone dies.
Those who accuse others of *tfu yibi* make the explicit claim that
those who practice it kill their victims to eat their flesh. Arens
(1979) pointed out that the literature on the subject is dense. Although he makes the distinction between cannibalism and "witchcraft," because witchcraft involves "supernatural evil doers," his
conclusion that the phenomenon exists only in the minds of the
creators still operates under a certain Western bias (Arens 1979,
150). Arens denied that witches exist. He claimed, rather, that
confessions in some cases were made because of bribes. Furthermore, he argued that anthropologists create cannibals (Ibid., 174).
One can understand Arens's frustrations that led him to this conclusion. "I have been unable to uncover adequate documentation of
cannibalism as a custom in any form for any society. Rumors, sus-
picions, fears and accusations abound, but no satisfactory first hand
account" (Ibid., 21). I do not claim to have any more insights into
the matter than the accounts that are given by other people, but
I think Arens overstated his case in the above statement. The claims
people make about *tfu yibi* must remain puzzling, because those
claims are based on exclusive knowledge not open to all people. I
now turn to a consideration of *tfu yebu,* which lacks the negative
connotations of *tfu yibi*.

Tfu Yebu

The Wimbum people believe that *tfu yebu* is positive. The claim
that people make regarding *tfu yebu* is that some have the ability
to "see" the evil practices of people who are involved in *tfu*, hence
the term *tfu yebu*. *Yebu* is the *Limbum* term that means to "see
things." Thus *tfu yebu* is used for positive purposes. This category
of *tfu* is large. What will be most helpful at this point is to discuss
briefly the different characters involved in this group.

The first group of people who have *tfu yebu* includes leaders, especially the *fons*. Goheen points out that, among the Nso, the *Fon's sem* is believed to be the most powerful (Goheen 1993b, 146). For an ordinary person who does not have this power, it is difficult to know if *fons* actually have this power or not, but there is some expectation that the one who occupies that office has the ability to "see" or at least to employ what Cyprian Fisiy calls "a second pair of eyes" (Fisiy 1994).[28] Although Fisiy addresses a broader set of circumstances, he demonstrates that both in the local and broader contexts what is involved in sorcery discourse is the acquisition of knowledge. This is knowledge used in a purposeful way, which means that the "sorcery idiom of acquiring a 'second pair of eyes' . . . permits the actors to see the invisible—to acquire new knowledge"(Fisiy 1994, 5). Among the Wimbum, it is expected that the one who is made *fon* should have this "second pair of eyes." Because the *fon*, or the *nkfu*, is responsible for the spiritual as well as the material well-being of the community, he needs to be able to "see things." Fisiy rightly argues that it would be wrong to imply a rigid reading of a binary opposition of the invisible and visible world here. This is a claim that, in spite of the ordinary nature of everyday complications, it would be wrong to "conjure images of banality and repetitiveness, as if these people were mere passive actors trapped in a structural cultural logic which is beyond their control" (Fisiy 1994, 5). When a person is installed *fon* among the Wimbum, although he has eyes just as anyone else, he is expected to have the powers that will enable him to see what other people cannot ordinarily see.

The investiture rituals will empower the new *fon* to be able to do things he could not ordinarily have done. Therefore, the Wimbum view the installations as events having cosmic implications. At the installation of the *fon,* all of the town's powers are supposed to be given to the new ruler, who in turn will take an oath to protect the people and will not use his newly acquired powers against them. If the new *fon* does not receive all of the powers expected, many people suspect that something must be wrong. For example, if other members of the royal family are competing for the position, it is possible that they could employ a more powerful *tfu* to make it difficult for the new *fon* to acquire the powers he needs. If this happens, the elders of the town will attempt to resolve the tension peacefully so that the person designated will succeed in his new position, acquiring the necessary powers.

The idea of a "second pair of eyes" brings up what the Wimbum call *mmir nkfu*, meaning "the eyes of the *fon*." This can be interpreted in two ways. First, used metaphorically, it means to possess the ability to see things or to be privy to things that may be out of the domain of an ordinary person. Second, *mmir nkfu* also is used to refer to a host of people who, because of their different abilities, have access to the *fon*. The insights offered to these people through the use of their special sight are reported to the *fon*. In the second case, *mmir nkfu* refers to the elders in the community who are responsible for the community's spiritual well-being. What is important to note here is that whether it is the *fon* who sees directly or someone else who sees for him, the *fon* is obligated to take actions to help the community deal with what is perceived as a danger.

The *fon* can do this by calling on the diviner, a medicine person, or *nwe nshep,* or through the employment of institutions that can take preventive actions. Such institutions include *nsingong* and *nwarong* associations. The towns of Ntumbaw and Njirong share one *nsingong*. It is such a powerful society that only a select few are known to be members. At the time I lived in Ntumbaw, I knew only one person who was a member of the *nsingong*. No one knew much about the society. Its activities were kept in strict confidence, perhaps even more strict than the powerful *nwarong* society. It was the duty of the *nsingong* society to go around the two towns to place protective medicines at all of the important entryways into the towns. The purpose was to protect the towns from evil influence. When that was done, it was believed that no evil influence could enter the town from outside. It also was believed that if people had gone out to practice *tfu* and the *nsingong* placed protective medicines at all of the key points, then they would be prevented from returning to the town. They could possibly die "outside," meaning die where they had gone to engage in occult practices.

An important question must be raised here: If the *fon* has *tfu yebu* so that he can see the "evil" others are practicing, could he then be called *nwe tfu*—that is, a sorcerer? As far as I know, Wimbum people maintain this ambiguity about the *fon* and his abilities to "see." What the *fon* has is considered neither bad nor morally wrong. Rather, it is thought of as a virtue if the *fon* has *tfu yebu*. To have the power and to use it in a harmful manner are distinct. If the *fon* practices *tfu yibi*, which involves cannibalism, then charges can be brought against that *fon* as they would be brought against any person. Indeed, this has happened in one Wimbum town. The people decided to depose one of their *fons*. One of the charges brought against him was that he was responsible for the deaths of many of the princes and princesses. Several sessions were held at the palace during which the *fon* confessed to all of the alleged activities. This confession was unusual because from the accounts of several people who took part in these meetings, the *fon* admitted freely that he had done the things he was accused of. The pattern of confession here seems to fit positions on confession elucidated by Max Marwick, where an individual confessed after an accusation (Marwick 1970, 17). However, it is important to indicate that there are times when this can be voluntary, as Wylie has demonstrated in his discussion on introspective aspects of "witchcraft" among the Effutu of Southern Ghana (Wylie 1970, 132ff).[29]

These confessions did not end the dispute. The people of the town decided to depose him. The local district administration intervened, arguing that it was unlawful for the people to depose the *fon*. A legal and administrative battle ensued, which was centered on the question, "Do the people have the right to depose the *fon*?" Implied in this question was another, "Who legitimately installs the *fon*?" The people argued that using *tfu* negatively was a crime for someone in such a high office, and that they had the right to depose the *fon*. Among the Wimbum, every town has its own *fon* makers who are responsible for selecting from among competing candidates when a *fon* dies and reporting this decision to the Clan Head. The Clan Head then joins the *fon* makers of the town to install the new *fon*. When the new *fon* has been installed, he is presented by the elders of the town to the Divisional Administration. British Colonial officers practiced indirect rule in this region of Cameroon. They respected the local *fons* and were not responsible for installing them. It is not clear at what point the practice of presenting newly installed *fons* to the Divisional Administration started, but it has become a regular practice. Thus, the people were right in arguing that it was their prerogative to install and depose *fons*. The administration was not willing, however, to accept their accusations of *tfu* against the *fon*, because members of the administration argued that, in this particular case, such accusations could not be demonstrated in a court of law. This incident illustrates that a *fon*, or for that matter, other members of the royal class, can be accused and punished for *tfu* practice. Their status and power do not shield them from the moral demands of the Wimbum people.

The *nwe mshep* also is believed to have this special power. *Nwe mshep* is sometimes erroneously called in the literature "witch doctor"—a term I believe to be mistaken. This person is not to be confused with *nwe seng*, who is a diviner. Rather, *nwe mshep* is someone who practices crafts such as taking away illnesses, which people believe *tfu* practitioners have maliciously planted in certain parts of the body or in an entire compound. *Nwe seng* is the person one consults to find out what is wrong. *Nwe mshep* also is different from a healer who uses local herbs.

An important distinction I make here is between the aforementioned types and the recent phenomenon of "traditional" doctor and "native" doctor that became popular during the 1970s. These doctors directed their activities toward a commercial enterprise unprecedented in Cameroon's history. While in the past healers were believed to practice their craft as a family tradition and accepted only very modest gifts, the recent trend of "traditional" doctors was more of a money-making activity. Given this implicit commercialism, they formed a national organization of "Traditional Doctors." Part of their practice involved the use of herbs, but they also employed chants and used religious books. Hence, Peter Probst points out, items such as "The Seven Books of Moses," believed to have magical powers, are quite common. The idea of "The Seven Books of Moses" indicates how Christianity is employed in this web of healing. They also imitated Western medical practices by bottling and labeling much of the medication they prescribed, setting up pharmacies, and advertising in newspapers and on billboards.

A large part of their practice is aimed at the so-called modern elite. Their area of practice covered many things, from medication for illness to protective charms that would protect their patients from harm. Within the bureaucratic framework of the modern state of Cameroon, some traditional doctors also claimed that they could give their clients medicines that would help them succeed in their occupations.[30] Janzen has pointed out that, in the Democratic Republic of the Congo, the practice of healers called *nganga* went through several stages. Initially, colonialists and missionaries opposed it. Gradually, however, an ambivalent relationship evolved through which some healers were recognized and allowed to practice. In time, some of these healers were used by politicians and administrators (Janzen 1978, 53).

A third group with this power of insight is a diviner known among the Wimbum as *nwe seng*. This function is carried out devoid of any of the publicity surrounding the *guérisseur traditionnel* (Fisiy and Gesehiere 1990, 146; Geschiere 1997). Among the Wimbum, the reputation of a *nwe seng* depends on the success of his or her predictions. The role of the *nwe seng*[31] is to help people determine the cause of their problems. If an illness cannot be treated either with medications from a healer or through biological medications, then a *nwe seng* is consulted. When people go to a *nwe seng*, the understanding is that they are entitled to other opinions.

If the relatives of the patient who have consulted one *nwe seng* are not satisfied, they will visit another. In some cases, if the *nwe seng* accuses someone of being the one who has made another person sick, the accused may prefer that he or she consult a different *nwe seng*.

Among the Wimbum, a *nwe seng* uses different objects to determine what is causing a patient's problem. Sometimes the objects for use may be as simple as the peelings from a kola nut, called *njooh*. Often these objects can range from sticks to pens and pencils to pieces of cloth. When people consult a *nwe seng*, they tell him or her what is wrong, the *nwe seng* then throws the objects on the ground, examines their position, and then diagnoses the patient's situation. At other times, the process is similar to consulting a psychologist who listens to information from the client, interprets what he or she has heard, and then suggests solutions to the problem. On occasion, the client gives the *nwe seng* few clues other than that someone has died, so the *nwe seng* has to figure out what is at issue.

In Ntumbaw, the foremost *nwe seng* by reputation was Tonga, from the town of Nsam. Simon Nfor from Ntumbaw remembers going to Nsam to consult with Tonga about *tfu* accusations involving members of the Warr family of Ntumbaw; however, because these cases were resolved amicably, Nfor did not want to give specific details. In most cases, he said that those who were accused were guilty and confessed to practicing *tfu*. The *nwe seng* usually tells the people who have come for consultation his interpretation of their problem. Sometimes the *nwe seng* tells them that the problem has arisen due to family members ignoring the performance of sacrifices to their ancestors, who are crying because they have been neglected. In that case, the clients are advised to go home to organize a celebration or in some cases to perform a special offering known in Wimbum as *tangsi*.

Philip Peek has argued appropriately that divination is not merely an aspect of a culture but a "means of knowing"; an institutional mechanism for stating the epistemology of the people (Peek 1991, 2). Although the practice of divination may involve the ideas of a sacred world, Peek observes that what is crucial is the practice of divination as the accessing of a dynamic system of knowledge, which is used by the people in ordering their world. I must restate that the claimed ability to see or know what or who is causing a problem implies that the *nwe seng* must share such a power with those who practice *tfu*. The *nwe seng*, however, uses this power for revelation and diagnosis of illnesses only, therefore the practice of *nwe seng* is seen as a community asset. Peek is therefore correct when he asserts that diviners are people of "exceptional wisdom and high personal character" (Ibid., 3).

The fourth group of people believed to have *tfu yebu* consists of healers. Many live in the Wimbum area. Sometimes their trade and practice is passed down along family lines. They are different from the new "traditional doctors" who now carry membership cards and all of the paraphernalia that makes them attractive to the urban class. Healers also claim to do the type of diagnosis that *nga seng* do, but usually the healer's task is solely to heal. Two examples from Ntumbaw will illustrate this distinction. The first is the healer Njong, who had the reputation for treating fractures. Sometimes he used medication, sometimes he did not.[32] I do not remember seeing Njong advertise anywhere, yet he was known in the entire district as *nwe nkup*, one who treats fractures. My second example, Pa Yeri Longka, was well known as a healer. Pa Yeri lived in Ntumbaw, but he was actually a member of the royal family of a neighboring town in the Bui Division. He came to live in Ntumbaw because his mother was from there. Pa Yeri was considered a healer par excellence, and he might be described as a general practitioner.[33] He, like many others, may have possessed some *tfu*, but that was *tfu yebu*, which the Wimbum consider positive.

Tfu Jarr

For lack of better terminology, I use the *Limbum* expression *tfu jarr* to refer to a category of *tfu* practice. In this context, *jarr* refers to destruction and discomfort. I offer three examples. First, *tfu jarr* destroys property. This kind of *tfu* is not practiced to kill a victim but to destroy property out of jealousy. Those who practice *tfu jarr* can do so individually or as a group. Practicing *tfu jarr* as a group is different from the practice of going to *njicang*, a name that the Wimbum use to refer to the *tfu* market. It involves the idea that when people reportedly make the occult pilgrimage to the market, they do so with the hope that they will bring back unnamed things that may help them get rich or acquire good luck and success. Fisiy reports that, in the past, one of the roles of the *fon* was to lead parties from his realm into *tfu* markets to bring back goods (Fisiy 1991, 15). Although these trips into the *tfu* market are not specifically considered destructive, they can be because it is sometimes believed that rather than bringing wealth, participants can bring back bad luck, which will destroy other people's property. The one distinction I should underscore here is that those who practice *tfu jarr* do so for the express purpose of destroying someone else's property, not necessarily because they missed out on taking good luck from *tfu* markets. Victims of *tfu jarr* may immediately become aware of their predicament, but sometimes they do not know until the person who did it confesses. Most of these confessions tend to be on a deathbed. The reason usually given for such a confession is that the person wants to have a clear conscience so that he or she can die in peace.[34]

Second, *tfu jarr* can be used to inflict illness on other people but not cause their death. In 1984, a prominent civil servant from the Wimbum area became ill and did not get well following medical treatment. He was flown to Europe, but his family suspected that something more than biological illness was the problem.[35] After divination, the head of the family, *Fai*, was accused of *tfu*. He confessed that he had caused the illness because he had asked this man to buy him a car and he had not done so. To observers this was disturbing because the individual had not refused to provide a car. He had only said that he did not have enough money at the time. Others believed that the request itself was out of order. The *Fai* could have asked this relative to provide money for the education of his children. What made it morally problematic to most people was the fact that, even if he had been given a car, it could hardly have been used for two years before being rendered worthless for lack of some part that could not be easily procured. At best, then, the car would end up being parked for birds to build nests in, or for younger children to play hide and seek in. The *Fai*, however, was not concerned about other problems that may have developed from owning and running a car; he wanted a car for the prestige. When he did not get it, he later admitted that he practiced *tfu jarr*, making his victim ill. Because those who claim to practice *tfu* do not always use charms or medicines, in a case such as this, only practitioners can explain exactly in what manner such knowledge works. When the person accused of carrying out the activity confesses, details usually are not given.

Third, *tfu jarr* can be used to cause another person to have nightmares, a practice the Wimbum call *nyo nwe* (Mbunwe-Samba 1989, 15). It is claimed that some people have the ability to plague their victims while sleeping. They do not actually cause severe pain or serious illness but make the victims have nightmares. Since in most cases the connection is money or a certain debt, the perpetrator usually is trying to get the attention of the victim to fulfill his or her obligations. A more severe type of *tfu jarr* consists of claims that people are able to direct lightening strikes toward an individual or his or her property. It is believed that this takes place in stages. Usually a warning is sent, which only does light damage; in that case, the person is being asked to put his or her house in order and to take care of all debts. An angry husband will use it when he believes that someone has been having an affair with his wife. Such a warning serves to inform the offender to stop. If the offender does not, then lightening strikes can cause severe damage, or even the death of the victim.

In my attempt to explain the idiom *tfu,* I have provided examples to distinguish *tfu* from the English term *witchcraft,* and to portray the ambiguity involved in this discourse. I also have focused on the moral dimensions of the discourse and examined what people perceive to be violations of intersubjective relations within the space of the community. In the following sections, I proceed to demonstrate that *tfu* is a dynamic discourse. This dynamism among the Wimbum can be illustrated by the fact that the Wimbum have appropriated new idioms from different parts of Cameroon in order to explain intersubjectivity in a constantly changing social environment. The bulk of the literature on Cameroonian "witchcraft" involves such terms, which previously were non-Wimbum words. Among the Wimbum, the non-domestic terms that have become popular are *nyongo* and *kupe,* which I now discuss briefly.

DYNAMICS OF *TFU*: APPROPRIATION AND INNOVATIONS AMONG THE WIMBUM

The Wimbum have recently employed the terms *nyongo* and *kupe* to speak about *tfu.* Pool's informants made the distinction between what they called *tfu,* family or local "witchcraft," and *nyongo* and *kupe,* which were considered "national witchcraft" (Pool 1994, 153). This suggests more than a simple creation of a distinction between local and national witchcraft but reflects the dynamism of *tfu* discourse and conceptualization among the Wimbum. Terms are no longer simply a depiction of what takes place in urban areas outside of Wimbum. The term *kupe* is actually the name of a mountain in the Kumba area in the Southwest Province of Cameroon. Originally the Bakweris (one of the peoples who inhabit the coastal areas of Cameroon) alleged that it was at this mountain that members of the *nyongo* society met to kill people. It also was alleged that members of *nyongo* used "witchcraft" to enslave their victims, thus making them work for the *nyongo* members on this mountain (Ardener 1970, 147). Edwin Ardener and Dickson Eyoh both trace the etymology of *nyongo* to the Douala people, who also live on the coast. *Nyongo* is derived from the Douala term *nyungu*, or "rainbow," used to refer to prosperous people "who have captured the magical python, which manifests itself in the rainbow" (Ardener 1970, 148; Eyoh 1998, 341).[36] Elsewhere, Luc De Heusch, in his groundbreaking work *The Drunken King or the Origin of the State,* demonstrates that the rainbow is a well-known Bantu mytheme which, among the Luba, provides a perspective on kingship as well as cosmology (De Heusch 1982). I argue in this section that the Wimbum people have appropriated and domesticated *nyongo* and *kupe* for their own *tfu* vocabulary.[37] This appropriation offers certain interpretations of the phenomenon of *tfu*.

First, *tfu* is seen as a means to riches. At the heart of the appropriation of *nyongo* and *kupe* is the belief that *tfu* is used to acquire wealth. People suspect that *nyongo* or *kupe* is involved when an individual becomes rich over a short period of time. People start suspecting that something out of the ordinary has happened. These fears usually are strengthened if someone dies in the family of the newly wealthy person, which fuels the speculation that the dead person has been offered to members of a *nyongo* or *kupe* group by the relative who has just become wealthy. If no one dies during the period of rapid accumulation, the suspicion develops that someone will in the future. When a well-known entrepreneur of Ndu died after a car accident on the Bamenda road, there were widespread rumors that he had been asked to pay for his wealth by the *nyongo* society but that he refused to sacrifice a close relative. For that reason, the members of *nyongo* took his life instead. Others claimed that it was his wife who had "given" him to the *nyongo* society so that she would inherit his wealth.

Second, *tfu* in this new form has become a highly transgressive enterprise. *Kupe* and *nyongo* make *tfu* a means of acquisition that defies the customary boundaries of *tfu*. It was once and is still largely believed that *tfu* takes place along consanguinial lines, thus it can be argued that if there is no blood relationship, personal *tfu* has no power over strangers. However, the expansion of *tfu*, now understood also as *nyongo* and *kupe*, can equally involve the gift of a relative or a non-relative in order to acquire wealth. All that is needed by practitioners is the establishment of some link between himself or herself and the victim. Thus it is widely believed that practitioners do this by presenting gifts of money to the intended victim or dropping money for innocent victims to pick up. Anyone who picked up money dropped by a *nyongo* practitioner could become a victim. Toward the latter part of the 1970s, I heard much discussion of this conceptualization of *tfu*. Fear and panic ensued in many Wimbum towns as word spread that warned children in particular not to pick up anything they found.

Probst reported other evidence of this conceptualization of *tfu* in his discussion of a serious traffic accident that happened at Sirngwa in the town of Ndu, in which several schoolchildren were killed (Probst 1992, 151). Rumors spread immediately that the headmaster, who was a prominent member of the community, had given the children to the head of a *nyongo* to pay the debts that he owed to that society for his riches. In the ensuing dispute, *ngambe* (*nga seng*, plural form of *nwe seng*) people, brought in from out of town, claimed that they had uncovered a pot containing all kinds of objects, including evidence that the headmaster of the school had given the schoolchildren to *kupe*. The anger of the people was so fierce that the divisional officer had to step in to protect the head-master. School was closed for awhile, and the conflict was resolved only with the transfer of the headmaster to the divisional head-quarters. This incident illustrates the belief that these new forms of *tfu* are transgressive because victims do not have to be members of one's family.

Third, this new use of the term implicates elites in the practice of *tfu*. Both Probst and Fisiy indicate correctly, I believe, that at the heart of the suspicion of *nyongo* and *kupe* are the elite and prominent members of society. To that extent, the understanding that these new forms of *tfu* are national ones, as Pool's informants claimed, makes sense, because some people assume that only those who have experienced urban life and its modern wealth practice it. Since members of the elite and urban dwellers have inserted themselves into the exploitative set of capitalist relations by pursuing an extravagant lifestyle, this new *tfu* fuels the suspicion that these urban elites will do anything to become wealthy. Fisiy notes that, in the Bui Division, it is suspected that the *fons*, while not tacitly endorsing these practices, at the same time appear to give their blessing by receiving gifts from people who have become wealthy through what others consider suspicious means. Furthermore, by bestowing titles on these people, the *fons* seem to be legitimizing the new forms of acquisition, as long as it is something that has been accomplished outside of the realm (Fisiy 1991, 17). I agree with Fisiy that a certain ambivalence toward wealth acquisition is at work here and appears to function as long as nothing goes wrong within the community that could be linked to these new forms of wealth. If this state persists, then many people may continue to regard members of their communities who have acquired this wealth as heroes.

Fourth, these new terms have tainted some wealth-making institutions. *Tfu* as *nyongo* and *kupe* has given rise to negative interpretations of customary institutions when it is believed that members of new associations kill relatives to acquire wealth. People believe that *nyongo* and *kupe* activities take place in a range of structured *njangis* or *famla* associations. These are voluntary associations, originally created to respond to socioeconomic changes. People now, however, suspect these associations of carrying on negative *tfu* practices. Kenneth Little, in his study of these associations in West Africa, suggested that industrialization and migration were largely responsible for the establishment of these associations (Little 1965). He focused on particular associations such as different ethnic ones comprised of members from a particular region who located in an urban area. Another kind of association is a syncretistic cult, where members come together to protect each other in an urban setting (Ibid., 36). Little called a third association "mutual aid" societies, where members contribute money for different purposes, ranging from illness and funerals to initial capital for business ventures (Ibid., 48).

While urbanization in Cameroon has led to the formation of many associations or societies, it is important to acknowledge the existence of mutual aid societies before urbanization. The Wimbum call these associations *ngwa*. *Ngwa*, or *njangi,* as it is known in pidgin English, is an old association that brought people together to pool resources so that each member could lay his or her hands on a large supply of wealth at one time. In Wimbum, there are two forms of *ngwa*. One is the weekly savings *ngwa*, which meets on holidays. In Ntumbaw, these days, which were wrongly called "Native Sunday" by Christians, are *Seng* and *Ndvung*. They were selected because they are the days on which the *Fon* died. Today, however, most *ngwas* tend to meet on Sunday afternoons. The weekly savings *ngwa* tend to be organized in different neighborhoods. Occasionally one draws people from all over the town, such as the one started in the early 1970s in the small neighborhood of Ntumbaw, called Sansi. Most of its many members were young people. It was more than a *ngwa*, however—it was a place for romance, for copying the latest fashion trends, and for keeping up with the vocabulary that was in vogue.

The second type of *ngwa* among the Wimbum is *ngwa nwee*, so called because it meets once every month. *Ngwa nwees* tend to be organized along professional lines. For example, it is quite common for businesspeople or schoolteachers to have one. *Ngwa nwees* can have two kinds of financial transactions, the more important being the contribution, which each member makes to the one who has been designated to receive the money. This recipient provides the food and drinks for the gathering that month, and if the members do not have a fixed meeting place, then the meeting takes place at this person's house.[38] The other financial transaction in a *ngwa nwee* is a regular savings account, from which members can take out small-interest loans. At the end of the cycle, when every member has received the contribution, the savings account is divided according to what each member saved, with the interest shared proportionately.

These means of acquiring wealth or accumulating capital are being threatened by the new forms of accumulation associated with *nyongo* and *kupe*. Again, practitioners of these new forms are alleged to sacrifice members of their own families to make themselves wealthy. Ardener has demonstrated how, in changing economic circumstances, the Bakweri of Southwestern Cameroon went all the way to Manfe to bring members of a powerful society to get rid of these new forms of accumulating wealth. Although Fisiy and Geschiere have indicated that this accumulation of wealth, with its implications for the valuation of people and things, seems to have been condoned to a certain extent by some of the Northwest *fon*s, it is clear that the idea of sacrificing a relative in order to obtain wealth is something not taken lightly among the Wimbum.

TFU ANALYZED IN POSTMODERN TERMS

Comaroff and Comaroff (1993, xxiv) have set "witchcraft" discourse within the larger discourse of ritual identified as a reflection of malcontent. In this section, I discuss how *tfu* also could be interpreted from a postmodern perspective. By postmodern, I mean simply calling into question practices of modernity, and in Cameroon, cultural practices that operate within a given logic such as *tfu*. Within this context, *tfu* among the Wimbum can be understood by probing the meanings behind accusations and *tfu* cleansing sessions. If we are able to view these as part of a complex relationship, we can examine the moral issues implied in the negative aspects of *tfu*.

First, *tfu* is power discourse. This is a complex issue, and I can only indicate briefly how postmodern thought allows for a critique of *tfu* as power discourse. I must distinguish the way I am looking at the issues of power involved in *tfu* from the way others have interpreted "witchcraft" and power in other parts of Africa. The classic functionalist view on witchcraft and power portrayed witch-craft" accusations as a way of regulating growth and leadership in a community (Marwick 1963). Eva Gilles has noted that:

> Witchcraft belief is no longer seen as a simple social and moral regulator in an immobile society, but as a political dynamic, mobilized for the cycle changes periodically un-dergone by the system. When a small village reached, by natural population increase, a certain critical size (beyond the numbers its frail authority structure could encompass), mutual "witchcraft" accusations began to be flung about by rivals for dominance within it. When the accusations and counter-accusations had thoroughly poisoned the atmo-sphere, a point of fission would be reached: a part of the village would hive off some distance away, under the lead-ership of one of the rival claimants; and the remainder would settle down in a climate lightened (for the time be-ing) of suspicion (Gilles 1976, xxiv).

This functionalist formulation of the question needs to be supple-mented with the emphasis that *tfu* deals with the acquisition of secret personal power that individuals use for personal gain. It is power that gives those who have it advantage over others. Some people believe that the members of the community who possess *tfu* use it to enhance their power in many ways, both economic and political. While this view does not assume the results of function-alist readings, which seem to limit the application of *tfu* to the creation of separate but stable political groups, it is clear that *tfu* can be used to both interpret and act in local political issues. This includes the possibility of *tfu* being used for personal ambition (Turner 1957, 99, 218). In Ntumbaw, people believed that personal ambition was at the heart of a prolonged chieftaincy dispute, be-cause the *fon* was reportedly an ambitious, powerful *nwe tfu* who could neutralize the *tfu* powers of members of his family who had similar ambitions. It is believed that many members of the *fon*'s family employed *tfu* to promote their ambitions to become the new *Fon*. In a recent conversation with Augustine Safe and Abel Bongmba, *Fai* Kuh, head of *Kibais*, hence the de facto leader of the town outside of the *fon*'s family, claims that several people brought *tfu* into the dispute and died as a result.[39]

The postmodern question in the postcolonial society is why must some members of the community desire and need such pow-ers? The postcolonial state has imposed a different kind of economy

among the Wimbum and in most of the Northwest Province of
Cameroon. Perhaps a much more radical approach here would be
to call into question the need for such powers even among the
fons, who claim that these powers have been acceptable. Do they
still need to legitimize their office with such powers? Are there
ways of attaining political goals without resorting to such powers?
A critique of individuality and power arrangements among the
Wimbum today suggests that these powers tend to be excessive.
These are precisely the questions that *tfu* discourse enables people
to contemplate.

Second, *tfu* is gender discourse. Andrew Apter, Mark Auslander,
and Pamela Schmoll address gender issues involved in witchcraft
among the Yoruba, Ngoni, and Hausas of Niger (Apter 1993a).[40]
Apter's essay clearly indicates that Yoruba women were subjected
to harsh treatment because they were women. They were accused
and humiliated, their religious objects and shrines destroyed. Apter
argues that the women were singled out because they had taken
prominent and powerful roles in the cocoa trade (Apter 1993, 117).

Among the Wimbum, public *tfu* cleansing ceremonies, which
humiliated women, declined but have been resumed with a new
sense of fury in recent years.[41] Historically, both men and women
have been accused of practicing *tfu*, but this does not mean that *tfu*
is devoid of gender issues. I illustrate this in two ways. First, Pool
reports a conversation in which his informants refer to a certain
woman as "poison," because inheriting her would mean that an
individual would become a target of *tfu* brought by jealous relatives
(Pool 1994, 141). This raises gender issues, because if a woman's
husband dies, the head of that family decides who the woman's
next husband should be. In this hypothetical case, if several men
find her attractive, the new husband's brothers may become jealous
and kill him because they would have had liked to have had the
woman. If his brothers are not jealous, the first wife of the individual selected as the new husband can use *tfu* on him because she
too is jealous. Notice that in this transaction, the woman does not
decide who she wants to marry, or even if she wants to remarry
within the family; she is told to whom she will be remarried. The
woman thus becomes a battleground for *tfu*. One well-known reaction to this kind of marriage arrangement from a woman's perspective is *Une Si Longue Lettre* by Mariama Bâ (1979).

A second area where the issue of gender can be raised must be
approached in a subtle manner. Although the Wimbum acknowledge that both men and women are involved in *tfu*, there is a sense
that a woman's *tfu* is stronger and more dangerous than that of a

man's. A *Limbum* expression conveys this view, while at the same time essentializing the participation of women in *tfu:* O ki kupse mshep njinwe bu mbo ka. This literally means that a woman is always part of any powerful medicine when it is prepared. A woman's *tfu* is needed to make any transaction effective. She may not be part of the public transaction, but it is believed that she will have been influential behind the scenes, due to the potency of her *tfu.* Such was the case with a woman in Ntumbaw who was suspected of having strong *tfu* powers. Her story took place amidst great changes in the community.

During the 1970s, a mini-cultural revival swept Ntumbaw. Several new organizations were born under the umbrella of *Bong Abi*, in *Limbum* meaning a call for unity. *Bong Abi* is a term employed by the Wimbum to refer to cultural groups that have been formed by them. The National Party in Cameroon, at that time the Cameroon National Union, had unity as its goal. This was a theme preached by all in the state bureaucracy, from President Ahidjo to the *sous prefect adjoint* and, at the lowest level, by the Municipal Administrator. People decided that the only way they could start new groups was to do so under the guise of *Bong Abi*. Using this device, people were able to start many new cultural organizations without placing themselves under the scrutiny of the state, as they would have been if they had gone through the routine of getting permits to start organizations outside of the umbrella of the party.

These new organizations had different goals; some were self-help organizations, while others were started for "development" purposes. In the Wimbum area, these were generally championed by the elites of the different towns who were expected to return home and spend their wealth constructing buildings, water projects, and health centers. Other groups were formed for no specific purpose other than to dance. Thus, in Ntumbaw, people believed that a group of men and a well-known woman, suspected of having powerful *tfu*, created a new dance.

This was not the only dance created in the town, but it gained notoriety quickly. The members of this dance held weekly meetings organized in the form of a *ngwa*. The dance itself consisted of several quick steps, with the right hand held up in a tight fist and the left hand supported on the left hip. The music employed polyphonic rhythms, and drummers played complicated rhythms on a bass drum and long conga drum. The most important instrument for this dance was a kind of small hand-held horn, made out of reeds, which several players blew in different styles. These players were positioned in the center of the dance floor. A lead singer began the vocals, and the rest of the dancers answered as a massive chorus. This dance soon became very popular, featured in many of the usual "meet the people tours" of the divisional administrators—sometimes called "collect-the-chickens or cows tour."[42]

No one knew what lay behind such success. It was only when one of the leading members, the only female, lay dying that it was disclosed that members had used *tfu* to "take the dance." The term the Wimbum people use here is *lor*, which literally means to take something, and it is used frequently when the Wimbum talk of *tfu* people bringing something into the community, especially from the so-called witch markets, known as *nta tfu*. What I am concerned with here is the belief that this new dance was successful and influential because a woman was involved when the dance was "taken" by the leaders. Many of the leaders made similar confessions when they were dying. Thus we have a situation where a woman's power is publicly denied but where it also is claimed that a woman's *tfu* powers are dangerous.

Fisiy discusses the popular belief that women have powerful occult powers in another context in his account of the Kom women. The women of Kom are said to have marched to Bamenda to protest colonial administration policy. He also has pointed out that recently, in Bamenda, the women themselves exploited this belief to their advantage when they prepared to march naked to visit the imprisoned officials of the opposition party. The reason for marching nude lies in the belief that if women who have passed childbearing age expose themselves, they will bring bad luck to anyone who sees them. Word of this impending activity by the female members of the Takembeng beyond menopause made officers, who had erected barricades, flee because they believed that the "witchcraft" of the women was very strong (Fisiy, 1994).

Third, *tfu* is economic discourse. Wimbum *tfu* is economic discourse, in that it involves complex economic issues that include acquiring and dispensing wealth. Recent studies of witchcraft in Cameroon and in other parts of Africa have explored the implication of *tfu* discourse on economic issues.[43] The complexity of *tfu* discourse and economics among the Wimbum needs further study. A number of questions raised by researchers in other parts of Cameroon can be applied to the Wimbum area, which is experiencing the same economic tensions as the entire country. The major source of income for many people in the area, other than the Ndu Tea Estate, remains individual family farms and cattle farming. Most people depend on subsistence farming, with the additional cash crop of coffee. In Ntumbaw, Njirong, and Nsop, many people grow rice in the rich soil of the Mbaw Plain, which can be irrigated rather easily. There is a cooperative marketing union at Mbiyeh that provides employment to some people in the area through local branches. The other main source of employment is the civil service; the government maintains divisional and subdivisional offices at different locations that provide employment for a few people. Different religious groups provide employment to a few members of the community as well.[44]

The Cooperative Union, including its local societies, established at the peak of coffee production in the 1970s, is the most viable of all of these employment sources. This organization is called the Nkambe Area Cooperative Union, headquartered at Mbiyeh in the town of Tala.[45] Recently, as Probst demonstrates, some of the prominent members of the cooperative system have been linked to *nyongo* and *kupe* (Probst 1992, 151ff). Some people charge that the wealth acquired by some workers of the Cooperative Union is not only derived from salaries earned working for the organization but from their membership in powerful *nyongo* societies.[46] Thus a tension has been created, because the leaders are not only suspected of receiving bribes and tipping the scales to deceive the farmers but of getting wealthy through *tfu* and membership in the *nyongo* and *kupe* societies. The leaders of the Cooperative Union have consistently denied these rumors and have claimed that they are Faithfully executing their duties by marketing the fruits of the residents' labors.

Several things should be said about *tfu* as economic discourse. First, *tfu* discourse in this sense speaks to the improper acquisition of wealth. People complain about the negative aspects of *tfu* when they accuse others of employing *nyongo* and *kupe* to acquire wealth. However, unlike the claims that arose in the early 1960s among the Wimbum that did not specifically link *tfu* to wealth but to the complexities of family life in general, the new emphasis is on killing one's family members and even non-family members to acquire wealth.

When someone becomes wealthy in a very short time, people tend to attribute such success to *tfu* powers, now interpreted as *kupe* or *nyongo*. When people discuss such wealth, they talk of *mba majing*, *mba kupe*, or *mba blee*. *Mba* is the Limbum word for money, and *mba majing* means "magic wealth, *kupe* wealth." The third expression *mba blee*, is an interesting one. It means "blood money" and is used to designate wealth that a person has acquired because he or she reportedly used *tfu* to kill someone so he or she could become wealthy. This is similar to what happened among the

Bakweri people of Southwestern Cameroon, who could not enjoy or take advantage of wealth because they feared that any success would be linked to *nyongo*. Thus they had to go to Mamfe to employ the services of the powerful regulatory society called *Obansenjom* to eradicate their towns of what they believed was the negative employment of *nyongo* powers. What appears to be at issue in the new discourses among the Wimbum is that the Wimbum people are conceptualizing and discussing the implications of new forms of wealth and the means of acquiring it. Through *tfu* discourse, they lay explicit claim to the unacceptability of these forms and means in their definition of Wimbum life. This discourse enables them to discuss the issues involved, to educate members of the society, and to act to take the necessary steps to avoid the negative uses of power derived from *nyongo* and *kupe*.

Second, as economic discourse, *tfu* also protects one's legally acquired status. *Tfu* is interwoven with economic issues in a new way through the protection that the members of the community claim they are giving to prominent elites so they will not be harmed by the *tfu* of other people. The community acts to protect its people, but with modern elites, members claim that they are protecting them because the elites bring economic projects to their home-towns, thus they are seen as assets.

One example of the ambivalence and complexity of *tfu* discourse concerning elites was evident in the 1970s, when a prominent Baptist educator, who received training in England and taught at several Baptist institutions, became the center of concern among the Wimbum. The elders of the community charged that his wife wanted to kill him through *tfu*. This charge was raised several times, and public pressure eventually led to the dissolution of their marriage. The departure of this man's wife was seen as a victory for the community, because he was spared from her alleged activities. The woman in question was Wimbum herself. It is unclear why no one came to her defense. There are times when the accused person's relatives (in this case, it would have been her brothers) can rally to his or her defense against those charges. In this case, nothing was done to help her. The presumed benefits that would come to the community through the man's influence led the community to press charges that contributed to the breakup of this man's family. At one point, the town of Binka passed local rulings making it an offense to try to harm an elite through *tfu*. The members of the community see the elites as successful people who are supposed to bring home the financial rewards of their involvement in the state bureaucracy. Hence, in passing such a local ordinance and promising to punish any violators, the town was claiming that the leaders will employ, as in the case of the Bakweri, powerful forces to punish those who use *tfu* in a negative way to harm a successful person. *Tfu* is therefore economic discourse that can be employed in the creation of wealth and in the protection of those who have the potential of bringing their earned wealth back home and using it to improve their local communities.

Furthermore, *tfu* raises questions about the distribution of wealth. It is expected that when people become wealthy, or when members of the family have become successful, this will extend to the rest of the family. The Wimbum employ the expression *Nfero iko rtee, a yi mbang tombui*, which means, "If your brother climbs a palm tree, you will be the first to eat the fruit." The concept of sharing is deeply rooted in the community. Earlier I discussed the case of a *fai* who expected the elite, who was a member of his extended family, to buy him a car. This *fai* as well as other people in the town believed that they contributed to the education of the elite, therefore should rightly benefit from their wealth. One could ask if this would justify inflicting members of the elite with an illness that could possibly kill them. These questions are not asked among the Wimbum. Moreover, there are times when the people at home have boldly claimed that the elite are making progress be-cause their family members at home take different actions to ward off the negative use of *tfu* against the elite.

There are other times when members of the elite receive a reminder from their less fortunate relatives about their welfare obligations to kin. In the town of Ntumbaw, people use the word *tambeya*, in Hausa meaning "to ask." When employed in connection with seeking help in the form of medicine, *tambeya* is then a ref-erence to the activity of going either to a diviner or a medicine man or woman for consultation regarding the welfare of one's family and relatives who are away from the home. When members of the elite make money, they are expected to share it with their brethren back home, those safeguarding their well-being. When they do not, *tfu* can be used to force them to do so (Geschiere 1997).

Fourth, *tfu* is religious discourse. This is a very broad area, and I offer only very preliminary remarks here, centered on the Chris-tian church, since my argument is that Christian theological reflection can still contribute to the discussion if the questions are reformulated through the grid of philosophical ethics. Indigenous religious practices continue to adapt to changes in *tfu* practices. It will take a different project to map out such changes and adapta-tions, however, for now, Wimbum ritual processes still include invocations for divine help to deal with *tfu* problems—an indication that *tfu* certainly raises religious issues.[47]

Tfu raises religious questions about life and death. It is important to underscore here that the heart of the debate over the negative use of *tfu* often centers on a person's death. Wimbum people use divination to explore such issues. When there is a crisis in the town, the elders say prayers to the gods, present offerings, and solicit the help of ancestors to deal with such crises.

Tfu discourse also continues to challenge Christian practices in Africa. The efforts of missionary religions to eliminate these practices have not succeeded. Regarding the attempt to eradicate "witchcraft" beliefs, Evans-Pritchard offered a word of caution for missionaries when he told them not to attempt to destroy the beliefs of other people, even if the missionaries thought that those beliefs were misguided (Evans-Pritchard 1935, 417–422). Many people in the Wimbum area continue to seek help through the practice of Wimbum religious beliefs. The debate on this subject will no doubt continue. The historian of African Christianity, Adrian Hastings, while arguing that a change has taken place regarding Christian views of "witchcraft," admits that mission churches for a long time denied its existence (Hastings 1976, 60). Writing about this denial in Ghana, Debrunner quotes a student as saying, "The church preached that we have been victimized by the mere psychological conviction that witches do exist as supra-normal phenomena, influencing the life of man. So they force us to abandon the idea of 'witchcraft'" (Debrunner 1959, 135). Debrunner points out that, in certain cases, the person who made the accusation was thrown out of the church rather than the accused. However, in asking people not to believe anything about "witchcraft," the church also preached the power of Christ over witches, an indication that it believed that there were witches who could indeed be countered with the power of Christ. In the case that Debrunner cites, the response of the church was extreme, excommunicating members who sought protection from witch shrines (Ibid., 143, 144).

African theologians have recognized the need to come to terms with the reality of witchcraft, as is evident in the number of monographs and conferences devoted to this problem. Hastings rightly asserts that many issues such as African beliefs, biblical concepts, and Western ideas of health converge in a discussion of witchcraft (Hastings 1976, 61). *Tfu* serves as a potential critique of African Christianity, because missionary Christianity did not take it seriously. Second, it is the indigenous church that had long been marginalized by missionary Christianity, that attempted to address these issues.[48]

MacGaffey has shown clearly how indigenous Christianity worked with the concept of *kindoki* in The Democratic Republic of Congo. In the practice of the modern prophets, the priest assumes the role of the *nganga*, the diviner-healer, who detects witches and deals with them (MacGaffey 1983, 4). MacGaffey has demonstrated that the rise of these movements is linked not only to local medicine but also to cosmic forces from which the new prophets were able to claim that they could deal with witchcraft through the power of Jesus Christ (Ibid., 35). The Wimbum have not had anything similar to a prophetic movement, despite the fact that the Christian church has not always addressed *tfu* effectively. In my opinion, turning to the Bible for condemnations of these practices as diabolic has not been impressive.

Many Africans believed that Christianity would help them eradicate *tfu*. Among the Wimbum, some people complained that there were still people in the churches practicing *tfu*. The healer Pa Yeri Longka complained to me during the time that I served as pastor of Ntumbaw Baptist Church that there were deacons in the church practicing *tfu*. Before coming to Ntumbaw as pastor, a drastic and temporary shift in thinking occurred in Ntumbaw and Njirong. In 1965, the Reverend David Tangko came to the town as pastor. Rev. Tangko was a gifted musician and was involved in the development of what has become an important aspect of Wimbum Christianity—the church choir. What was significant about the Rev. Tangko's work at Ntumbaw was that he broke through the legalism that kept *fons* and *fais* from being members of the church. Prior to this, their role in the local religion, and the fact that they were polygamists, prevented them from participating actively in church life. Rev. Tangko preached the Gospel, and the *Fon* of Njirong accepted the message and his many wives were baptized and accepted into the church. Nearly all of the *fais* of Njirong and Ntumbaw followed suit. The *Ya*, Queen mother of Ntumbaw, started coming to church. Sunday services were a spectacle. Seated in the front row on the left-hand side of the pulpit was the *Fon* of Njirong and the *Ya* of Ntumbaw; by customary practice, the *Fon* and the *Ya* cannot sit among the people. At the back of the church hall, on the men's side of the aisle, three benches were reserved for the elders of the town and the *fais*, who attended regularly. On the women's side, the benches were reserved for the *bkinto* and the *wibahs*.[49] The *Fon* of Ntumbaw decided that he was going to become a Muslim. He explained his decision in pragmatic terms: President Ahidjo was a Muslim, and the *Fon* thought that he should become one as well. In carrying out his evangelism and incorporation of the local leaders into the church, Rev. Tangko did not carry out the burning of so-called "fetishes" characteristic of missionary Christianity; instead, he urged the new believers to abandon all old practices and to trust Jesus completely.

The impact of this kind of message was that the leaders who had embraced Christianity now employed a new language in dealing with *tfu*. They did not deny that it existed, but they decided that they would submit all questions to prayer. None of them would ever visit a *nwe seng* (diviner) again. Some of the townspeople were furious, but that did not change the new religious awakening. Individuals continued to practice *tambeya*—the Hausa term that means to ask, which in this case referred to activities similar to divination. This practice used to determine the future also was used as a sort of early warning system, because most of the elders of the town would not go out and talk to a *nwe seng*. When I became pastor of the church in 1973, this was very much the understanding. I regularly heard people talk, however, about the real and alleged practice of *tfu*. It was during this time that Pa Yeri Longka used to complain to me about the presence of *witfu*, the plural of *nwetfu*—a person who practices *tfu* in the church. I did not know how to deal with the situation.

Several years after this revival, people in the community started making open claims that some of the *fai*'s themselves were involved in *tfu*. In 1989, one of the most influential of the *fai*s was publicly reprimanded by the new Muslim *Fon* of Ntumbaw and was told that if he did not stop killing members of his own family through *tfu* that he would be deposed and exiled from the community. One member of this *fai*'s family, who had a reputation of being a healer, was exiled outright and told not to return to the town of Ntumbaw. He too was a Christian. The people involved used Christianity as a cover-up for *tfu*. This case further illustrates the claim that *tfu* is a critique of Christianity. It is clear from this illustration that the trumpets that heralded the extinction of the alleged "evil and satanic practices" were sounded much too early and without due consideration of religious issues and worldviews involved in conversations surrounding *tfu*.

Finally, *tfu* discourse invites us to a revision of theological discourse. I argue that a new theological approach can be attempted through the grid of philosophical ethics. The view that theologians needed to do something about the prevalent beliefs and practices of *tfu* and "witchcraft" was stated clearly by Archbishop E. Milingo of Lusaka, Zambia. When he became Archbishop in 1969, he was faced with a difficult problem.

I inherited the archdiocese of Lusaka in which the clergy were highly divided on a national basis, and the church very vaguely established. On the top of that there was little achievement in promoting local vocations. The missionary method developed was ineffective and certainly not in conformity with the missionary pronouncements of the church. . . . My mission was that of presenting the Christian doctrine "in a manner corresponding to the difficulties and problems by which the people are most vexatiously burdened and troubled." In this field, there was a lot to do in the archdiocese of Lusaka. The old traditional religion had such an impact on the people that those who had been baptized could hardly with pride carry the precious name of Christian. Their belief in an ancestral world constantly caused a departure from the church in time of personal difficulty . . . most of our baptized Christians had two religions. (Milingo 1984, 4)

The Milingo's ministry drew critics from inside and outside the church. His negative portrayal of what he calls "ancestral religions" is problematic. I believe that those religions will have to be partners in a new conversation taking up issues of *tfu*, healing, and power in Africa. I echo his views, however, because the situation he encountered in Lusaka, as well as that encountered in other parts of Africa, calls for new thinking. Theological reflection can rejoin the conversation on *tfu* by employing some of the categories of philosophical ethics. It is with this in mind that I pursue the philosophical ethics of Levinas so that interpersonal relations that are impacted negatively in *tfu* can be analyzed through a radical critique of the Other.

I have demonstrated in this interpretation of Wimbum *tfu* that it is a complex phenomenon that Wimbum people perceive to have both good and bad qualities. Indeed, *tfu* is moral discourse. I also have shown that the complexity of interpreting Wimbum *tfu* requires the development of new terms and a search for conceptualizations beyond "witchcraft." This approach makes it possible to understand the dynamics involved, especially when one considers the appropriation of new terms. It also makes it possible to understand and address the politics of *tfu* discourse and practice when analyzed in light of modernity and postmodernity.

In my reading of *tfu,* I maintain that it has a complexity to it that tends to leave the student in a state of perplexity. In a personal communication, Emmanuel Eze calls attention to my perplexity by pointing out that he agrees that it is complex. But he also points out that I convey to him (and the reader) my understanding of *tfu* as a discourse about gender, postcolony, and religion in a convincing way. He expresses concern that I still insist that only those who have it know what *tfu* is. He then wonders if I have *tfu* or should do away with the mystery in which I want to enclose it. Furthermore, he wonders if I am claiming like Tempels that the practitioners have knowledge that they do not know they have and are waiting for me to give them an account. Eze also raises the question that those of us who study *tfu* often raise. What if it turns out that there really is no secret knowledge such as *tfu*? He points out that I indicate that the diviners and specialists address *tfu* problems in a variety of ways but that I do not seem to make clear to the reader the fact that they are aware of their knowledge. These concerns reflect the complexity of the subject matter.

I wish I could write away the idea of knowledge about *tfu*. I still do not know how that power works. I only interpret what I have been told and interpret social relations that are governed by that discourse. I do not have any *tfu*. Second, the people who claim to have this power sometimes boast about it. The power is not dormant in them waiting for the researcher to awaken it. I have questions about some of the claims they make, but I have not reached the point where I can write off their claims. It remains a mystery to me, and I am willing to study and comment on information that is available. Finally, what if it turns out that there really is no secret knowledge? We will then be able to write a history of *tfu* indeed and at that time probe why a false idea has held generations of Africans hostage. We would like to know why some have defended it, calling it "African science."

I proceed in the next chapter to address the issues of the rationality of and belief in *tfu*. I return to that debate in order to indicate that in light of this interpretation of *tfu*, an ethical critique of its practice can be attempted. In Chapter 3, I propose that we move beyond the rationality debate and engage in contextual ethics. The ethical approach that I draw from is that of Emmanuel Levinas's. I provide the basis for a critical contextual ethics and follow up with a sketch of Levinas's ethical philosophy. I end the chapter by proposing ways to apply Levinas's views on intersubjectivity to *tfu* discourse. When such groundwork has been laid, I then argue that Levinas's phenomenology of eros offers a rich approach to building intersubjective relations.

Chapter 3

Beyond the Rationality Debate
to Contextual Ethics

The subject of rationality and relativism has received consider-
able attention in the philosophical and anthropological literature.[1]
The debate in its various forms has addressed issues of translation between two cultures, and interpretation, explanation, commensurability, and incommensurability. Surrounding these issues
is the nagging question, are standards of rationality universal, or
are those standards relative? Taking a relativist position, I return
to this debate to argue that communities such as the Wimbum
ought to transcend this debate and focus instead on contextual
ethics.

I take a relativist position because the totality of human experience demonstrates that one cannot impose universal standards of
rationality. Cross-cultural studies demonstrate that a uniform set
of standards is undesirable and impossible, since people continue
to live with what Mary Douglas has called "our cognitive precari-
ousness" (Douglas 1975, xviii). The early Richard Rorty[2] articulates
in a novel fashion positions held by philosophers such as
Wittgenstein, Quine, Sellers, and Davidson. Rorty states that we
should get away from the view that "there are foundations [that
can] serve as common ground for adjudicating knowledge claims
and that the philosopher is 'guardian of rationality'" (Rorty 1980,
317). In each situation and at each moment, what we consider
objective truth for Rorty "is no more than and no less than the best
idea we currently have about how to explain what is going on"
(Ibid., 385).

Second, the relativist position better accounts for decisions in the realm of morality, politics, and religion. In these domains, the interpretation of reality is not made with the neutrality that anti-relativists claim. I advance only what Steven Lukes calls "perspectivism," meaning a "closely related set of beliefs, attitudes and assumptions that specify how social reality is to be understood" (Hollis and Lukes 1986, 301ff).[3]

What is at issue here for me is a broad view of reality. This is different from Charles Taylor's perspective, because he links rationality to articulation and explanation. Taylor, who is sympathetic to Winch's contextualism, calls into question the claim that rites have a relation to crops and can make them grow (Taylor 1986, 93). He advances a view of rationality that stresses order and attunement, and he argues that science has been able to do better than magical activities. The problem I see with Taylor's view is that what counts as order for him is always what is measurable. No one would argue that science does a more precise job with measurement than magic. The problem is that not all of life's experiences are quantifiable. The broader implication of Taylor's position is limiting, because what counts for order is cast necessarily in positivist terms. Furthermore, Taylor is clearly offended by what he calls "the anti-imperialist liberal conscience, wary of ethnocentrism, in a view, which assimilates magic to pure symbolic activity" (Ibid., 99). For Taylor, the West has won the quest for a view of reality that is orderly, therefore, we should quit trying to soften the blows on other cultures. Taylor makes a much bolder claim when he says, "We may want to argue that *our* science is clearly superior. We point to the tremendous technological spin-off it has generated in order to silence many doubters" (Ibid., 100).[4] Clearly, Taylor sees nothing ethnocentric in his position. "They," those who abide by the scientific perspective, have won the battle, and the rest of the world should apply the same standards of rationality that the West has used. Robin Horton, in his many writings and comparison of African thought and modern science, makes a similar argument in a kinder, gentler way by focusing on what he calls "universal rationality," conditioned by different technological, economic, and social settings (Horton 1993, 200ff).

A broader view of reality must reject the comparison made between science and symbolic actions such as belief and magic. It also must reject the view that makes rationality the domain of the West. What is needed is a contextual approach in adjudicating conflicting claims to rational activity. To do this, I return to Peter

Winch's perspective stated in his classic essay "Understanding a Primitive Society," because in that essay he addresses issues that bear directly on witchcraft (Winch 1970). I follow up Winch's position with Richard Bernstein's approach for overcoming the impasse between objectivism and relativism in his work *Beyond Objectivism and Relativism* (1988). Bernstein's hermeneutical approach is particularly useful because it validates contextualism without leading to irrationalism (Bernstein 1988).[5] Bernstein's call for dialogue within communities offers a much more fruitful path to overcoming the impasse on rationality. I conclude that one should focus on contextual ethics rather than on the debate that questions whether *tfu* beliefs are rational or not.[6] This chapter then is mainly a reconstruction, an exposition, and an excursus of the main ideas that validate contextual ethics rather than a new constructive approach. The views of the authors I discuss here provide an important bridge to critical contextualism, a notion I discuss in the next chapter. Since this discussion has a particular bearing on African thought, I introduce it with Mudimbe's reflections on the discourse on Africa (Mudimbe 1988).

MUDIMBE ON THE DISCOURSE ON AFRICA

Mudimbe's book, *The Invention of Africa* (1988), is part of the growing literature that analyzes the representation of Africa in Western discourse and by African scholars in what Mudimbe has called the African *prise de parole*.[7] Mudimbe's archaeology, in the Foucauldian sense, stands out because it is a brilliant, encyclopedic analysis of Western discourse on Africa, encompassing anthropological, philosophical, and theological perspectives. His account provides a provocative *entrée* into the debate on rationality. Mudimbe clearly outlines the epistemological ideology behind Western discourse and the resulting double consciousness (borrowing Du Bois's expression) that it has created in African intellectuals engaged in the *prise de parole*.

Furthermore, Mudimbe's "deconstruction" is important because he raises the question of Otherness, directed first toward its construction by Western discourse and second toward Otherness as understood by African intellectuals who, working largely within the epistemological legacy of the West, are attempting to reclaim a marginalized Otherness. These attempts now constitute a growing and critical library of Africanisms.

WESTERN EXPLORATION OF AFRICA

Mudimbe argues that Western penetration into Africa was a brief exercise of power and construction of Otherness, that left a dualism characterizing precolonial Africa in Hobbesian terms, in contrast to the Romantic view of African thought in Rousseauian terms (Mudimbe 1988, 1). Mudimbe reads colonialism as a project of organization and arrangement, consistent with the interest of the colonizer, who constructed a subject to fit those aims. To realize such goals, colonial industrial projects created structures of marginalization (Ibid., 4).[8] According to Mudimbe, a "dichotomizing system emerged," setting apart "traditional" and "modern"; in literature, "oral" versus "written"; about communities, "urban" versus "industrialized." Colonialists created cultural and religious institutions to cement these dichotomies. These contradictory institutions paved the way for a new marginality that turned out to be "the intermediate space between the so-called African tradition and the projected modernity of colonialism" (Ibid., 5).

Africa became a means of discursive representations that demarcated the boundaries of white and black, "civilized" and "savage." According to Mudimbe, even a new appreciation for African art and studies is an invention of "Africanisms" and, as such, is a naming, an ordering, and an analysis of Otherness in terms of "identity and difference." This ordering depicts Africans as inferior and incapable of any good taste, because what is good in Africa must have come from outside of Africa. The specific examples that Mudimbe cites are claims that, "Yoruba statuary must have come from Egyptians; Benin art must be a Portuguese creation; the architectural achievement of Zimbabwe was due to Arab technicians; and Hausa and Buganda statecraft were inventions of white invaders" (Ibid., 13). Furthermore, Dogon's astronomy, if genuine, was taken there from the outside. Imperialism propelled the genesis of modern Africa, and the science of anthropology facilitated the comparison of "primitive" societies.[9] Mudimbe offers a critique of Western *episteme* to establish the condition of the possibility for an African gnosis. He borrows Foucault's thesis of a disappearing subject and Levi-Strauss's relativism, as well as Foucault's archaeology of knowledge that challenges the *episteme* of the Same through a process of "reversal, discontinuity, specificity," and "exteriority," demonstrating that knowledge functions as power.[10] "Foucault's enterprise remarkably explains the conquering horizons of this history" (Ibid., 27–28).

Mudimbe draws from Levi-Strauss's "diffuse relativism," thereby appealing to a "non-Western *Weltanschauungen*." Levi-Strauss's self-analytical anthropology rejects the notion of a normative human culture (Ibid., 33).[11] Levi-Strauss presents this relativism in three principles. First, "Each human language is particular and expresses in an original way types of contacts that exist between 'man' [the producer of culture] and his environment [nature]" (Ibid., 30). Second, Levi-Strauss proposes a "science of the concrete versus science of the abstract" to replace the opposition established between magic and science. Finally, Levi-Strauss also believes that science and magic are not two levels of thought on the evolutionary grid but rather are "different and parallel systems of knowledge."

Mudimbe rightly sees invitations to a transformative history of the same (and I might argue of other cultures) in Foucault's analysis, in Levi-Strauss's position, and in Ricoeur's appropriation of "Plato's great class which associates the Same and the Other. The similar is the great category... or better the Analogue which is a resemblance between relations rather than between simple terms" (Ibid., 34).[12]

AFRICAN RESPONSE TO WESTERN DISCOURSE

African intellectuals have been influenced by the critique of Western thought offered by Levi-Strauss, Foucault, and Ricoeur. They also have argued that there is more than one path to truth.[13] Their critique of anthropology has included questions on the nature of African humanity and comparative studies of humanity, in a self-reflexive approach that interrogates the "credibility of their own *prises de parole,* challenging the evaluative scale and ideological presuppositions of the social sciences" (Mudimbe, 1988, p. 39).[14] This is an attempt to subvert colonial discourse and anthropological amplifications in what Eboussi-Boulaga calls a "way of survival" (Ibid., 41). Mudimbe argues that although African projects present "the intelligence of the Same," it is possible to see through them "the promises of Kant's old question on the possibility of an anthropology: how pertinent is it to speak about humans" (Ibid., 43).

Masolo points out that while Levi-Strauss's *menage* involves science and *bricolage*, Mudimbe's praxis engages anthropology and philosophical practice (Masolo 1994, 185). A future path that will avoid Western signification of Africa lies in the critical analysis of African culture and languages, and given Mudimbe's philosophical orientation, I must add critical philosophy. This critical analysis must present not only an African alternative but a contribution to human gnosis. While Mudimbe provides a context for looking at the debate on rationality, it will now be helpful to revisit the debate from a Winchian perspective before I turn to Bernstein's alternative for dealing with the impasse represented in the debate on the rationality of witchcraft.

PETER WINCH ON UNDERSTANDING ALIEN SOCIETIES

Sir Evans-Pritchard's work on Azande witchcraft provoked a debate on rationality and the understanding of different cultures. Winch's (1970) essay, "Understanding a Primitive Society," is significant because he addresses epistemological concerns in relation to an understanding of a different culture and the issues raised in Evans-Pritchard's "progressive" anthropology.[15] Winch examines Evans-Pritchard's account that the Azande believe that some of their people are witches (*tfu* people, as we have seen in the discussion of Wimbum *tfu* beliefs). Such people use occult influences to cause trouble for others. The potential victims respond to the activities of their fellow Zande by performing certain rites intended to enable them to overcome the power of witchcraft and magic. They use magic and medicine to protect themselves and to punish those who are using witchcraft in a negative way (Winch 1970, 78, 79).

Winch argues that Evans-Pritchard remains in the *episteme* of the Same because his text is laden with remarks such as "obviously there are no witches," and because of his claim that, during his days of fieldwork among the Azande, he had a hard time shaking the Azande from their "unreason" (Ibid., 79). Although Evans-Pritchard, in opposition to Levy-Bruhl (1966), admits the validity of other forms of belief and the difference between scientific reasoning and mythical reasoning, he chose to make a distinction between scientific and logical thought. Evans-Pritchard thereby presented the scientific as that which is in accord with objective reality and logic as that which is in accord with rules of thought (Winch 1970, 80).

Dismissing the correspondence of scientific notions and objective reality, according to Winch, is necessary because there are forms of reality outside of the parameters of science. Furthermore, the concept of "real" and "unreal" is linguistic, and Evans-Pritchard elucidates them through a Western linguistic form and its logic,

hence, that language usage and its structure determine the notion
of rationality. "We could not in fact distinguish the real from unreal
without understanding the way this operates in the language. . . . If
then we wish to understand the significance of the concepts, we
must examine the use they actually do have in the language" (Winch
1970, 82).[16] Evans-Pritchard bases his appraisal of the Azande view
of reality on scientific language and its usage in the scientific community. Therefore, appealing to the "established universe of discourse" cannot be used to dismiss Azande notions of reality (Ibid.,
83). Furthermore, Winch contends that a system such as Zande
magic is a coherent universe of discourse. He is careful to point out
that even where Evans-Pritchard accepts mystical knowledge, he
does not want to attribute it to the Azande, because the criterion
for the mystical is set by Evans-Pritchard's Western context.

To illustrate further the inappropriateness of Evans-Pritchard's
approach, Winch criticizes his evaluation of the poison oracle. This
practice involves giving poison to a fowl and asking certain questions. If the fowl dies from taking the poison, then the answer is
affirmative or negative, depending on how the question is framed.
It is on such a basis that guilt is positively or negatively determined. Sometimes, a postmortem examination is used to detect
witches. The practice of *Benge*, the oracle, is so important to the
Azande that Evans-Pritchard compares it to the equipment of an
engineer. According to Winch, there is no reason for Evans-Pritchard
to compare the *Benge* with a technological instrument; rather, for
Winch, the question is: "What criteria have we for saying that
something does or does not make sense?"[17]

Winch's essay continues to attract attention, because he also is
critical of MacIntyre's position. MacIntyre charges that Winch, in
his 1963 work *The Idea of a Social Science*, espouses relativism.
Furthermore, MacIntyre charges that Evans-Pritchard takes a similar relativist position in *Nuer Religion* (Evans-Pritchard 1956), and
that both do not uphold standards of rationality.

I do not think Winch advocates that standards of rationality
should be ignored. However, he calls into question the kind of standards that MacIntyre and Evans-Pritchard want to establish. Winch
argues that MacIntyre desires a new

> unity for the concept of intelligibility, having a certain re-
> lation to one old one and perhaps requiring a considerable
> realignment of our categories. . . . Seriously to study another
> way of life is necessarily to seek to extend our own—not
> simply to bring the other way within the already existing

boundaries of our own because the point about the latter in their present form is that they ex hypothesis exclude that other (Winch 1970, 99).

Winch states further that the very notion of rationality may not be as important in other societies as it is the West. MacIntyre is correct in observing that by requiring such notions as rationality in one language, the observer is already employing his or her standards. The problem for Winch, however, is not that MacIntyre has standards but rather that standards applied to society "S" also should be applied to society "T." By advancing his case in English and arguing for standards that reflect European culture in the twentieth century, MacIntyre is espousing an extreme form of relativism, because he fails to recognize that criteria have a history, namely, the history of the society in question.

> But if we are to speak of difficulties and incoherence appearing and being detected in the way certain practices have hitherto been carried on in a society, surely this can only be understood in connection with problems arising in the carrying on of the activity. Outside that context, we could not begin to grasp what was problematical (Winch 1970, 101).[18]

Winch asserts that MacIntyre, in his analysis, focuses on issues of consumption and therefore tends to miss the worldview in which witchcraft and magic are mechanisms for coming to terms with misfortune and explaining human existence. Rather than emphasize rules and conventions, as MacIntyre does, one should instead focus on human life. In that way, what we learn from a different culture is the variety of ways in which culture makes sense of human life (Winch 1970, 106).

> This dimension of the matter is precisely what MacIntyre misses in his treatment of Zande magic; he can see in it only a [misguided] technique for producing consumer goods. But a Zande's crops are not just potential objects of consumption: the life he lives, his relations with his fellows, his chances for acting decently or doing evil, may all spring from his relation to his crops. . . . Magical rites constitute a form of expression in which these possibilities and dangers may be contemplated and reflected on—and perhaps also thereby transformed and deepened (Winch 1970, 106).

Winch proposes that in order to understand a different society, one ought to examine what he calls "limiting notions" such as birth, death, and sexual relations—notions that provide one with a conception of life and the right way to live. By examining these areas of human life as they are understood in different societies, one can have a better perspective and a better chance of expanding one's understanding of a different society. Standards of rationality, even on issues such as witchcraft and magic, operate in a concrete, historical situation. This position need not commit anyone to believing all that is said about witchcraft or magic. I must state also that even within a particular society, standards should be open to scrutiny. For example, my own emphasis in this work is that dimensions of individuality among the Wimbum people ought to receive more emphasis so that individuals can continue to highlight the ethical problematics of *tfu*. One way of doing this is to be open to a human Other, which Levinas articulates. The call for contextual standards articulated by Winch reflects the perspectives advanced by Richard Bernstein (1988) in *Beyond Objectivism and Relativism*, to which I now turn.

BERNSTEIN'S MEDIATION: HERMENEUTICS AS DIALOGUE

Bernstein addresses the uneasiness in intellectual and cultural life caused by "the Cartesian anxiety." By this he means the search for some algorithmic position that can serve as a foundation for rationality, and he argues that since we cannot establish such a foundation, we need to abandon such a search and engage in a social praxis by moving "beyond Objectivism and relativism." By "objectivism," Bernstein means the view that, "There is, or must be, some permanent, a-historical matrix or formula to which we can ultimately appeal in determining the nature of rationality, knowledge, truth, reality, goodness, or rightness" (Bernstein 1988, 8). For those who hold such a position, the task of philosophy then is to find that matrix and argue from such a foundation, supporting their claims with strong arguments. By relativism, Bernstein advocates the position that if we examine the "concepts that philosophers have taken to be the most fundamental—whether it is the concept of rationality, truth, reality, right, the good, or norms—we are forced to recognize that in the final analysis all such concepts must be understood as relative to a specific conceptual scheme, theoretical framework, paradigm, form of life, society or culture"

(Ibid.). The relativist position stresses pluralism against a universal standard of rationality to which we can all turn.

Bernstein demonstrates that a new way of looking at human experience and practice is emerging from three dimensions: science, hermeneutics, and praxis. First, in *The Structure of Scientific Revolution* (1970) Kuhn argues that the sciences also employ hermeneutical strategies of understanding and reason. He indicates that there is "no neutral algorithm for theory of choice, no systematic decision procedure which, properly applied, must lead each individual in the group to the same decision" (Kuhn 1970, 200; Bernstein 1988, 23). Kuhn is not espousing irrationality, but a "more open, flexible, and historically oriented understanding of scientific inquiry as a rational activity" (Bernstein 1988, 23). Kuhn highlights conflicting positions and calls upon us to recognize the historical situatedness of scientific activities and how they are affected by nonscientific values.

Kuhn's revolutionary idea is that paradigm shifts in science occur when theories become inapplicable and unilluminating. Such a process of shift involves the examination of competing theories, with scientists advancing claims in persuasive ways. This process continues until one of the theories gains acceptance. Positivists argue that, in such a struggle to establish a leading paradigm, meaningful discourse is done through basic analytic and synthetic propositions. In contrast, in ethical debates, participants use the language of persuasion rather than analytic and synthetic propositions. Bernstein correctly asserts that, by stressing the role of persuasion and argumentation in scientific communities, Kuhn comes close to the "good reasons" approach often taken in ethics (Bernstein 1988, 53). Kuhn's language is similar to the idea of *Phronesis*, which emphasizes choice, deliberation, and openness to differing opinions, and makes room for the general and the particular. Such a process is not based on any set of specific rules; instead, what is required is "an interpretation and specification of universals appropriate to the situation" (Ibid., 54). Thus Kuhn demonstrates that what others may see as universally fixed criterion is indeed open-ended and interpretive.[19]

It would be a mistake to assume that Kuhn's perspective has solved the debate. Bernstein notes that Kuhn does not address the epistemological status of values that one should take when considering different options. For example, do scientists pick values arbitrarily, or is there a criterion that determines the choice of specific values that influences the selection of a theory? This kind of question puts into play nonscientific and interpretive elements when changes in paradigms take place. Thus Kuhn's arguments constitute a response to the Cartesian anxiety, because Kuhn is critical of the search for some firm foundation on which to ground rationality or to test and evaluate competing claims.[20]

Bernstein argues that recent developments in the philosophy and history of science indicate an increasing appreciation for the practical character of science. "Practical" here implies the role of reason, choice, deliberation, and a process that considers conflicting, variable opinions, bringing good judgment to bear on the rational process. This process deemphasizes method, if by method we mean fixed rules. Scientific communities need to develop and share criteria in addition to a hermeneutical process to balance the weight of cumulative evidence with argumentation and persuasion.[21]

The question about incommensurability should be seen from the perspective that Bernstein is advocating.[22] There is no permanent, algorithmic foundation on which to ground rationality. Kuhn allows for comparisons that can enable people to see which successor theories are dropped and which are carried over.

> For Kuhn rival paradigm theories are logically incompatible (and, therefore, really in conflict with each other); incommensurable (and, therefore, they cannot always be measured against each other point-by-point); and comparable (capable of being compared with each other in multiple ways without requiring the assumption that there is or must always be a common fixed grid by which we measure progress)[23] (Bernstein 1988, 86).

Second, the movement beyond objectivism also is at work in the social sciences, evident in the work of Peter Winch and Clifford Geertz. Geertz brings an important anthropological perspective to this matter (Geertz 1973). Geertz argues that an anthropologist should not try to achieve an "inner correspondence of spirit" with the people and at the same time understand and interpret what people think and do by examining their modes of expressions and symbol systems. This process demands what Geertz calls "experience near" and "distant concepts." The first refers to what the researcher observes, a description of what the researcher sees, feels, thinks, and imagines; the second refers to the interpretation provided by a researcher who brings to bear formal scientific and philosophical notions to make sense of the data (Ibid., 95, 96). Geertz argues that when both approaches are employed, one gains an understanding more analogous to "grasping a proverb, catching an illusion, seeing a joke, reading a poem—than achieving communion" with the people.[24]

Bernstein points out that incommensurability is an issue in Geertz's work, although the topic is not mentioned explicitly. Geertz shows how a kind of comparison can be done by using a hermeneutical practice to understand differing views on the concept of "person" in Western and non-Western societies.

The western concept of a person as a bounded, unique more or less integrated motivational and cognitive universe, a dynamic center of awareness, emotion, judgment, and action organized into a distinctive whole and set contrastively against other such wholes and against a social and natural background is, however incorrigible it may seem to us, a rather peculiar idea within the context of the world's cultures[25] (Geertz 1976, 229).

According to Bernstein, Geertz rightly concludes that what Westerners think is a universal idea, as in this case their view of a person, turns out not to be one.[26]

Bernstein returns to Winch's position and argues that Winch has not explored the Geertzian notions of "experience near" and "distant concepts." Furthermore, Winch has not explained what he means by reflective and nonreflective understanding. In addition, he seems to accept some distant concepts in the Geertzian sense, such as psychoanalytic theories. According to Bernstein, however, Winch does not tell us which distant concepts are employed: Weber's, Durkheim's, Freud's, or Marx's? (Bernstein 1988, 105). In place of universals and particulars, Winch borrows from Vico the idea of "limiting notions," determinative of the ethical space that humans occupy. These "limiting notions" are birth, death, and sex. Bernstein notes that one could add to the list the concept of "person" that Geertz tackles. One also could counter that Winch's limiting notions are constitutive of personhood and include the concept of person by default. I do not see how adding the notion of personhood changes or modifies Winch's proposition on understanding a different society. Bernstein contends that Geertz overcomes the either/or impasse by showing how we can understand human variety, and through the "distant concepts," he shows us how to reconstruct what the statistics indicate. By failing to do this, Winch misses the spirit of his work. I must say that the extent to which Bernstein expects Winch's text to be programmatic is debatable, because I find Winch's position on contextual standards persuasive.

The third field, which demonstrates par excellence the movement from objectivism and relativism for Bernstein, is philosophical hermeneutics. Bernstein devotes the bulk of the argument in *Beyond Objectivism and Relativism* (1988) to analyzing the proposals of Hans Georg Gadamer, Jürgen Habermas, Richard Rorty, and Hannah Arendt.[27]

Bernstein calls attention to Gadamer's call for a fusion of praxis and *phronesis*, Habermas's grounding of praxis in communicative acts,[28] Rorty's non-foundational pragmatism,[29] and Arendt's *vita activa* as the means to liberation and freedom.[30] From these thinkers, Bernstein appropriates the notion of dialogue and practical judgment, both of which should guide human effort toward praxis, pointing the way toward the resolution of the Cartesian problematic. He argues that we ought to create "dialogical communities" where we can exemplify "*Phronesis* and practicable discourse." The work of the thinkers he has reviewed contains "incommensurable languages but a coherent powerful conversation that has direction. Each contributes to exorcising the Cartesian anxiety and the movement beyond objectivism and relativism—not only in our theoretical endeavors but in conducting our practical lives" (Bernstein 1988, 225). From Gadamer's perspective, we can revitalize *phronesis* in what seems to be a fragmented society, and to the extent that we have not yet entered the cosmic night, this is a laudable goal. In contrast, Arendt sees public action as the sort of miracle that is possible because individuals and communities have been engaged in public actions in the past. Rorty, for his part, wants us to advance toward human solidarity by claiming what is good in each tradition's heritage. Habermas wants clear communication and unconstrained understanding to facilitate that emancipatory exercise (Ibid., 225–226).

These insights contribute to the move beyond objectivism. For Bernstein, these can further be supplemented by a study of Hegel's notion of *Sittlichkeit*. By this, Bernstein refers to Hegel's attempts to appropriate Hellenistic ideals with full recognition that there can be no return to that period. Bernstein notes that Hegel's ambiguity and his all-encompassing objective spirit make it difficult to say if an *Aufhebung* can truly do justice to the particular and the universal. Bernstein calls our attention to the fact that Hegel himself, in showing the movement toward objective spirit, also pointed to the contradictions that prevented *Sittlichkeit* (Bernstein 1988, 227). He argues that one ought to avoid Hegel's tendency toward homogenization, even if one considers certain aspects of Hegel's themes appealing. We should attempt to retrieve "a sense of significant differentiation so that partial communities, be they geographical, or cultural, or occupational . . . can become again important centers of concern and activity for their members in a way which connects them to the whole" (Ibid.). For Bernstein, this calls for dialogical communities where conversation and persuasion are the modes of approach.[31]

I have devoted much attention to Bernstein because his thesis and mode of argumentation present a viable option for going beyond the Cartesian anxiety and an "either/or mode" of thinking.[32] I should emphasize that in addition to arguing that rationality is a contextually bound concept, Bernstein calls for a recognition of difference. Part of my goal is to call for such a differentiation in communities such as the Wimbum, where personhood is articulated even through protests against the negative use of *tfu* powers. Such differentiation can be strengthened with Levinas's notion of Otherness, which I turn to in the next chapter. In the meantime, I respond to a critique of Winch's position on witchcraft, offered by Colwyn Williamson.

Williamson (1989) argues that as an idealist, Winch holds that our conceptions settle our experience of the world. He observes that Winch entertains "realms of discourse, . . . categories of action," and modes of "social life." According to Williamson, "The struggles between peoples, tribes, nations and classes appear in Winch's scheme of things only in the attenuated form of the competition between rival ways of 'making reality intelligible'" (Williamson 1989, 445–446). Winch's philosophy therefore threatens the possibility of social science, a claim I believe Williamson does not justify adequately (Ibid., 445). Williamson attacks Winch's "claim that religion has a special concept of rationality," arguing that Winch does not defend this claim with clear historical examples (Ibid., 446). Instead, Winch indicates that irrationality occurs in religion and even dwells in the fiction of the "Black Mass," which he cannot show was practiced in Europe.

Williamson indicates repeatedly that Winch presents no evidence that black masses were held or that they derived from religion. Williamson is so sure of his position that he can claim,

> We know from genuine sources that the practices depicted in the witchcraft ideology also inverted quite different aspects of respectable social life, reversing the roles of men and women, liberating repressed impulses, sexual and otherwise, and mocking conventional behavior generally (Williamson 1989, 453).

Williamson not only denies that there is any evidence for black masses, but he calls them "Winch's black masses"! He places the discussion of witches and cannibalism on a progressive grid, with the organizing principle being class wars. Thus the early Romans accused the oppressed Christian groups of cannibalism; in turn, Christian persecutors accused the witches of cannibalism; and in modern times, colonialists have accused the colonized of cannibalism.[33]

Williamson raises four objections to Winch's position on black masses and cannibalism. Winch gives no proof that there really was such a phenomenon, makes no distinction between witches and witch mongers, and fails to see that some of these so-called witch practices were inversions having no relationship to the orthodox mass; and the fourth point reiterates the third in a different way: even if one accepts that there was such a thing as the black mass, its practices were not parasitic on anything (Williamson 1989, 454). Therefore, Winch's position is an invitation to share in the illusion of the witch-hunter.

Furthermore, Williamson takes Winch to task for claiming that Western observers who view practices such as the black mass as unorthodox have the weight of the culture behind them. To Williamson, this is "intellectual patriotism," which claims that witchcraft is a parasite of religion. Furthermore, Winch seems to place "criteria of logic" and "intelligibility" on the same plane. Williamson says that someone could accept the intelligibility of witchcraft and Christianity, as he does, but still think that such practices and beliefs are irrational. Finally, Williamson faults Winch for not defining what "our culture" is and for not spelling out his concept of rationality, which according to Winch is "current in different societies" (Williamson 1989, 460). It is this critique that is presented to the reader as "Winchcraft."

Rather than engage in a point-by-point rebuttal of this highly polemical piece, I simply indicate that Williamson has forsaken the spirit of Winch's work. Winch could accept all of the charges that Williamson has labeled, but his views on the ideas of social science and a contextual approach to the rationality of witchcraft beliefs would still hold. Furthermore, Winch could agree that the so-called black mass was a fiction, and that we do not have evidence for its existence, but that would still not take away from the views that he has advanced about the standards used by different societies to judge what is and is not acceptable. Winch's discussion and defense of the rationality of black magic do not commit him to accept that it actually existed nor force him to argue that witchcraft is a reality.

Winch is concerned about how these practices and beliefs mirror human existence as well as human praxis. One need not agree with Winch on all of the issues he raises, but in his dispute with MacIntyre, Winch argues that one can only understand a social practice within the context of a particular society. What counts as rational then is not a set of standards set elsewhere. Indeed, those standards may have no relationship to the way of life of the people whose social practices we are studying.

I have demonstrated that Mudimbe and other African scholars have joined the discourse on Africa, seeking to raise the issue of Otherness in their own way and to assert their right to difference. I also have reviewed Winch's perspective on understanding a different society to establish that he correctly argues that the standards of rationality should be those of the particular society that one wants to understand. Bernstein invites us to move beyond the rationality debates and to focus on ethics to be determined by standards of practice and judgment that prevail in a given context. This does not mean that one cannot do cross-cultural ethics. If ideas are borrowed from a different context, they must be subjected to scrutiny along with the ideas of the context in which one is working. What is needed is a recognition that in a global context, postmodern critiques of power illuminate humanistic practices in societies such as the Wimbum, which have not been taken seriously in the past. In highlighting their beliefs, one also can draw insights from other perspectives. What I hope to accomplish is an opening up of an ethical conversation on *tfu*, which draws from Levinas's articulation of difference and Otherness. This is a radical approach that has as its aim a rigorous engagement with subjective and intersubjective discourses that could limit the totalizing tendencies in *tfu*. To accomplish this contextual cross-cultural task, I turn in the next chapter to Levinas's argument of the Other.

Chapter 4

Levinas on the Ethics of the Other

In this chapter, I present a contextual critique of *tfu* by drawing on Levinas to argue that the employment of *tfu* powers in a negative way constitutes a violation of Otherness. I find Levinas's post–phenomenological personalism a forceful meditation for posing the question of the Other in light of *tfu* discourse and practice. This appropriation does not argue that Levinas offers the only option. Neither is the use of Levinas an indication that through him I have found the key to Bantu philosophical ethics—if indeed there is any Bantu philosophical ethics in the Tempels' sense. I am simply appropriating Levinas's notion of the radical Other to illuminate my argument that negative *tfu* practices are a violation of the Other. I approach the problem through Levinas's critique of the ontological tradition, for to raise the issue of *tfu* through the philosophical tradition as revised by Levinas offers a viable option for ethics.

I first discuss critical contextualism; by this I mean doing ethics in context. This is followed by a discussion of the question of personhood in Wimbum as well as in other African communities. I argue that there are dimensions of individuality in Wimbum society that validate the use of Levinasian categories to provide a philosophical critique of *tfu*. I follow this with a critique of negative *tfu* practices using the ethical philosophy of Levinas.

CRITICAL CONTEXTUALISM

In the debate among African philosophers, Hountondji and others argue that philosophy in Africa needs to take a critical approach.

71

Everyone who turns to philosophy to articulate a concern subscribes, to a certain extent, to Hegel's view that philosophy is a reflection on the thought of the era. In this case, a reflection on *tfu* is an issue that concerns the Wimbum people and some African communities. I am convinced that all conceptual tools should be brought to bear if they contribute to a greater understanding of Otherness. Levinas's radical Other does that because it addresses a human question that defies provincialism.[1]

I characterize my argument as critical contextualism, because it draws from Levinas's philosophy to provide a critique of the negative aspects of *tfu*. Critical to the postmodern approach is an unveiling of the ideological building blocks on which the discourse on Africa has been constructed. Furthermore, it is critical because I locate this work within a tradition of discourse by African intellectuals, thus I provide an ethical critique of intersubjective relations. Third, this is a critical undertaking because I appropriate, from phenomenological discourse and the growing library of "Africanisms," aspects that are germane to African philosophical thought.

Contextualism here simply means that I join with others to address issues that are relevant to the Wimbum people and, by extension, to other areas in Africa. In this sense, context is not geographical but refers to the subject matter of reflection.[2] This view of critical contextualism raises another important methodological question—who can practice African philosophy? There is a sense in which Africans themselves bring a different kind of *Einfühlung* to the issues that arise, not only in African philosophy but also in anthropology and other disciplines that concern Africa. However, I have no doubt that anyone with training in philosophy and sensitivity to African issues can do African philosophy. Said differently, anyone trained to do critical philosophy can do African philosophy as a contextual philosophy.

OTHERNESS AND THE DEBATE ON PERSONHOOD AND COMMUNITY

Levinas proposes a radical Other whose claim subverts my agenda. Such radical singularity seems contrary to what some perceive to be the predominant communitarian mode of African thought. Furthermore, readers of Levinas wonder if his radical Other does not present a new kind of tyranny—the tyranny of a singular Other who now is posited in confrontation to the Same. This fear has grounds because, as I point out later, Levinas does not develop a detailed social and political philosophy, thus there is a danger that in appropriating his critique for Wimbum thought I may be imposing radical individualism on a society that some think is primarily communitarian. To be more specific, the question is—how appropriate is it to posit a radical Other in societies scholars have claimed have a communitarian outlook? To answer this question, I consider the debate on personhood in African society as I argue that there are dimensions of individuality in Wimbum society that justify positing a radical individual for contextual ethical analysis.

MENKITI ON THE COMMUNITARIAN VIEW

Ifeanyi Menkiti (1984) argues that in Africa the community has priority over the individual. He contends that personhood is acquired through an individual's lifetime (Menkiti 1984, 171ff). To justify the claim that personhood is acquired, Menkiti uses a linguistic analysis of the neuter pronoun "it." He argues that a child is referred to as "it" when he or she is born. It is only as this child grows up, matures, and takes his or her place in the community that personhood is attained. Menkiti further argues that funeral rites demonstrate this claim. The funeral rites of an adult who has attained personhood in a community are more elaborate than rites performed for a child. As Kwame Gyekye and others point out, Menkiti's analysis of the English neuter pronoun "it," denying personhood to children, is problematic. Furthermore, Menkiti's analysis of funeral rites in one community may be inappropriate for others.[3]

It is true that funeral rites for adults are elaborate. Indeed, among the Wimbum, they reflect the life that the individual has lived. Regarding the funeral rites of children among the Wimbum, however, the ceremony's brevity and accompanying sadness cannot be associated with lack of personhood. This usually is due to the grief associated with the fact that children have not had a chance to live out their lives. Personhood is taken for granted. During funeral celebrations among the Wimbum, it is common for people to cook corn, beans, and groundnuts for people to eat. If the dead person is an adult or an older person, the celebrations, known in pidgin English as "die cry," take on a festive mood as members of the family spend elaborately to provide food and drinks. Depending on the individual's status, masked figures from the palace perform and entertain people. The individual who has led a full life and who has contributed to the good of others and the community is celebrated. However, when a child or a young person dies, no such celebration takes place. When a young person dies, Wimbum people describe such a death as *rkwi bipsi shu*, literally meaning "death that spoils the mouth." There are two ways of looking at this. First, such a death has shocked people to the extent that they can hardly talk about it. Second, it also means that death has killed any appetite for food or drinks. The thought of the one who has died numbs any desire to eat. It is the tacit recognition that the person has not had a chance in life that causes such grief and leaves mourners with no appetite. In this respect, the personhood of the deceased is taken for granted.

Such a death took place when I was pastor of the Wimbum town, Wanti. One afternoon, I heard a strong cry from the valley community below my house. This certainly was a cry of distress. I ran out to find out what the problem was, but before I got to the compound, many people had arrived there and the grief of the entire area was carried up in a mournful chorus that left everybody paralyzed. I was told that Johnson Nginyui, a young man from the town who had gone to the Mentchum area of the Northwest Province to work in a logging and timber industry, had died mysteriously. His body was being brought home.

The quarter head, *Fai* Ngamudoh, expressed disgust and contempt at death for stealing such a young man. *Fai* Ngamudoh told me that he would die on *Mruh*, the sacred day of the town, so that all of the people would come together to celebrate his death and make up for the celebration that could not take place because the young man's death was *rkwi bipsi shu*. Furthermore, he indicated that dying on *Mruh* would put death to shame. The people could not celebrate Nginyui's death because he died at a young age, not because he had not earned personhood. (Among the Wimbum, personhood does not have to be earned.)

GYEKYE ON MODERATE COMMUNITARIANISM

Gyekye proposes moderate communitarianism by arguing that other things such as rationality, virtue, moral judgments, and choice should be considered when defining personhood in different African communities. Furthermore, the community does not set all of the standards adopted by individuals, nor is it such a superstructure that the individual merely hides behind it. Furthermore, Gyekye argues that the community does not always prevent its members from taking a radical perspective on contested values in the community (Gyekye 1997, 112). The individual person can reevaluate the standards of the community, and this indicates that the person *qua* individual is not lost in society.[4] The possession and exercise of autonomy, a radical and an assertive will that allows an individual to take positions contrary to the communal structures, confirm individuality and moderate communitarianism. This view of personhood provides the conceptual tools to take a critical look at personhood and the burning issue of human rights in the African context. Gyekye states the well-known thesis that postcolonial African leaders have stressed communitarian views. The erroneous assumption made by some thinkers is that a communal spirit would translate easily into the structures of a nation-state inherited from the so-called metropolitan states. It is such an assumption that prompted some leaders to champion different forms of socialism. This is not the place to deliver a full analysis of such ideologies. African communities recognize individuality. The essentialism that has promoted absolute communitarian perspectives tends to stifle debate on human rights in Africa. The very question of human rights suggests that individuals have certain rights and are entitled to self-determination.[5] Gyekye indicates that although John Rawls argues from a Western liberal tradition, his work *A Theory of Justice* takes community seriously (Rawls 1971). It is clear to me that the communitarian position gives only a partial portrait of some African societies. Personhood and community should be considered in an ongoing dialectic in which individual and societal notions of the good and the pursuit of that good are constantly being negotiated and reformulated. It is within this context that I locate critical contextualism. To do this I must articulate Wimbum respect for personhood and individuality, which will permit me to borrow Levinas's radical critique of intersubjective relations.

PERSONHOOD IN WIMBUM SOCIETY

The Wimbum conception of personhood is captured in several ways, but I highlight the expression *Fo Ni Nwe,* meaning "pride in a person," as an example of intersubjective relations.[6] This expression is employed in speeches and is used as a name. When it is used as a name, it is called *Nfoninwe.* The first word, *fo,* refers to human dignity, satisfaction, and a sense of self-confidence. It also can mean pride, but in this context, it does not mean pride as in a haughty spirit. The Wimbum expression for pride as haughtiness,

an attitude and feeling that one is more important than others, is
yu nyor. Another expression for a sense of dignity, respect, and
satisfaction is *sa fo*. The Wimbum people believe that *Fons*, nobles,
and other leaders of the community, or even individuals who carry
themselves in a dignified manner, express *sa fo*. The other word in
the expression *fo ni nwe* is *nwe*. This word is the singular for
person.[7] The entire expression indicates that one derives satisfaction from another human being. The implication is clear—a person
as an individual is important. In addition to this expression, there
are other ways Wimbum people show respect for people as individuals. The first usage relates to Wimbum attitudes towards
"strangers," the second to marriage practice, and the third to *tfu*
discourse and practice.

The Wimbum people demonstrate pride and the value of a person
as an individual through the welcome extended to strangers. In
Wimbum society, the unwritten code of conduct is that residents of
a community welcome a guest who moves into their town. Where
it is possible, residents give the guest a piece of land on which to
build and farm. If this person is single and has good character, he
will be encouraged to marry a wife from the community. This is not
an economic transaction. Residents do not expect the guest to bring
something to the community. Rather, the practice is a recognition
of the importance of the newcomer and a communal expression of
the pride surrounding his or her coming into the community. To
underscore the importance attached to the recognition of the individuality of the sojourner among the Wimbum people, I explore a
common political praxis in Wimbum society.

The head of the town, the *fon*, generally informs the community of important events and gives warnings through public announcements at the marketplace. The messenger the *fon* sends to
make such announcements is usually accompanied by a masked
figure from the closed association *nwarong*—an association that
has been mislabeled a "secret society" in earlier anthropological
literature. In Ntumbaw, proclamations are usually made on market day, which takes place, according to the Wimbum calendar, on
the eighth day of the week, *Lih*. When such an announcement is
to be made, the spokesperson of the *fon* will arrive at the market
accompanied by the masked figure at a time when there is a large
number of people at the market. When the spokesperson arrives,
he invites the people to gather for the proclamation. Although he
speaks for the *fon*, the spokesperson always states that the message issues from *nwarong*, as it is a regulatory society. These proc-

Strangers —& converts— may get extra attention.

Nail sticks rat — Also concentrates on individual.

lamations generally concern seasonal activities such as the planting and harvesting of crops or important festivities. Sometimes
they warn people about danger the *fon* believes is about to come to
the town. A critical element of these pronouncements is a conclud-
ing reminder such as, "Do not destroy someone's property," "A son
of the soil should not hurt a stranger and vice versa," or "A son of
the soil should not touch a stranger's wife and children." The ex-
hortation that members of the community should not violate the
stranger's property and family indicates a healthy sense of respect
for the individual.[8] What is clearly implied here is that a person
qua individual is important, hence a violation of the stranger disrupts intersubjective relations.

A second example in which individuality is valued is in marriage transactions. The Wimbum people believe that no person
should be denied the experience of marriage. Marriage transactions among the Wimbum involve the giving of the bride wealth. If
an individual cannot afford bride wealth, there are provisions that
will allow the person to marry without it. The Wimbum's belief in
the importance of the individual is again expressed when *fo ni nwe*
overrides bride wealth. No individual should be denied the experience of marriage on the grounds that he cannot afford the bride
wealth.

The third area in which *fo ni nwe* is demonstrated is in *tfu*
discourse and its alleged practice. I interpret *tfu* as an intersubjective
transaction, because at the heart of the discourse about the negative use of *tfu* powers are claims that a person has done something
harmful to another person. The accusations focus on individuals.
When the head of a family wants to know why the treatment given
to an ill member of the community has not worked, he is demonstrating concern for an individual. I do not deny the communal
dimension of *tfu* discourse, which sometimes involves communal
cleansing rituals, however, what I want to emphasize is that when
members of the community accuse someone of killing another person through *tfu* powers, they are acting in defense of an individual
who has been stripped of the right to live by a *tfu* person.

Upholding a rigid communitarian perspective would make it
difficult to apply a Levinasian critique of intersubjective relations.
These three examples validate my intersubjective critique of the
negative deployment of *tfu* powers using Levinas's idea of a distinct
Other. Having established the place of intersubjective relations in
Wimbum society, I now discuss Levinas's ethics of the Other, presenting its implication for an ethical approach to Wimbum *tfu*.

LEVINAS AND THE ETHICS OF THE OTHER[9]

Emmanuel Levinas articulates the distinctiveness of a human Other in his philosophy, and in so doing he proposes a radical ethic that is both bold and inviting.[10] Levinas presents his thoughts in several works, but for this argument I focus on *Totality and Infinity* (1969), where the broad outline of Levinas's articulation of an irreducible "Other" is presented in detail.[11]

Levinas argues that war brings about the absence of morality. "War does not manifest exteriority and the Other as Other; it destroys the identity of the same" (Levinas 1969, 21). War is grounded in the concept of totality, which dominates Western thought. He proposes "Infinity" as the only way of bringing peace into the state of immorality and war. Peace is accomplished when beings exist in relationships that shun totality and embrace dialogue, departing from the anonymous utterance of history (Ibid., 23). Levinas also articulates an eschatological vision that breaks totality and retains the face of the Other as a context for ethics. This visage challenges a totalizing spirit, a spirit that focuses on knowledge and objectivity. Thus Levinas writes to defend a subjectivity that he grounds in the notion of infinity (Ibid., 26). He argues that it is in the human face that justice lingers and the idea of truth is born. I follow this intriguing argument to provide a critique of negative *tfu*.

I have provided a hermeneutics of *tfu*, which makes it possible for the reader to appreciate the negative aspects of *tfu* as immorality and war. The abuse of *tfu* power constitutes war within the family, since it is understood that the negative, destructive practices of *tfu* operate only along consanguinial lines. The image of war is apropos, because *tfu* accusations tend to divide families and make resolution and reconciliation difficult. The story of John, the university student cited in Chapter 2, whose death was blamed on *tfu*, demonstrates that such accusations can lead to verbal warfare and the separation of families. Members of the family settled the conflict, but later more problems emerged, continued, and intensified over a period of time. New but related charges were leveled against members of the family. This time it also was alleged that John's mother was practicing *tfu* to seek revenge for the death of her son. She was forced to leave the town.

This state of "war" that occurs among families and has intensified in the wake of massive economic difficulties in Cameroon requires a new approach to ethics. Levinas's work, proposing transcendence as a desire for the "Other," offers this new approach. In the overthrow of "totality," Levinas demonstrates the transcendence of another human being as separate, exterior, and never merely a correlate of the Same. The other is not an alter ego "but is prior to every initiative, to all imperialism of the Same" (Levinas 1969, 34, 38–39).[12] Levinas underscores transcendence when he declares that "the absolutely Other is Other." This is an invitation to replace identity with strangeness, exteriority, and an absolute Other who is not a divine being but a human Other. Thus the breach of human totality is achieved by recognizing a genuine human Other who resists objectification and whose face resists my control because "he escapes my grasp by an essential dimension even if I have him at my disposal" (Ibid., 39).

TOWARD A LEVINASIAN CRITIQUE OF *TFU*

In analyzing Wimbum *tfu*, I have argued that philosophical ethics should be employed to create a space for a theological conversation on *tfu* that does not demonize the individual. I have presented a sketch of the Wimbum society and have analyzed *tfu* from a Wimbum perspective, pointing out that *tfu* belongs to a class of terms that deals with the Wimbum outlook on life and on meaning-making events. When isolated and analyzed as I have done, *tfu* itself is rendered a dynamic concept. The Wimbum people have borrowed new terms and concepts from other parts of Cameroon to express activities that have a resemblance to what they consider the negative aspects of *tfu*. I also have argued that *tfu* can be studied as part of the African discourse of modernity and postmodernity. The concerns of modernity with *tfu* center around the debates that have taken place about its rationality. I have argued that the question of rationality ought to be considered in a context where the beliefs and practices take place. Using Bernstein's hermeneutical approach, I have demonstrated the necessity of considering *tfu* within a contextual ethics. The postmodern questioning spirit enables us to understand the various discourses on *tfu* as a construction of conflicting relationships. These conflicting relationships demonstrate that *tfu* can be regarded as power, gender, economic, and religious discourse. I also have stated that there are dimensions of individuality in Wimbum society that make it reasonable to articulate an ethics that focuses on the individual.

The ideas I present here are preliminary and provisional. My critique refers only to the negative application of *tfu* powers. I also do not claim that Wimbum moral thought employs similar categories as philosophical ethics. Yet Wimbum moral values and its rituals provide rich resources for ethical reflection and praxis that should be subjected to critical scrutiny. The goal of such an inquiry is not harmonization with philosophy but the development of a critical understanding and utilization of Wimbum ideas for moral thought. The fact that I do not seek harmonization with academic philosophy does not rule out the possibility of using philosophical categories to do a critique of those values. Those who engage in an ethical critique should take time to see the convergence or divergence of these ideas and to incorporate them into ethical reflection. I now present highlights of Levinas's ethics, suggesting how those ideas can be appropriated for a critique of *tfu*.

ETHICS IN THE CONTEXT OF *TFU* SHOULD PRIORITIZE THE PERSONAL

Levinas articulates a "post–phenomenological personalism" that stresses the priority of the personal and proposes a new relationship with people enacted in a conversation, which is marked by goodness and desire (Surber 1992). Conversation and dialogue recognize the foreignness of the Other and provide an opportunity for the Same to offer an apology for past wrongs. "Transcendence designates a relation with reality infinitely distant from my own reality, yet without this distance destroying this relation and without this relation destroying this distance, as would happen with relations within the Same" (Levinas 1969, 41).

The breach of totality implied by the emphasis on the personal challenges ontology and opposes the philosophy of Hegel, Heidegger, and to a certain extent Descartes. Western philosophy has privileged ontology, emphasizing the freedom of the thinker, and in so doing, has reduced the Other to the Same. This has obscured the Other and has enhanced the grasping powers of the subject, even if he or she is not portrayed as the all-knowing, self-actualized, self-conscious subject manifested in the historical development of the powerful Hegelian *Geist*. Ontology as *prima philosophia* (first philosophy) exalts power and its conceptualization, thematization, and cultivation. The primacy of ontological questions has totalized human beings as well as nature. Despite Heidegger's protest over the dominance of technology, in the end, the subject returns to "the pre-technological powers of possession" (Levinas 1969, 46).[13] Thus ontology as first philosophy is ultimately injustice, because it reduces the Other and rediscovers war, thereby reducing ethics to opinion.

At the heart of Levinas's project is a genuine human Other that cannot be analyzed, fully thematized, objectified, ridiculed, tortured, or murdered. The Other that Levinas wants us to recognize is an Other that is already there as one who addresses us. The Wimbum debates about the negative uses of *tfu* take place because people value a human Other who should not be violated or totalized. The imagery of totality in Levinas represents anything from political manipulation to racial annihilation. I take negative *tfu* to represent totalization to the extreme. I have already discussed dimensions of individuality in Wimbum society, which refer to a person as *nwe*, a human other qua individual. If this human Other is a victim of the negative use of *tfu,* he or she, in Levinasian terms, has been subjected to "totalization." A critique of *tfu* therefore elevates the personal rather than seeks to establish a system of ethics. *Tfu* practitioners who are accused of causing others ill harm, violate the personal well-being of another individual. If such claims are true, an individual Other's physical and mental health has been attacked, and the deliberations that the Wimbum people conduct stress the dignity of the individual person, even though they do not construct a particular system of thought or theory.

A CRITIQUE OF *TFU* SHOULD STRESS TRANSCENDENCE AND INFINITY

Levinas presents transcendence as the idea of infinity.[14] He reinterprets the Cartesian idea of the infinite to designate a relation with a being that is totally exterior to the thinking subject. Infinity and exteriority signify strangeness. The "I" is invited to think the good, to turn toward the Other, and to accept the Other as a gift in a face-to-face relationship where conversation is enacted. The face of the Other brings truth and teaching. The face-to-face conversation is a nonviolent moment in which meaning is not established through my initiative or the truth of history, which only amalgamates the Other. Meaning must arise by my speaking with him or her.

According to Levinasian formulations, the Same is invited to a notion of exteriority, which recognizes individuality and society. Levinas emphasizes a separate "I," who is not a cognate of the Same but different, who transcends the Same. This reformulation of the transcendent being in Descartes's "Meditations" (1969) challenges the Same to assume responsibility. As Theo De Boer points out, "The transcendence, the absolute distance from God, is thus converted or reverted to my responsibility" (De Boer 1995, 170).

Wimbum thought does not formulate the question in these terms, but the Wimbum recognize that one takes pride in another person. Thus rituals carried out to pronounce judgment on those who practice *tfu* negatively are a reminder that they violate the dignity of other people when they do so. Put in Levinasian terms, the Other transcends me, and if I encounter that transcendence, I will not use my *tfu* powers to force them to do what I merely want them to do.

Levinas presents a transcendent Other as an attempt to overturn the project of ontology. In *Totality and Infinity*, he shows that the process of assimilation of the Other is a life of enjoyment. Again, one cannot fail to notice parallels to the critique of *tfu* discourse. The practices of groups where *tfu* people meet, offer other people, and collect material wealth for themselves should be challenged, because such activities subvert the transcendence of the Other. In the practice of what I have described as *tfu jarr,* Wimbum discourse claims that *tfu* is employed to destroy property. Where human transcendence is recognized and stressed, one could make the case that their property also cannot be violated.

In Chapter 2, I referred to the argument advanced by Arens, that the idea that a person can kill another person and consume their flesh through "witchcraft" is a myth. He further argues that, historically, such myths were constructed in different communities and that anthropologists have perpetuated them through their own fascination with this idea. In a paper at the African Studies Association meeting in Chicago in November 1998, Emmanuel Eze questioned this fascination of anthropologists with the occult. He suggested that both the anthropologist and the sorcerer seem to be chasing the same thing. My concern is not to question whether this actually happens but to point out that in the situation where charges of *tfu* are brought, the words alone can have a powerful, destructive impact. The Wimbum people recognize the power of words, which is why they have social rituals through which they can resolve disputes. One such ritual is called *susi bshu,* or "washing of the mouths." People do this often because if they neglect it, unresolved discussion will poison present relationships. One does not have to believe that people literally "eat" other people. Poisonous words can cause many of the problems associated with the negative powers of *tfu.* At the same time, I am not reducing the notion that people can and do consume human flesh to mere emotional distress. This study does not have the medical, psychological, and occult insights to make such a claim. However, if it were true, the one who consumes another person's flesh commits capital totality.

When he presents a critique of Martin Heidegger's notion of care, Levinas uses language that people working with concepts such as *tfu* can appreciate. He rejects an ontology that possesses (Levinas 1969, 109). Thus, the Same establishes a relationship with the world that Levinas describes as a monism, characterized by an autonomy that strives for gratification.[15] In language reminiscent of the language used to describe the alleged activities of *tfu* people, Levinas describes the Same sinking its teeth into another person. It is a process of consumption that results in "the transmutation of the Other into the same, which is the essence of enjoyment: an energy that is Other, recognized as Other, recognized, we will see, as sustaining the very act that is directed upon it, become in enjoyment, my own energy, my strength, me" (Ibid., 111).

I must of course point out the limitations of this kind of comparison. People accused of *tfu* hardly describe how human flesh is consumed, let alone describe this act as "enjoyment." However, the graphic metaphors of "sinking one's teeth into another person" provide an image of what happens in the *tfu* realm where human flesh is supposedly eaten. A further difference here is that in ontological thinking, the "need" of the subject can influence him or her to totalize, consume, and create his or her own identity, while in *tfu* beliefs and alleged practice, the "need" of the *tfu* person can cause him or her to eliminate the Other person. Both are totalizing processes.

This process requires a base or a "dwelling" that signifies the domain of control for the same. Adriaan Peperzak makes an interesting connection between what Levinas calls the house or dwelling and what Heidegger designates as the tool—it is a place of action. The one who occupies such a dwelling place is familiar with it and from it carries out the controlling activities (Peperzak 1993, 157). Levinas uses religious language to describe the process of consumption and enjoyment as "pagan" sensibilities. These images can only be compared to *tfu* in a partial way. The image of dwelling denotes the life and practice of someone who exercises control over his or her environment. In *tfu*, this is similar to so-called "markets" where practitioners gather mostly to get things and to trade human flesh with one another. These markets and places where Others as victims are tied like tethered goats waiting for their day of slaughter are similar to "dwelling" places where *tfu* people enjoy and consume human flesh.

People who reflect on ethical issues in Wimbum society must insist that the Other, who is at risk of assimilation or obliteration through the economy of dwelling, is a distinct individual who should not be subjected to such treatment. Levinas directs his critique at the phenomenological process, which is why he argues, "The Other signals himself [herself] but does not present himself [herself]" (Levinas 1969, 176). The claims made about *tfu* are more powerful. If *tfu* powers are used, it is difficult for the victim to escape in the manner that Levinas suggests that the Other can refract from the phenomenological process. In most cases, the elders of the community or members of the family would intervene in the interest of the ones that have been subjected to such control. The issue here is not if the Other actually succeeds in escaping from the control of someone who has *tfu* powers but the fact that the distinctiveness of the Other constitutes an injunction on the consuming powers of the one that exerts control.

I probe this issue of consumption in *tfu* a bit further. In my analysis of nondomestic terms in Wimbum society, I argued that such words clearly suggest a widespread belief that people kill others through *nyongo* and *kupe* societies (specific dwellings) to obtain wealth. If this is true, it represents absolute control in which a genuine Other is not only manipulated but is supposedly annihilated to satisfy the financial desires of another person. Those who possess *tfu* powers according to this logic would make it difficult for others to compete. However, in most Wimbum communities, those who have a reputation of possessing negative *tfu* powers are not the wealthiest members of the community. When you ask people why that is so, they say that it is because they have misused what should be good power. The Wimbum complaints about *nyongo* and *kupe* are a resounding rebuff of such use of *tfu* powers.

Another objection that could be raised here is that it is wrong to stress transcendence in the Levinasian sense in Wimbum society where only elders are held in high regard. Such an objection is not correct, because respecting another person and considering him or her transcendent should not interfere with cultural norms such as paying respect to elders. The notion of transcendence, as Levinas argues, limits totality and tyranny. In Wimbum society, people, including elders, show deference to twins who themselves may not be elders. They do so because they believe that they have special abilities. One could argue that I am calling the extension of the relationship to twins to include all people, so that *tfu* powers might be limited. Stressing views of human transcendence that make human life inviolable strengthens Wimbum ethics.[16]

ETHICS IN *TFU* CALLS FOR TRUTH AND JUSTICE

In the third section of *Totality and Infinity*, Levinas defines truth and justice in three theses. This is an important moment in Levinas's thought, and I spend some time here tracing his argument. The first thesis calls into question the traditional notion of freedom. The second traces the investiture of freedom, or what Levinas calls "critique." Finally, Levinas argues that truth presupposes justice, a conclusion that will become clear as I trace out his argument.

First, Levinas questions the wrongful use of freedom to totalize others and instead proposes the cultivation of "desire" (Levinas 1969, 82). This is a desire for the Other expressed in discourse, which Levinas argues makes justice possible "in the uprightness of the welcome made to the face" (Ibid.). Truth, for Levinas, is linked to intelligibility. Knowledge, however, is comprehension in a radical form, subordinating knowledge and comprehension to justice. Levinas also is critical of the use of freedom to suspend ethical action. "The first consciousness of my immorality is not my submission to facts, but to the infinite Other. The idea of totality and infinity differ precisely in that the first is purely theoretical, while the second is moral" (Ibid., 83). Thus, freedom, which becomes ashamed when confronted with its failure to respond to a genuine Other, finds truth not in theoretical deductions but in an encounter with another person. The implications are clear; the Other is not a fact as it is in Kant and the critical tradition, nor is the Other an obstacle or a threat as it becomes in Sartre. Rather, the Other is a human person who helps us know our own imperfections (Ibid., 84).

Upon a first reading, it seems that Levinas has placed the Other in a privileged position. This is true. Levinas, however, also speaks of a mutuality that is worth noting: "And if the Other can invest me and invest my freedom, of itself arbitrary, this is in the last analysis because I myself can feel myself to be the Other of the Other. But this comes about only across very complex structures" (Levinas 1969, 84). Here is where desire comes in. Desire is important, because now my conscience "welcomes the Other." As in Buber, one goes out to meet the Other, an activity that questions "the naive right of my power. . . . Morality begins when freedom, instead of being justified by itself, feels itself to be arbitrary and violent" (Ibid.).

Second, Levinas discusses the investiture of freedom, or "critique." Knowledge as critique, even in the Kantian tradition, is possible in a rational being who also is self-critical. According to Levinas, this procedure of identifying the foundation with "an

objective knowledge of knowledge is to suppose in advance that
freedom can be founded only on itself, for freedom, the determination of the Other by the same, is the very movement of representation and of its evidence" (Ibid., 85). This ignores the arbitrariness
of freedom "which is precisely what has to be grounded." Levinas
argues instead that proper critical knowledge should lead to the
Other. "To welcome the Other is to put in question my freedom"
(Ibid.).

This journey takes the reader beyond Cartesianism represented
by the *cogito*, where *cogito* is understood as the commencement of
knowledge. Any awakening or commencement takes place in front
of the Other (Ibid., 86). In opposition to the philosophical tradition, the Other is not the master who reawakens what the ego
already has. This is a human Other who eludes attempts to
thematize him or her. In other words, this Other is not an object
of my speculation and control. To welcome the Other is to be aware
of my injustice toward him or her, because I have dominated or
totalized the Other and such awareness should prohibit my control of the other. In a statement highly critical of the philosophical
tradition, Levinas says:

> If philosophy consists in knowing critically, that is, in seek-
> ing a foundation for its freedom, in justifying it, it begins
> with conscience, to which the Other is presented as the
> Other, and where the movement of thematization is in-
> verted. But this inversion does not amount to 'know one-
> self' (as in Socrates) as a theme attended to by the Other,
> but rather in submitting oneself to an exigency, to morality
> (Levinas 1969, 86).

Thus the Other measures me. The freedom of the Other does
not come from me but is an inherent part of the Other. Levinas
calls for an inversion of the prerogatives of the Same in order to
terminate imperialism wrongly construed as freedom.

> In this inversion, the Other imposes himself [herself] as an
> exigency that dominates this freedom, and hence [is] more
> primordial than anything that takes place in me. The Other,
> whose exceptional presence is inscribed in the ethical im-
> possibility of killing him in which I stand, marks the end
> of powers. If I can no longer have power over him it is
> because he overflows absolutely every idea I can have of
> him[17] (Levinas 1969, 87).

Thus justice takes place only when one realizes that the Other is not constituted by thought. The Other is independent and should be welcomed as such. "The term welcome of the Other expresses a simultaneity of activity and passivity which places the relation with the Other outside of the dichotomies valid for things: the *a priori* and the *a posteriori*, activity and passivity" (Levinas 1969, 89). Levinas contends that, while the Other can and indeed should be known, justice, which he sees as the condition of knowing, is not "a *noesis* correlative of a *noema*" (Ibid., 89, 90).[18] Levinas takes us through the role of language to indicate what justice is.

Husserl made an important contribution by positing signification in his notion of auto-representation. (Husserl 1970, 1982) However, this self-representation has no meaning in and of itself, because signification takes place only with the break of ultimate unity of the satisfied being. Signification "is posited in a discourse, in a conversation [*entre-tein*] which proposes the world. This proposition is held between [*se tient entre*] two points which do not constitute a system, a cosmos, a totality," as in Hegel (Levinas 1969, 96). For Levinas, the signifier is a concrete individual who manifests himself or herself in speaking about a world in dialogue. In the dialogical encounter, the interpretive key does not lie with the Same but in the presence of the Other, "who can come to the assistance of his [her] discourse, the teaching quality of all speech. Oral discourse is the plenitude of discourse" (Ibid.). In further discussion of the significance of language and speech, Levinas states emphatically that "language is not one modality of symbolism; every symbolism refers already to language" (Ibid.).

How is this related to justice? Levinas argues that the origin of justice is the action of the Other, who through dialogue calls into question the freedom of the Same. Conscience and desire are conditions of consciousness constituted in the welcoming of the Other, a response to the judgment he or she passes on my action. "Association, or the welcoming of the Other is conscience" (Ibid., 100). A moral relation with the one who judges limits my freedom. Since this is where language begins, Levinas insists that the speaker must remain foreign, although he or she proposes a world. It is this foreignness that judges me and also places him or her outside of my knowing. All of this is possible through the use of language.

For language can be spoken only if the interlocutor is the commencement of his discourse, if, consequently, he remains beyond the system, if he is not on the same plane as myself. The interlocutor is not a Thou, he is a You; he reveals himself in his lordship. Thus, exteriority coincides with a mastery. My freedom is thus challenged by a master who can invest it. Truth, the sovereign exercise of freedom, becomes henceforth possible. (Levinas 1969, 101)

One can thus conclude that truth and justice are not attained in solitary thought but become clear in a face-to-face conversation with the Other (Levinas 1981, 45).[19]

Truth for Levinas involves a different kind of knowing than merely an accumulation of fact. It involves a direct engagement in ethics, which starts with a basic act such as engaging in dialogue with the Other. To know truth is to recognize that the face of the Other limits and prohibits injustice. To practice truth is to welcome the Other. The act of welcome initiated in dialogue is what Levinas calls justice.

A critique of *tfu* requires that truth and justice be grounded in conversation between members of the family and the community. It is in such a conversation that one can say emphatically that the truth requires welcoming and having a dialogue with another person. The Other is not and should not become "meat" for consumption. To know the truth is to recognize him or her as a person with whom one can have and should have a dialogue. That dialogue is predicated on the realization that we cannot kill the Other. To knowingly hurt another person through *tfu* is to live in untruth and injustice. In dialogue, the Other proposes a world that calls into question any control that I may exert over him or her through *tfu.*

For example, the story of John, the university student, shows the need for open dialogue. John's father had several wives, each of whom had their own children. Family resources often were pooled together. Although the wives had their own farms, they also were expected to work on the farms owned by John's father. The other wives and their children felt that by pooling their resources they were contributing to John's education. There is nothing wrong with this, as families often do so. In my conversation with members of the family, I had the sense that there was some concern that their resources were being used to educate John as the future head of the family at the expense of the other children. The idea that John could possibly be the future chief and that they were contributing to his education may have provoked some jealousy. This is not a unique situation among the Wimbum people, however, when such problems come up, they can be difficult to resolve. I am convinced that open dialogue could have provided an opportunity for the entire family to address some of these concerns and to solidify family relations with ethical relations. The absence of such a dialogue may have tempted some family members to turn to other powers to redress what they perceived as injustice. Of course, since I have no *tfu* powers myself, I cannot state categorically that the events happened in the way in which they were conveyed to me. I am suggesting, however, that justice could have been achieved through a face-to-face dialogue and negotiation.

THE ETHICS OF THE FACE INVITES RESPONSIBILITY

According to Levinas, the structures of language announce the "ethical inviolability of the Other and, without any odor of the 'numinous,' his 'holiness'" (Levinas 1969, 195). This is not a consciousness that originates with the "I," but rather one that puts the "I" into question. "The first revelation of the Other, presupposed in all Other relations with him, does not consist in grasping him in his negative resistance and in circumventing him by ruse. I do not struggle with a faceless god, but I respond to his expression, to his revelation" (Ibid., 197).

The phenomenon of the Other's face then, as Levinas understands it, resists possession and invites one into a "relation commensurate with a power exercised, be it enjoyment or knowledge" (Ibid., 198). This open invitation can be negative, because "the Other is the sole being I can wish to kill" (Ibid.). However, Levinas envisions a transcendence of the face that is stronger than murder with a resistance whose primordial expression forbids the commission of murder. "Infinity presents itself as a face in the ethical resistance that paralyses my powers and from the depths of defenseless eyes rises firm and absolute in its nudity and destitution" (Ibid., 199–200). What occurs in the epiphany of the face is that I am invited to ethical responsibility.[20]

The expression of the face of the Other does not come from an assemblage of terms but is an exchange that incorporates a word of honor from the Other. It goes beyond the mystical, or a relationship in which the original being overwhelms people and interlocutors play a role that originates outside of them (Ibid., 202). The expression of the face through language discards violence, proclaims peace, and brings something new to me which, according to Levinas, is teaching.

The idea of infinity in me, implying a content overflowing
the container, breaks with the prejudice of maieutics without breaking with rationalism, since the idea of infinity, far
from violating the mind, conditions non-violence itself, that
is, establishes ethics. The Other is not for reason a scandal
that puts it in dialectical movement, but the first teaching.
(Levinas 1969, 204)

In this new relationship of responsibility established in the
face of the Other, discourse conditions thought. Levinas challenges
the Husserlian and the Heideggerian understanding of words. He
departs from the view that the sign forms signification and builds
thought through interaction with Others as the only possibility for
understanding meaning. One could argue that Husserl and
Heidegger do the same thing. The difference here, however, is that
for Levinas, meaning is grounded in the face of the Other, in which
"all recourse to words takes place already within the primordial
face-to-face of languages" (Levinas 1969, 206). Infinity in this case
does not present itself as transcendental thought or meaningful
activity but rather as the face of the Other putting me into question. "It is the ethical exigency of the face, which puts into question
the consciousness that welcomes it. The consciousness of obligation
is no longer a consciousness, since it tears consciousness up from
its center, submitting it to the Other" (Ibid., 207).

In stressing exteriority over interiority, dialogue and welcome
over totality, Levinas argues that the Other invites the Same to
responsibility. The idea here is that the Other is foreign yet close
enough for us to render service to him or her. The Other in this
case can be the homeless, the widow, or the weakest in the society.
We are commanded to be responsible for them. There is a deliberate double meaning in Levinas's Other that makes his call for
responsibility toward the Other very challenging. The Other is at
once destitute and helpless, yet foreign, transcendent, and appear-
ing from a height.

I find the ideas that Levinas works with applicable to a critique
of *tfu* in an intriguing way. The Other who is affected by *tfu* is
destitute because he or she is at the mercy of the one that is privy
to some power and knowledge. Yet on the grounds of Levinasian
ethics, the Other should be treated by the one who has *tfu* power
as a transcendent human Other who resists violence and offers
peace. Family obligations are quite important for the Wimbum
people. Caputo's (1993) claim that we are obligated to one another
communicates what I know of the Wimbum. Family members take

these obligations seriously. I want to spell out different areas of responsibility that present themselves in this connection when we consider the whole picture of *tfu* and the related terms that I laid out in the hermeneutics of *tfu*.

First, those claiming to have any *tfu* are obligated to use it responsibly. Responsibility rules out personal ambition that is pursued at the expense of the Other. The Wimbum believe and expect *fon*s and other leaders in society to have a "second pair of eyes." If they do, these "pair of eyes" should be used to promote the welfare of the Other and the society. When an individual uses this "pair of eyes" to subvert the succession procedure in the event of the death of a *fon,* for example, a proper application of Wimbum thought requires that this be challenged as an irresponsible use of the power.[21]

I do not wish to imply that employing *tfu* power for the good of whoever has it is necessarily evil. As Geschiere points out, the Maka people are not primarily concerned with moral evaluations, but there are indications that certain expressions of *djambe* are negative (Geschiere 1982, 102). Geschiere also points out that sometimes these forces paradoxically serve to preserve the moral order. The Maka people expect leaders especially to seek protection in the realm of the *djambe.* Furthermore, the main reason people concern themselves with this power is their desire to have power (Ibid., 103, 104). Perhaps the strongest claim that Geschiere makes for the ambiguity of *djambe* is that the weak can turn to it in order to redress the excesses of those who possess it (Ibid., 104). Such powers should not be used to violate the dignity of other people. They should be used to build, as Levinas points out, a "relation with the Other as a relation with his [her] transcendence—the relation with the Other who puts into question the brutal spontaneity of one's immanent destiny—introduces into me what was not in me. But this 'action,' upon my freedom precisely puts an end to violence" (Levinas 1969, 203).

What counts as responsible use of this power is open to debate. There are some families in the town of Ntumbaw whose members have succeeded and are now part of what the anthropological literature calls the "elites." Other inhabitants of the town claim that they have special powers that allow them to protect these successful elites. In one particular case, the people who claim to have such powers continually bombard the parents of some of the elites with demands for money, claiming that they could perform certain rituals to protect their children. The mother of these children has no rest because of these demands. The frequency and amount of money and gifts they demand make this practice an extortion and for that reason constitutes a violation of the family. While the family may have initially established a client relationship with these people, it now is complaining that the relationship is out of hand. They cannot make any decision as a family without the intervention of these people. It is clear that the negative use of *tfu* does not have to involve killing someone. This kind of pressure and control over a family constitutes an irresponsible use of power.

Responsibility also includes looking out for the economic well-being of the Other. In the discussion of Wimbum society, I have shown the interrelatedness of that society to the extended family system. The *fon* is the head of the town, but the *fais* who head the large families are the ones who run the day-to-day activities of the town. The Wimbum people say, when your brother climbs the palm tree, you will be the first to eat the palm fruit. What is implied in this expression is that when a member of the family succeeds, he or she should help other members. Where there has been neglect of this principle, the doors are opened for *tfu* people to express their discontent through the negative use of such powers.

The issue of responsibility here is a very difficult and challenging one for Wimbum elites. The time has come for them to accept this responsibility in a critical manner. In carrying out their responsibility to members of their families, they should invest in the future of their relatives by providing gifts and bequests to them through voluntary associations, sponsoring attendance at schools and universities. What makes this difficult is that one elite cannot do this for all of his or her relatives. Furthermore, some of the elites themselves do not have enough to live well in a society such as Cameroon, where the economy has declined. Thus the challenge here is to be able to do something with and for the Other while doing something for themselves as well. Carrying out such a responsibility should not force the elites, who are expected to support the less affluent members of their families, to become corrupt in order to provide for their families.

Assuming responsibility for family and members of the extended family is a difficult task. Some elites prefer to stay away from their places of origin. They build a token house in their towns of origin but spend most of the time in urban areas where they may be employed in civil service or in the private sector. Sometimes certain elites stay away because their relatives have advised them not to come home, suspecting that someone may use *tfu* to hurt them. Thus some elites remain in urban places and do not return home, except in cases of death in the family.

There are no easy answers to what people should do to carry out their responsibilities in these circumstances so their relatives will not use *tfu* against them. Rather than avoid the Other, one ought to establish an engaging, critical dialogue with the home base. If this dialogue is open and allows the Other to be heard on his or her own terms, truth will emerge and justice can be done, both to the Other and to the elite. Such an open dialogue will reveal the truth, and the elite will not fear that some members of the family will milk them dry of whatever resources they may have. The ethical responsibility is clear. One does not turn away from the destitute. The obligation to help the widowed or the poor implies working with them to improve their economic condition. In the case of the Wimbum society, this means that elites sometimes have to assume responsibility for the education and apprenticeship of extended family members. It is an obligation that should be undertaken not out of fear of *tfu* but because one recognizes their ethical responsibility to the Other. The hope here is that, in open dialogue, those who prefer to use *tfu* negatively to force others to supply their needs will be willing to work with other members of the family to improve their own economic condition.

The responsibility here is enormous and continues to be a burden to the elites. The challenge is for those who have been successful either through education or business to use their power and freedom in a direction that recognizes exteriority in Levinasian terms. Recognition of exteriority then implies deemphasizing consumption, assimilation or a more positive feeling of being at home in one's dwelling, which Levinas has attacked as the interiority of Dasein. Wimbum thought obviously does not speak in these terms, but a critique of consumption and assimilation, by those who have knowledge—the so-called modern elite—is inherent in the expectations placed on them by their society. Their financial obligation to their communities, which may be carried out when they contribute money for projects at their homes through self-help organizations, voluntary associations, and urban organizations, is a step toward deemphasizing the assimilating project of the Same. Such activities will not eliminate all jealousy, nor will they eliminate all *tfu* practice. Rather, if a genuine, open, and critical dialogue is established, and people recognize and carry out their responsibility to the Other, first of all, in the economic arena, it could be possible to mitigate some negative aspects of *tfu* that occur when these obligations are ignored.[22]

Finally, responsibility involves a humane treatment of those who allegedly are guilty of *tfu*. The literature is full of different

ways in which those accused of *tfu*-like activities have been mis-
treated in different parts of Africa. Wimbum society itself has re-
sponded to *tfu* accusations in a variety of ways. There are times
when leaders reprimanded those accused of *tfu* publicly and invited
members of the public to "shame" them in a public ritual of "sham-
ing." Other forms of punishment include fines, which have included
payment of fowl or goats. These are never cash transactions. Severe discipline in the past included banishment from the community. In fact, in 1989, one member of the Ntumbaw community was
exiled and told not to return to the community. There also are
claims that in the past, people who were accused of serious *tfu*
violations were executed.

All of these are avenues available in Wimbum society to examine and rehabilitate individuals found guilty of the negative use of
tfu. I stress that an ethical approach demands that in cases where
individuals deserve some kind of punishment, responsibility toward the Other implies that the "guilty" party be treated in a
humane way. The colonial enterprise in most African societies attempted to eliminate executions of people who were accused of
engaging in activities similar to *tfu*—activities that could harm or
destroy others and their property. In most cases, colonial reaction
backfired. O'Neill (1991) has argued that the suppression of the
sasswood ordeal among the Moghamo of the Grassfields reportedly
increased rather than diminished "witchcraft" activities. The colonial authorities abolished such practices, because many people who
were given the sasswood died. It is difficult to say whether they
died because the dosage was too potent or whether they were guilty
of practicing witchcraft. The local people who administered the
ordeal believed that individuals guilty of "witchcraft" would die,
regardless of how potent the ordeal was. In a similar ritual, the
Wimbum people once administered a substance called *ngurr*. Anyone accused of practicing *tfu* was given this mixture to drink. If
they survived, they were innocent of the accusations brought against
them. If they died, it was presumed that they were guilty. It is
clear to me that this is not a humane way of establishing guilt.
Responsibility for the Other demands that any individual guilty of
tfu should be treated with compassion and not be given a substance
that may cause their death. Several people died in the Wimbum
area in 1999, and in most of these cases, their relatives were accused of using *tfu* powers to cause their deaths. I was recently in
Cameroon and it was reported that a woman was beaten to death
at Mbah. Another woman was beaten and sent away from the town
of Ntumbaw. It is reported that she died some weeks later, and

some suspect that her death may be connected to that beating. What is important to me here is not whether these people were guilty—what is important is the responsible, humane treatment of another human being, which is clearly lacking when people are paraded in the streets and beaten to death.

ETHICS IN THE CONTEXT OF *TFU* SHOULD BALANCE INDIVIDUALITY AND SOCIETY

The thrust of Levinas's ethics is that ethics prioritizes the personal. He maintains this focus on the person and does not provide a detailed discussion of relations in society, except for a few important hints (Peperzak 1993, 166). These gaps in Levinas's account remind one that perspectives on social philosophy and communal thought in African society are ignored, at a great price. There is a need to carefully negotiate the relationship between the individual and the community, because the discourse of *tfu* involves individuals as well as communities. Levinas recognizes multiplicity as a given, and he states that the task of politics is to ensure justice within that multiplicity.

Levinas argues that the language that establishes a relation between the Same and the Other should not be understood as an "I-Thou" relationship that ignores other people, but rather that it should be seen that "in its frankness it refuses the clandestinity of love, where it loses its frankness and meaning and turns into laughter and cooing" (Levinas 1969, 213). Beyond the "clandestinity" of love, the expression of the face also implies a third party who looks at me and observes my relationship to the Other. Levinas spells a relation that exceeds the human-divine relationship, the relation between lovers, and includes the community and society. "The epiphany of the face *qua* face opens humanity" (Ibid., 213) The scenario is not one in which there is first a face, which manifests a being who then reflects on justice. For Levinas, the face as face opens humanity.

Levinas does not ground society in biological terms but rather in ethical terms. Biological terms cannot convey the kind of relationship he proposes. "But the human community instituted by language, where interlocutors remain absolutely separated, does not constitute the unity of genus. It is stated as a kinship of [men]" (Levinas 1969, 214). For Levinas, brotherhood, and I would add sisterhood, is not determined by resemblance or a common cause but by the "phenomenon of solidarity."

Levinas structures society around the idea of guilt and inno-cence. To talk of guilt and innocence is to presuppose a third party. One is guilty in respect to another person or a certain principle. This presupposes a free ego that is not part of totality (Ibid., 29). In other words, guilt can only be established in the presence of another person who is Other than the Same, who is free. Further-more, Levinas compares the notion of society he is attempting to sketch to the ontological structure of monotheistic religions, where there exists a transcendent God. For Levinas, this transaction between a transcendent God and people presupposes a society. The idea here is that it is in this society that one can legitimately gain pardon (Ibid., 30).[23] Justice is validated by the laws of society: "And we do not put into this activity our concern for justice except for being assured that the general laws of society are just, and all effects of our action on third persons have been allowed for in conditions where our everyday acts will be done" (Levinas 1987, 32).[24] For Levinas, the very idea of "human" implies fraternity ca-pable of displaying two aspects: the individual who is separate and cannot be reduced to the logical status of genus, and the kind of relationship that can be likened to the commonness of Father. Thus there is a kinship that Levinas argues must exist for society to be a fraternal community where the face presents itself for a welcome. What takes place through this relation is asymmetrical. It is so because the Other is a stranger, a widow, an orphan, and the most vulnerable in society to whom one is obligated.

One can gain insight from Levinas on the idea of community, although he has not discussed it at length. A community is not merely a "professional organization." The structure of "we" is not made up of a common task—although there is nothing wrong with individuals coming together for a common task. These kinds of common-cause groups do provide some sense of community and do meet some needs. What makes Levinas's formulation powerful is the notion that a community is not grounded merely on common interest but on the infinity, the destitution of the Other. This im-mediately puts one under obligation (Lingis 1994).

AN ETHICS OF *TFU* SHOULD BE PLURALISTIC

I assume that the Wimbum people who have demonstrated that certain concepts can be borrowed from other parts of Cameroon will choose other ways of addressing questions posed by the act of *tfu*. In terms of methodology, no single approach, not even Levinas's, which I have used as a basis for this study, can claim to speak with finality. Levinas himself rejects idealist philosophy and claims without expanding that idealism reduces ethics to politics where society runs like a system. Against Kant, he argues that in the kingdom of ends, people are defined as wills capable of being affected by universals. In this structure, multiplicity rests only on the hope that there can be happiness. Levinas instead focuses on the "interdiscoursivity" made possible by language rather than on the idealist notion of the kingdom of ends.

It is important at this point to ask if Levinas does not ignore something important. If his goal is to reject Kantian idealism, the question remains whether "will" can always be reduced to reason. One would argue that by opting for a deliberate relationship with the Other, Levinas could advance a strong view of the human *Wille*, perhaps in the Kantian sense. I am not convinced that if Levinas were to argue that there is a definite act of the will involved in the movement he has posited, he would have to recoil to an idealist position or fall back into Husserlian intentionality. In other words, has Levinas not invited us to undertake a will to desire? Can one not separate this will to desire the Other from the trappings of idealist philosophy and still retain Levinas's bold project? This is a tension in Levinas's work that needs further probing. Furthermore, one also could question why Levinas thinks political society is a system. Since his point is to offer a critique of idealism, one can only assume that Levinas opposes a position that totalizes the relationship between the "Other and I" by deriving it from an idealist premise as a calculus, approaching each other on the basis of what Levinas characterizes as "ideal necessities" (Levinas 1969, 216). The tension here is whether one can posit a society where the *politea* is not organized as a totality, or does not end that way. It seems to me that by taking this path, Levinas can still posit a sociality that gives priority to the personal, in which the human will is operative in a conscious effort to relate to the Other in precisely the manner that Levinas has argued.

Levinas's proposals call for recognition that a person should not impose his or her will on another person. This anti-idealist view of the will, where the will represents the possibility of violence, can be corrected by an emphasis on a different understanding of the ability and the will to the good—beyond even our idea of the good. This calls for boldness in *willing* dialogue rather than violence. Those who have *tfu* have to will the good and move toward others without using the negative *tfu* powers they possess. This opens possibilities for a new kind of discourse on the negative use of *tfu*.

A CRITIQUE OF *TFU* REQUIRES RETHINKING RELIGIOUS ETHICS

No one religious or philosophical tradition can monopolize a discussion of *tfu*. In the Wimbum society, the resources of indigenous religion, as well as Christianity and Islam, have to be employed to address *tfu*. My background in the philosophy of religion and Christian theology has influenced not only my language but also the categories I have employed throughout this work. I do not claim that only philosophical ethics and Christian theology can deal adequately with this issue. Rather, I contend that Christian theology has failed to deal with it and needs the categories of philosophical ethics and Wimbum moral discourse to reenter the debate. A religious conversation on *tfu* should utilize all religious avenues open to Wimbum society.

Writing specifically about Judaism, Levinas has argued that one can only experience God through a relationship with another person (Levinas 1990). Levinas is clear that human freedom and self-consciousness are means to reach the Other. It is this moral dimension of human consciousness that is united with the consciousness of God. Given this perspective, a religious ethical view is not something ancillary.

> Ethics is not the corollary of the vision of God, it is that very vision. Ethics is not an optic, such that everything I know of God and everything I can hear of His Word and reasonably say to him must find an ethical expression. . . . To know God is to know what must be done. Here education—obedience to the Other will—is supreme instruction: the knowledge of this will which is itself the basis of all reality. In the ethical relation, the Other is presented at the same time as being absolutely other, but this radical alterity in relation to me does not destroy or deny my freedom (Levinas 1969, 16).

In the next chapter I propose that Christian theology should utilize Levinas's phenomenology of *eros* as a point of departure for ethical relations. This means that relationships between people should be based on the sort of metaphysical desire articulated by Levinas. The cultivation of this kind of desire means that people will demonstrate a genuine desire for other people but will be willing to "let go" as well. Thus, people may possess certain powers, but they will not use them at the expense of someone else. As part of the religious approach, I also propose that we stress human transcendence. There is no indication in Levinas's texts that he wants to elevate human beings beyond a divine being. When he refers to another human being, he talks of transcendence. In the Christian tradition, where people are taught that only Christ is Lord, this may seem to pose problems. But Levinas is simply saying that the Other person should rise above our own interest and schemes. Moving in this direction will strengthen existing human relations in the Wimbum society and will allow religious ethics to focus on a genuinely human Other. I now turn in Chapter 5 to the phenomenology of *eros* proposed by Levinas to argue that it is an appropriate basis for community relations. Those relations are anchored in an intersubjectivity that should be grounded in the alterity, infinity, and transcendence of a concrete, historical, human Other.

Chapter 5

Toward a Philosophical and Theological Critique of *Tfu*

In this chapter, I propose a philosophical and theological critique of *tfu*. One of my central assumptions is that theological reflection in Africa should take a "felt need" such as *tfu* seriously. I review the search for an African theology in the first section, and I argue in the second section that agape is an inadequate motif for contemporary theological reflection. In the last section I propose that *eros*, interpreted phenomenologically by Levinas, be appropriated as a motif for philosophical and theological thinking by the Wimbum and other African contexts to address a felt need such as *tfu*.

THE SEARCH FOR AN APPROPRIATE
THEOLOGY FOR AFRICA

For over three decades, African theologians have engaged in a quest for a postcolonial theology that will respond to the human condition in Africa. In his discussion of Africanisms, Mudimbe argues that theologians who have integrated linguistic and cultural expressions into theological reflection have raised questions about the compatibility and difference between Christianity and African religions (Mudimbe 1988, 171).[1] Liberation and reconstruction theologians continue to focus on socioeconomic, and religio-cultural issues and sociopolitical and ethical problems. Fabian Eboussi-Boulaga, in his critique of Christianity, argues that revelation is God's gift of liberation concretized in the event of the incarnation. The task of theology, therefore, is to enable the community to work for human

101

liberation and the reconstruction of relationships within and the structures of society (Ebousi-Boulaga 1981; Villa-Vicencio 1992; Mugambi 1995).

Mudimbe argues that the missionary enterprise confronted Africa with a discourse that had political, economic, and religious implications (Mudimbe 1988, 45). The colonial mandate received papal blessings through *Dominator Dominus Terra Nullius*, a bull that sanctioned the colonization, marginalization, and enslavement of non-Christians facilitating the Western adventure into other lands. This activity ignored the possibility of dialogue with so-called "pagans," who were required by the missionaries to convert to Christianity on missionary terms (Ibid., 48).[2] Eboussi-Boulaga points out that the missionary enterprise employed language and practices that sidelined African realities and compelled conformity to a new worldview. The missionaries presented this worldview as divine revelation.[3]

The missionary project in Cameroon, issuing from its symbolic seat of power the "mission compound," is regarded by some as an invading civilization. In the southern regions of Cameroon, Mongo Beti's novels, *Le Pauvre Christ de Bomba* (1956) and *Le Roi Miraculé* (1958), are critiques of the mission compound model. Although the missionaries depended on the people for the success of their message, the mission compound model emphasized the virtue of minimal contact with local people (Beti 1956, 1957).[4] Thomas Beidelman's *Colonial Evangelism* is another powerful critique of the missionary enterprise, specifically the mission compound model (Beidelman 1982).[5]

In addition to this spatial separation, engaging in indigenous cultural activities was frowned upon. In the towns of Ntumbaw and Njirong, Christians were asked to renounce their membership in cultural organizations that would require participation in masked dances such as *mkung* and *toh*.[6] More recently, in the early 1970s, these towns, in spite of a bitter chieftaincy dispute in Ntumbaw, went through a cultural renaissance. New cultural organizations were formed, and new dances were created to revive masked performances. Even with such a massive reorganization, aided at times by the then Cameroon National Union Political Party, Christians were apprehensive about participating. I remember vividly the days when inquisitorial "Christian meetings" were held in town to examine Christians who were caught participating in masked performances. The Muslims in Ntumbaw did not forbid their followers from participating in these dances. Generally, they were more tolerant of the local culture than were the Christians. Today, Wimbum churches as well as other African churches and their theologians continue to struggle with the problems of being an African and Christian. The task of articulating a theology that is sensitive to the local culture of the people remains a felt need.

African theologians have used different methods to achieve this goal. Mudimbe points out that Vincent Mulago of the Democratic Republic of Congo and John Mbiti of Kenya have forged a path that adapts the Christian message to African institutions (Mudimbe 1988, 27). Alexis Kagame of Rwanda, Bolaji Idowu of Nigeria, and Engelbert Mveng of Cameroon have all championed a nationalist appropriation of Christianity. They propose a theology that will incarnate the faith in African realities. Since the 1970s, African theologians have accelerated their growing discontent with classical theological reflection. According to Mudimbe, in the 1980s theologians intensified their quest for a relevant theology by looking for areas of convergence between Christianity and African religions (Ibid., 61). Bénézet Bujo's book, *African Theology in Its Social Context* (1992), and the collection of essays *Faces of Jesus in Africa* (1991), edited by Schreiter, reflect such a quest and critique of the classical theological tradition (Schreiter 1991; Bujo 1992.). This emphasis on the reality and relevance of African religions provoked discussions on "Christo-paganism" and syncretism in mission societies. In Africa, the discussion yielded works such as Byang Kato's *Theological Pitfalls in Africa* (Kato 1975). In this work, Kato misrepresented the spirit and mission of the All Africa Conference of Churches and missed the focus and spirit of Idowu's classic work *African Traditional Religion: A Definition* (Idowu 1973). Mudimbe correctly affirms the claim of these theological projects that the African must be thought of as "Other"; an Other who evaluates past ideologies and looks to the future. Their quest for theological relevance in Africa celebrates the diversity of human experience, challenges relative "cultural grammars," and asserts "the African will to truth" (Mudimbe 1988, 63).

Jean-Marc Ela from Cameroon, in his search for a theology that addresses felt needs, focuses on socioeconomic issues (Ela 1986, 1988). His praxis-oriented theology involves participation in the life-world and struggles of the poor in northern Cameroon. This experience convinced Ela that poverty in many parts of Cameroon is linked to exploitation and led him to adopt a theological method that frees him from being a "manager . . . of doctrine and discipline," because such an approach does not relate to the lives of the people. Theologizing at the margins and what Ela calls "the cutting edge of the gospel" is a new conversion experience for Ela, who states, "Everything [has] impelled me to abandon the traditional Christian questions, and patiently let another language of the gospel burst forth from the life of the people" (Ela 1988, 5).[7]

South African theologians provided sustained critiques of the apartheid system and called for a reflection and praxis to uphold human dignity.[8] A paradigm shift has occurred in the post–cold war and post–apartheid eras. Charles Villa Vicencio, Jesse Mugambi, and John de Gruchy, for example, stress reconstruction as the compelling theological task (Vicencio 1992; De Gruchy, 1995; Mugambi, 1995). These attempts to construct an African "Other," and for my specific purpose here, an "Other" whose theological engagement addresses the felt need in Africa, are not and should not become provincial projects.[9]

African theology is generally grouped in two broad categories. The first is a "theology of culture," which seeks to make African culture relevant to theological thinking. The second is the "the theology of liberation," articulated in the southern part of the continent as part of the liberation struggles of Zimbabwe, Namibia, and South Africa. Emmanuel Martey (1993) locates the genesis of African theological reflection in the revolutionary movements that launched the critique of colonial discourse: Pan-Africanism, négritude, and the revolutionary and political philosophies of the founding leaders of contemporary Africa, such as Kwame Nkrumah, Julius Nyerere, Amilca Cabral, and Albert Luthuli. According to Martey, African Diasporan thinkers, such as W. E. B. DuBois, Edward Bleyden, and George Padmore, and several socioreligious and theological organizations joined African thinkers to champion the cause of African liberation.[10]

These African theologians and organizations participate in what I call a multi-vocal emancipatory discourse, which started with the publication of reflections by a group of priests published in the collection Des Prêtres Noirs S'interrogent (Abble 1956).[11] Grand syntheses such as négritude, consciencism, and African socialism have been scrutinized.[12] For example, Ela is critical of the discourse that comes from this era because it was formulated under the epistemological model of négritude, which has since proven inadequate in dealing with contemporary African realities.

Martey himself calls for a synthetic approach that incorporates the themes emerging in the post–apartheid era: liberation and reconstruction. The implication is that the struggle for emancipatory discourse in its philosophical and theological dimensions needs to take place on two fronts. On the sociopolitical front, the theological task should be contextual and critical of the structures of oppression in all of its forms.[13] On the religio-cultural front, Martey argues that: "It is on the pillars of both culture and politics that a meaningfully relevant theological hermeneutics would emerge that can radically face the challenges of the future" (Martey 1993, 131). This hermeneutics should stress cultural, political, linguistic, social, and historical pluralism in order to develop a transformative theology (Ibid., 55). Martey echoes Ricoeur when he argues that hermeneutics should begin with suspicion, an activity that uses doubt as a force that transforms "intentionality into kerygma, manifestation, proclamation . . . a tearing off of masks, an interpretation that reduces disguise" (Ricoeur 1970, 30; Ibid., 56).

Hermeneutics is gaining influence in African theological and philosophical reflection.[14] Mudimbe refers to a growing hermeneutical school in African theology and philosophy that has gained ground since Theophilus Okere published part of his doctoral dissertation on hermeneutics.[15] In that work, Okere explores and appropriates the work of Heidegger, Gadamer, and Ricoeur to establish the condition for the possibility of philosophy in Africa.[16]

A similar project is evident in greater detail and depth in David Tracy's work *The Analogical Imagination*. There, Tracy lays out a hermeneutical and pluralistic theological agenda.[17] I highlight Tracy's argument that is germane to this work. He argues that theology is a threefold public discipline necessarily relating to society, the academy, and the church (Tracy 1988, 5). These disciplines are not closed monads but entities with fluid boundaries. The theologian is called to carefully negotiate the interrelationship between these boundaries.[18]

Tracy claims that theological discourse within and between these public disciplines involves two constants. The first is the interpretation of the religious tradition. Theologians should use rules that are spelled out clearly and should have well-defined criteria for appropriate interpretation when working with the texts of their tradition.[19] The second is the need to provide a religious interpretation of the contemporary situation. Tracy points out that the shock of World War I forced Karl Barth to ground his theology in the Word of God, while Ellul and Yoder articulate their theological position in response to the impact of technology. In pursuing such an interpretation, the theologian needs to clarify his or her "truth claims." The implication here is that the general religious situation that comes under the sociology and philosophy of religion should become theological data and partly constitutive of the theological agenda.[20]

CONTEMPORARY THEOLOGICAL
REFLECTION IN AFRICA

In this section, I make a case for a hermeneutical approach to contemporary theology in Africa. I follow Tracy's argument that theological reflection involves two constants: the constant of a tradition and the constant of a contemporary situation as an entrée into an issue such as *tfu* among the Wimbum. Tracy's notion of tradition is broad and encompasses different religious traditions. If one limits the notion of tradition to a specific Christian one such as Reformed, Anglican, Methodist, Baptist, and Catholic, there are many possibilities, since the Christian tradition was transplanted into Africa in multiple forms. Alton Templin demonstrates in *Ideology on a Frontier* that a theological tradition can easily be transformed into a destructive ideology, as the Dutch Reformed Church has done in South Africa (Templin 1984). In response to the corruption of that tradition, John De Gruchy argues that the Reformed tradition also has a long history of liberating hermeneutics. Citing examples of theological shifts inspired by the work of Calvin, Schleiermacher, and Barth, who applied their theology to the needs of their day, De Gruchy likewise draws from that tradition to speak to a contemporary situation. In this case, his task is to free the Reformed tradition in South Africa from the "myths of racial superiority and oppressive powers" (De Gruchy 1991, 39).[21]

Among the Wimbum, where one strand of the Baptist tradition is in the majority, no significant theological tradition has developed. The North American Baptist missionaries, who work in the Wimbum area and at the Cameroon Baptist Convention, established a theological school that was upgraded to a seminary in 1984 to train pastors for local churches. They focus on church planting, elementary and secondary education, and health care. Some members of the mission continue to view higher theological education with a great deal of suspicion, and they tell Cameroonian pastors who seek higher education that they do not need such an education because they already have what is necessary to preach the Gospel. Meanwhile, when some of the missionaries return home on leave (a number that has been increasing in recent years), they enroll in universities and seminaries for advanced degrees. It is clear that those who discourage Cameroonians from obtaining higher education believe that such training may be good for missionaries but not for Cameroonians. Thus missionaries have planted, in the case of the Baptist Church in Cameroon, a church that is bereft of critical theological reflection.[22] This narrative is important to the argument I make about using philosophy and theology to address *tfu* problems, because the lack of sophisticated training renders pastors ill equipped to bring much-needed subtlety and depth when approaching issues such as *tfu*.

Furthermore, what is curious about Baptist mission work among the Wimbum and in Cameroon is that missionaries of the North American Baptist General Conference, who work in Cameroon for theological reasons, do not teach the progressive theology of one of their most distinguished theologians, Walter Rauschenbush. Such neglect of their own distinguished theologian, involved in emancipatory reflection, also has occurred outside of Cameroon. At the North American Baptist Seminary in Sioux Falls, South Dakota, the only reminder of the great prophet of "Christianity and the Social Crises," besides an occasional mention in lectures, is the picture of Walter Rauschenbush, which hangs in the hallway along with pictures of former faculty members.

The work of the North American Baptist Conference in Cameroon, particularly among the Wimbum people, has so far produced no critical theological tradition. The Catholic Church in Cameroon has developed a significant theological voice, as is evident in the work of theologians such as Ela, Mveng, Eboussi-Boulaga, and Hegba,[23] who incorporate in their theology Tracy's two constants: tradition and the contemporary situation of the Cameroonian and African church.[24]

I have argued that no significant theological tradition that follows the Baptist heritage has emerged from the Wimbum area and Cameroon Baptist Convention. In addition, no theology has been developed to deal with social upheavals such as *tfu*. There also is a need for a socioeconomic critique directed toward insights into the possibility of instituting responsible economic policies. These insights also should help people develop a clear understanding of what is needed in order to live in a society where people battle constantly with changing realities. The simple polarization into "tradition" and "modern" is therefore inadequate in understanding and articulating the complexity of life in a postcolonial, postmodern, underdeveloped world. Members of the Christian community in Wimbum land still struggle with their fellow Wimbum to find a working position on *tfu*. There is a clear need to come to grips with the religious reality of the time. This need calls for a serious encounter and dialogue with Wimbum religious heritage and *Weltanschauung*, without which theology will be unable to properly or effectively contribute to any conversation on *tfu*. To satisfy Tracy's proposals, a theologian should seek to come to terms with the religious, cultural, and textual tradition out of which he or she comes. Here, *la chose du text* should be extended beyond what is written to include, what Okanda Okolo calls, "the text as a fact of tradition" (Okanda 1991, 204).

To advance such a conversation that encompasses a wide conception of texts to include material culture, oral tradition, works of art, and literary works, it is imperative that theological discourse must proceed in a pluralistic and an interdisciplinary manner, utilizing much of the literature in the humanities, social science, and African studies. The moral imagination of different African communities shines in some works in African studies, and it is necessary that both philosophical and theological reflection involve a critical appropriation of this material.[25] Works such as Thomas Beidelman's *The Moral Imagination in Kaguru Modes of Thought* (1993), Monica Wilson's *Religion and the Transformation of Society* (1971), and Meyer Fortes's, *Religion, Morality, and the Person* (1987) provide an entry point.

THEOLOGY, PHILOSOPHY, AND ETHICS: THE INADEQUACY OF AGAPE

The preceding background to hermeneutics and theology opens the door to a theological and philosophical response to *tfu*. I presented a critique of *tfu* in Chapter 4 based on Levinas's argument for the Other. I now discuss and appropriate his argument on *eros,* arguing that this is a viable philosophical and theological motif that should be employed in a reconstruction of human relations affected by the discourse and practice of *tfu*. Such an engagement is apropos because Levinas reflects on God and philosophy. He states clearly that God can only be known through the face of the Other. His position is consistent with various New Testament teachings on interpersonal relations. Jere Surber is correct in pointing out that, for Levinas, infinity should be seen not just as an idea that lies beyond but within subjectivity itself. The "saying" of the Other awakens the subject to respond to the Other.[26] Surber rightly claims that this "is the key to any attempt to develop the theological implications of Levinas's view as well as to ascertain the relations between theology and ethics" (Surber 1994, 312). Levinas argues that following God is constituted in relation to a human Other.[27]

> Yes, and it is essential to point out that the relation implied in the preposition towards (a) is ultimately a relation

derived from time. Time fashions man's relation to the other, and to the absolutely other or God, as a diachronic relation irreducible to correlation. . . . Going towards God is meaningless unless in terms of my primary going towards the other person. I can only go towards God by being ethically concerned by and for the other person. (Surber 1994, 312)[28]

Although Levinas is critical of aspects of nineteenth-century thought, especially Hegel's grand schemes, he echoes a certain spirit of that era: the insistence by many of the thinkers of that time that religion is not primarily dogma but a life of ethical relationships. *Tfu* complicates ethical relationships, and any philosopher and theologian among the Wimbum would do well to rethink these issues carefully.

In light of *tfu*, one theological motif that should receive attention among the Wimbum is love. The Belgian theologian Verhaegan advocates "a theology of charity that will address the issues of social inequalities and poverty and offer radically new solutions" (Mudimbe 1988, 179). I want to go beyond charity, because I agree with Edith Wyschogrod that charity can become the activity of the Same, something that comes out of the "good feelings" of Dasein (Wyschogrod 1990, 80ff). In contrast, "The saintly gift is a response of the saint's total being to the sheer animal destitution, the vulnerability, of the Other. The hand of the saint that gives, welcomes, blesses, heals, and redeems is, by synecdoche, a condensation of the total charismatic power of the saintly body" (Ibid., 82). Before I turn to Levinas, I highlight the inadequacy of agape as a dominant theological motif.

NYGREN ON AGAPE AND EROS

The significant study of eros was undertaken by Anders Nygren in his book *Agape and Eros* (Nygren 1953).[29] His study is a landmark work because of the scope of the subject matter he covers. Nygren's burden in this work is to demonstrate that agape is a new, distinctly Christian understanding of love. This argument is problematic because he sanctifies agape. Furthermore, Nygren's methodology is problematic because he distinguishes between agape, and eros, compartmentalizing agape as God's love and eros as human love (Ibid., 53). Given this framework, Nygren argues that agape is spontaneous love that is not motivated by anything. It is "indifferent to value" and creative because it gives a sense of worth to that which formerly had no worth. Finally, Nygren interprets agape as that love which brings about fellowship between God and people (Ibid., 75ff).

Nygren argues that Plato's *Phaedrus* and *Symposium* portray eros as acquisitive love (Nygren 1953, 175ff). Plato thinks eros is a means to the divine, thus making it instrumental because it is a means for one to acquire what one lacks (Ibid., 177). There is such an element in eros. What is problematic with Nygren's interpretation is that love, or eros, is interpreted as a flight from the world, and I see no justification for such an interpretation. Furthermore, Nygren characterizes eros as egocentric love based on his interpretation of friendship from the *Lysis* (Ibid., 179).[30] There are elements of self-love in eros, but it is also a desire that reaches out to the other. Paul Tillich presents a richer interpretation of eros than does Nygren.[31]

Before I present Tillich's perspective, I should point out Eberhard Jungel's astute work *Gott als Geheimnis der Welt,* in which he proposes the possibility of thinking God. This work can be read as a phenomenology of love, although he does not focus primarily on eros and agape (Jungel 1983). Jungel argues that this possibility lies in language, in particular the language that God has already spoken through the crucifixion of Jesus. Love is selflessness, affection, and surrender, and according to Jungel, love's character of giving and dying transcends the ego and replaces it with something new (Ibid., 323). Jungel distinguishes between eros and agape: "*Eros* is to be understood as the process of attraction to another person without which a person knows that he is not complete. That beauty which is lacking for one's own completion appears worthy of love and desirable. And so one wants to have it" (Ibid., 337). Jungel prefers agape because in the *Symposium*, eros represents a deficiency and lack but Johannine agape is superior to eros because it is a selfless, pure love (Ibid., 338).

The comparison that Jungel makes between agape and eros sells eros short and does not reflect the complexity involved in the platonic understanding of eros. Without necessarily endorsing everything that Feuerbach wrote, I argue for the reality of human love, because it is not always deficient. Jungel fails in this work to focus on human love, he compartmentalizes love, and he adopts a theological approach that lacks pluralism. We need to focus on the richness of human love if we are going to use love as a solution to *tfu.*[32]

TILLICH ON EROS AND AGAPE

Paul Tillich grounds his understanding of love in the ontological structure. In *Love Power, and Justice,* he argues that Plato's eros should be seen "as the power which drives to the union with the true and the good itself," qualities that one needs to understand and respond to negative *tfu* (Tillich 1954, 21, 22). Furthermore, Tillich argues that there is in Aristotle a "universal *eros* which drives everything towards the highest form, the pure activity which moves the world not as a cause (*kinoumenon*) but as the object of love (*eromenon*)" (Ibid., 25). Tillich underscores the view that love is one and that its different aspects should not be construed as kinds of love as we have seen in Nygren and Jungel.

The moralists have misinterpreted *epithymia* and naturalists have overvalorized it by subjecting other dimensions of love to it (Tillich 1954, 28).[33] Tillich finds, in the ontological structure, a solution to this impasse.

First, he employs the Latin term *libido* to subvert the hedonistic, Freudian interpretation of pleasure. In doing so, Tillich does not deny that there is pleasure in the movement of desire. However, he points out that it is not pleasure for pleasure's sake only. Pleasure is found in the union of being with what it is separated from. Contrary to Freud, Tillich argues that libido is not perverted but seeks that which is high and noble (Ibid., 29, 30). The image of pleasure in Tillich is important, because this pleasure seeks the Other and the good rather than the kind of pleasure that people imagine *tfu* practitioners must have when they allegedly destroy other people and consume their flesh.

Second, Tillich rejects the sharp contrast between eros and agape, arguing that eros includes but transcends *epithymia* (Tillich 1954, 30).

> It strives for a union with that which is a bearer of values because of the values it embodies. This refers to the beauty we find in nature, to the beautiful and the true in culture, and to the mystical union with that which is the source of the beautiful and the true. Love drives towards union with the forms of nature and culture and with the divine source of both (Tillich 1954, 30).

Tillich rejects moves by theologians, who despise culture because such moves negate the mystical elements involved in the relationship with God. Tillich is convinced that "without the *eros* towards truth, theology would not exist, and without the *eros* towards the beautiful, no ritual expressions would exist" (Tillich 1954, 30). The extraction of the notion of *eros* from human love to God has turned love directed toward God into mere obedience and a meaningless concept.

Third, Tillich posits a necessary relationship between eros and *philia,* because eros has a transpersonal dimension while *philia* has a personal one. The creative and religious force of eros can be experienced if self-centeredness is separated from one's understanding of the erotic. The relationship between eros and *philia* is manifested in personal relations: "It is the desire to unite with a power of being which is both most separated and most understandable and which radiates possibilities and realities of the good and the true in the manifestation of its incomparable individuality" (Tillich 1954, 32).

This relationship also is demonstrated in community life where people relate to one another. Here Tillich is clear that saintly lives come with the libido (Tillich 1954, 33). Accordingly, agape is not the highest form of love as some interpret it, even though it is an aspect that adds depth to the experience of love because it puts one in touch with the ground of being. Tillich does not subvert agape. In *Morality and Beyond,* published in 1963, nine years after *Love, Power, and Justice,* Tillich argues that love, or agape, is needed to transform concrete individual and social demands without giving up its "eternity and dignity and unconditional validity" (Tillich 1963, 89).[34]

Although I find Tillich's perspective rich, one must be mindful of recent feminist and womanist critiques of Tillich's work. Carter Heyward writes that Tillich's theology portrays "an amoral, individualistic God-man as constitutive of being itself" (Heyward 1989, 63). Furthermore, Tillich does not adequately demonstrate relationality and sociality, since he understands being as "the inner life of the individual agent." He fails to highlight the material body and make the connection between the devaluation of sex and women in Christian history. Tillich's new being is one who grasps through the divine spirit in the God-man structure, and Tillich does not consider the "collective, relational, sensual and embodied ground on which he stood with others" (Ibid., 66).[35]

I now turn to Levinas, whose phenomenology of eros provides a way forward. I do not claim that Tillich and Levinas are engaged in the same project. It is not clear if they were familiar with each other's work, although they were contemporaries. Levinas first proposed his interpretation of eros in a lecture, *Le temps et l'autre,* later published in the collection *Le Choix, Le Monde, L'Existence* in 1947 by Jean Wahl (Wahl 1947). Tillich published, *Love, Power, and Justice* in 1954. Both Tillich and Levinas present ethical reflections on love, and both retrieve the rich dimensions of eros to articulate their understanding of love. Furthermore, both were part of the two great catastrophes of the twentieth century, the two World Wars, and experienced the difficult loss of family and friends. This experience changed their perspectives on human responsibility in theology and philosophy. The difference between them lies in the fact that Tillich explores the subject of love through the ontological structure, whereas Levinas prefers the path of phenomenology and attempts to go beyond Husserl, whose intentionality and call to return *Zu die Sachen Selbst* provoke Levinas to transcend Dasein's *Befindlichkeit* and *Sorgen* to point to a human face that confronts and summons us to responsibility. I prefer Levinas's approach, because Tillich's ontological approach leads to the *aporias* of ontology that Levinas attempts to correct.[36] Both offer signs of hope in their recovery and interpretation of eros, but Levinas's phenomenology of eros recovers human desire in a radical way that can be appropriated to develop new ways of thinking on the question of *tfu.*

LEVINAS'S PHENOMENOLOGY OF EROS: POSSIBILITIES FOR ETHICAL RELATIONS

Levinas presents eros as human desire operational in the intersubjective relation of the face-to-face encounter, which calls for a human response. This desire does not originate from above as some argue agape does (Levinas 1987, 82ff). The broad outlines of his discussion of eros in *Totality and Infinity* were formulated for the series of lectures that have now been published as *Time and the Other.* In his fourth lecture in *Time and the Other,* Levinas focuses on power and the self's relationship with the Other.[36] He calls for a relationship with the Other that rejects mastery and restores decency (Ibid., 83). Levinas challenges the kind of vision that can only know the Other as an alter ego. "The Other as Other is not only an alter ego: the Other is what I myself am not. The Other is not this because of the Other's character or physiognomy, or psychology, but because of the Other's very alterity" (Ibid.).[37]

These early formulations contain some of the key ideas that one finds in *Totality and Infinity.* For instance, the Other always has a human face, which Levinas identifies with the poor, the widow, and the orphan. The "I" is the rich and the powerful. The reality of such a social imbalance explains Levinas's claim that, "It can be said that the intersubjective space is not symmetrical. . . . .The relationship with alterity is neither spatial nor conceptual" (Levinas 1987, 83–84). Levinas introduces eros in *Time and the Other* with the following question: "Does a situation exist where the Other would not have alterity only as the reverse side of its identity. . . . where alterity would be borne by a positive sense, as essence? . . . [where] . . . alterity . . . does not purely and simply enter into the opposition of two species of the same genus?" (Ibid., 85). He declares, "I think the absolutely contrary (*le contraire absolutement contraraire*), whose contrariety is in no way affected by the relationship that can be established between it and its correlative, the contrariety that permits its terms to remain absolutely Other, is the feminine" (Ibid.). I follow Levinas's discussion in *Totality and Infinity,* although he sketches the broad outlines of that kind of alterity also in *Time and the Other.*

Levinas argues that eros as desire and love is directed toward a human Other. This Other is frail, vulnerable, sets limits on being, and takes flight into its own manifestation (Levinas 1969, 256). He calls the beloved a materiality that denotes "nudity of an exorbitant presence coming as though from further than the frankness of the face, already profaning and wholly profaned, as if it had forced the interdiction of a secret" (Ibid.). What Levinas presents is one who presents himself or herself to light yet remains out of the realm of signification by the Same and thus rejects subjection or scrutiny. Hence what is opened up as a secret also defies profanation. According to Levinas, the erotic and its pathos constitute itself through love as modesty and oppose virility and pride. The question at this point is, what, for Levinas, is a good representation of this kind of relationship?

Levinas calls this fragility and femininity (Levinas 1969, 256).[38] He argues that the feminine as the beloved should be approached with compassion, the complacency of a caress, and a sensibility that is not sensible. The emphasis here is on caress, and for Levinas this caress is devoid of the kind of assimilation that he repeatedly characterizes as consumption. Instead, he upholds and highlights a spirit that solicits what escapes into the future.[39] Levinas also characterizes this particular relationship to the feminine as desire. He contrasts *desire* with hunger, because hunger consumes, but desire is insatiable and does not possess what it seeks. This distinction allows Levinas to highlight the material. He argues that the body of the beloved is not a place for the Same to demonstrate the "I can." Levinas states unequivocally:

> The Beloved, at once graspable but intact in her nudity, beyond object and face and thus beyond existent, abides in her virginity. The feminine essentially violable and inviolable, the eternal feminine; is the Virgin or an incessant *recommencement* of virginity, the untouchable in the very contact of voluptuousity, future in the present (Levinas 1969, 258).

What Levinas paints is the picture of a relationship in which one desires and seeks the Other but does so with a caress that respects the virginity of the Other. The futurity into which the lover escapes is an act that neutralizes the subject. Such action is consistent with Levinas's argument regarding the recognition of a radical, independent Other. Levinas says "an amorphous non 'I' sweeps away the 'I' into an absolute future where it escapes itself and loses its position as a subject" (Levinas 1969, 259). The play of voluptuousity is contrasted to the act of profanation that wants to discover and master. Love is not reducible to knowledge, and eros is not an act of discovery and intentionality, directed at the object by the searching subject. The experience of eros is not a conceptualizing act.

> Love is not reducible to a knowledge mixed with effective elements which would open to it an unforeseen plane of being. It grasps nothing, issues in no concept, does not issue, has neither the subject-object structure nor the I-Thou structure. *Eros* is not accomplished as a subject that fixes an object, nor as a pro-jection, toward a possible. Its movement consists of going beyond the possible (Levinas 1969, 261).

The motif of eros that Levinas employs offers hope for those concerned with *tfu* discourses and practice, because it restores desire to intersubjective relations and to the human community. The employment of eros in interpersonal relations among the Wimbum should stress difference. It is this difference that should be the springboard upon which one can reject the imposition of violence and invite an attitude of compassion. Negative *tfu* contains the language of desire, but this desire does not affirm. On the contrary, erotic desires should seek the best in interpersonal relations and

promote respect for other people. When we bring to intersubjective
relations our passions, we truly touch and impact on one another
in a meaningful way, because eros awakens the desire that lies in
each of us. Audre Lorde indicates that we need to go beyond our
fears of desire in order to reclaim the erotic and the spiritual that
is within each one of us (Lorde 1984, 76). Such love, according to
Sheila Briggs, seeks self-fulfillment as well as the good of the other.

> As such it shares the structure of compassion, for compas-
> sion is not disinterested love nor love without a self-refer-
> ence. Compassion is an act of empathy in which one is moved
> to connect the sufferings of another to one's own feelings, to
> link the material and the emotional needs of another to
> one's own desire for happiness. (Briggs 1987, 274)

Those who protest against the wrongful use of *tfu* powers among
the Wimbum do so because such actions destroy desire for the
Other and instead unleash violence on interpersonal bonds and
interconnectedness. There is a need to retrieve the idea of eros, to
stress its pathos and strength, in order to bring this eros to bear
on one's relationship with another. This is important, as theologians think about one-on-one relationships in the community. Rethinking human relations, especially in *tfu*, where its idioms and
negative praxis spell totality to the extreme, calls for a full expression of desire toward the Other. Returning within to rekindle the
fires of eros is a homecoming that tacitly owns the *imago dei* that
humans embody. As one recognizes that image in another and works
to realize its full potential, one replaces what Levinas calls hunger,
which consumes and destroys in its totalizing enterprise, with a
desire that builds and nurtures hope in the Other.

Beyond recognizing the *imago dei,* when we reinstate eros we
concretize the possibilities for people to love God. It is only when
people express this desire, in the face of the Other that they can
truly say that they love God. Stressing human love as a condition
for loving God does not abandon agapic love. Ricoeur argues that
on ethical grounds, biblical faith adds nothing to what should be
good and obligatory and should rightly be part of human action
(Ricoeur 1992, 25).

> Biblical *agape* belongs to an economy of the gift, possessing
> a meta-ethical character, which makes me say that there is
> no such thing as a Christian morality, except perhaps on

the level of the history of mentalities, but a common morality . . . that biblical faith places in a new perspective, in which love is tied to the "naming of God." (Ricoeur 1992, 25)

In addition to restoring desire into intersubjective and community relations, eros as a philosophical and theological motif could promote justice in the community. Levinas argues that justice takes place when one listens to the Other and realizes that he or she is guilty for past sins. For justice to become a reality in interpersonal and communal relations where *tfu* remains an issue, one needs to consider the erotic as an empowering relationship. In recovering eros, feminists and womanists reject male power and domination. Erotic power demands the eradication of all things and strategies that totalize at all levels. This means that people who claim to have *tfu* and operate with knowledge unavailable to others in the community should develop erotic desires that will empower others. The misuse of such powers constitutes an act of injustice. To explain, recall that the bulk of discourse on the wrongful use of *tfu* involves accusations that someone has caused another to become ill. Seen from that angle, this wrongful use of *tfu* power and its discourse involves negative difference. I call it negative difference because what happens in negative uses of *tfu* powers puts people at odds with one another. In such relationships, the Other is not strengthened but weakened and, in extreme cases, eliminated.

I also find images of hunger and desire intriguing when one considers how applicable they are to the world and language of *tfu* among the Wimbum. Some aspects of *tfu* are loaded with images of hunger—the hunger that leads to the control of others through some hidden power, or the hunger that leads to a determination to possess what others have. There also is the claim that some people have a hunger to "consume human flesh" through *tfu. Tout court,* or the negative elements of *tfu,* involve an excessive hunger to control an Other distinct from the one that possess *tfu* powers. One may suspect that such hunger to control may have been at work in the case of a parent who is alleged to have caused the death of his son, who was a successful civil servant. He wanted his son to buy him a vehicle, but the son did not have the money to do so at the time. It is alleged that the father used *tfu* to make him sick. Although attempts were made to reconcile the two, the son died of complications from cancer of the liver, according to hospital sources. However, most people claim that the father was responsible for his death.

When he was confronted with the situation, the father reportedly confessed before elders of the village that he was angry with
his son. Members of this area generally take such an assertion as
a confession of guilt. It is not helpful in some of these incidents to
try to psychoanalyze the confession of the father. I was not present
when this confession was reportedly made. As a minister to the
deceased, I had assisted in arranging for him to be moved from a
public hospital to a church hospital where the quality of care was
better. Two days after he was taken to the church hospital, I sent
a message by radio to find out how he was doing. I was shocked
when the hospital operator told me that he had died that morning
and when they asked me to arrange for his children to attend his
funeral. I still cannot comprehend how this could have happened.
Even in cases where the person does not die, such accusations can
be very difficult for the family. Levinas rightly argues that eros
implies redirecting human energy away from consumption to a
desire for the Other, which transcends selfishness. The limitless
energy of eros provides an opportunity to admire, respect, and work
for the well-being of the Other because we desire him or her so
much. Erotic desire also invites people to a deeper level of commitment that opens up possibilities for the respect of persons that
could eliminate the "hunger" for the flesh of others.

Levinas also argues that, through desire people can create a
beloved community that restricts totality. Such a community prohibits its members from causing the demise of other people in the
community. Although Levinas uses the principle of femininity,
members of the Wimbum community should not find that strange.
Perhaps what needs to happen is that the respect that the Wimbum
people claim they give to mothers should indeed be given not because they bear children but because of who they are as individuals. Eros, as articulated by Levinas, demands it. When eros
flourishes in a community, its members will not be governed by the
schemes of *tfu* people who, in secret meetings, express a selfish
hunger at the expense of the community. Levinas's community is
not even a community of coinciding comprehension or, viewpoints.
It is a community that grounds morality on "the fact that in existing for another I exist otherwise than in existing for me [which] is
morality itself" (Levinas 1969, 261).[40]

The erotic in Levinas also can be seen as the realm of transcendence. As Wyschogrod notes, the metaphysical event of transcendence that overturns reduction to the same takes place, according
to Levinas, through language and desire (Wyschogrod 1974, 115).

One is confronted with transcendence in the face of the Other, where exteriority begins (Levinas 1969, 261–262). "Language, source of all signification, is born in the vestige of infinity, which takes hold before the straightforwardness of the face making murder possible and impossible" (Ibid., 262). Levinas's picture of transcendence is characterized by nudity, and temptation, yet such transcendence resists murder and all forms of subjugation. The signification of erotic nudity is not artistic, poetic, or exhibitionist.[41] Rather, Levinas characterizes erotic nudity like the laughter and playfulness of Shakespearean "witches," who display an obscene seriousness and tell ambiguous tales, yet throughout there is a childlikeness enacted in play. It is important to note here that beyond this playfulness is what Levinas calls equivocation in the face of the feminine.

[The feminine is] at the same time interlocutor, collaborator and master superiority intelligent so often dominating men in the masculine civilization it has entered, and woman having to be treated as a woman, in accordance with rules imprescribable by civil society. The face, all straight forwardness and frankness, in its feminine epiphany dissimulates allusions, innuendoes. It laughs under the cloak of its own expression, without leading to any specific meaning, hinting in the empty air, signaling the less than nothing. (Levinas 1969, 264)

Furthermore, Levinas portrays eros as a revelation in which voluptuousity is enacted. Revelation ordinarily is considered an unveiling, yet for Levinas such unveiling that takes place between two lovers exceeds expectations, because this erotic revelation also is a refusal to surrender completely to the control of the Same. The Other does not engulf her will in this act of revealing.[42] Voluptuousity refracts from public view or universalization and opens one to the Other, yet keeps them separate (Levinas 1969, 265). In voluptuousity, the beloved keeps her freedom intact. The masculine does not possess the feminine, because where there is control, both lose their freedom.

There is a clear distinction between this view of love and a consideration of friendship. Levinas calls eros an asymmetrical relationship and applies its power to the feminine. Eros is different from friendship, because erotic love does not seek another self in the same way that Aristotle defines friendship.

Love seeks what does not have the structure of an existent,
the infinitely future, what is to be engendered. I love fully
only if the Other loves me, not because I need the recognition of the Other, but because my voluptuousity delights in
his voluptuousity, and because in this unparalleled conjec-
ture of transubstantiation, the Same and the Other are not
united but precisely—beyond every possible project, beyond
every meaningful and intelligent power—engender the child.
(Levinas 1969, 266)

Levinas does not deny self-love. He is aware of the dimensions of
self-love because he speaks of the self returning to itself through
this encounter with the Other, which for Levinas is a pleasurable,
dual egoism that "moves away from itself; it abides in a vertigo
above depth of alterity that no signification clarifies any longer a
depth exhibited and profaned" (Levinas 1969, 266).[43]

Two ideas are presented in the preceding paragraphs—transcendence and revelation. We have already stated that Levinas
uses transcendence to refer to the distinction that exists between
the Other and the Same. Furthermore, he uses revelation to mean
a manifestation of the face of the Other. If we combine these two
theological motifs, we can take them further by arguing that it is
when one recognizes transcendence and allows the Other to manifest himself or herself as such that solidarity is born. Liberation
and reconstruction theologians of all trajectories have written an
enormous amount about the notion of solidarity. Solidarity implies
an awareness of the face that unveils itself yet refracts from view.
Such solidarity involves affirming the Other as well as sharing in
his or her pain, poverty, powerlessness, and marginality in all of
its forms. Solidarity calls for an engagement that goes beyond
charity. It is a commitment that calls for total involvement in the
lives of others. Restoring eros into interpersonal and communal
relations offers an opportunity to recover and renew solidarity,
making sure that it does not become another cliché. This is a very
powerful concept when one reflects on it in relation to *tfu*. The
wrongful use of *tfu* disrupts harmony and shatters the spirit of
solidarity. A genuine erotic spirit can restore that solidarity among
individuals and in the community. In certain cases where solidarity has been broken, family members do not speak to one another,
do not go into each other's homes, and do not eat food or drink
beer prepared by another person. In cases where this is extreme,
they do not even attend public gatherings at the same time. The
Wimbum people call such a complete boycott *dzini*. It is believed

that for those families who at a certain stage of their lives are carrying any form of *bzini* [plural], any violation can cause illness and even death. Such a boycott constitutes a complete shattering of solidarity. The cultivation of eros can provide a way out of these situations.

The employment of eros to articulate a theology and philosophy that builds and restores solidarity requires the practice of pardon. When things go wrong and people accuse others of using *tfu* in an incorrect way, the erotic as desire empowers people to give the gift of pardon. This calls for a philosophy and theology of forgiveness. Among the Wimbum, people sometimes quote popular expressions such as "to ere is human but to forgive is divine." What is needed is a counter discourse of pardon that locates forgiveness at the heart of human relationships. How this is constructed may vary, but what I stress here is the conviction that forgiveness is a human capacity that should be used even in difficult times of *tfu* accusations. I emphasize forgiveness as a human capacity but want to point out that forgiveness does not erase the past, which would be a wrong understanding of and use of pardon.

To pardon another person accused of using *tfu* to hurt others is to recognize that one cannot merely erase memories of the past. I do not expect that theologians will join *tfu* cleansing ceremonies where charges and countercharges usually are presented then resolved, and where pardon or punishment is given to the guilty party. But I hope that theologians and those who address these issues can create an atmosphere where open conversation addresses the past and paves the way for pardon. This calls for wrestling with uncomfortable yet necessary issues. These memories do not go away. Bringing them out in open dialogue, however, opens the door for pardon. Pardon helps those involved in *tfu* disputes to move into the future. Hannah Arendt points out that persons reach into the future because pardon frees the hold that the past places on us (Arendt 1958, 147). Arendt argues that pardon is an original, unexpected way of responding to the action of another person (Ibid., 241). According to Arendt, responding to the transgression of the other person with pardon is grounded on plurality. It is a gift exchanged with another person rather than counter *tfu* or magic. It involves community, which is always the terrain of human transaction. I believe that the community plays an important part in this pardon, because individual actions affect others that are part of the web of relations in the Wimbum community, anchored in the extended family. Arendt dismisses the notion of self-forgiveness and emphasizes that neighbors are the ones who remind people of their past sins (Arendt 1929, 358). Put differently, pardon and forgiveness are ideals that function in a human community. This does not mean that individuals cannot forgive one another. However, in light of the conversation on *tfu,* where such transactions tend to involve very public rituals, pardon also is an important public ritual with profound theological significance. When pardon is extended from one person to another, both people open themselves up in a new way (Ibid., 237). The giving and receiving of pardon also brings a new freedom into the realm of the intersubjective, making it possible for people to start over again (Ibid.).

Pardon should take place in the "present," as people bring charges and countercharges about *tfu.* Levinas argues that pardon is a present act that conserves and purifies the past and leads to what he calls a "surplus," which becomes available for happiness and reconciliation (Levinas 1969, 283). Pardon, therefore, is a transaction in time that rescues the past, points to the future, and opens up freedom and alterity.[44] The face of the Other that is encountered may have inflicted harm on one through *tfu* in the past. It is necessary in the present to extend pardon and to prepare for the future. To pardon does not mean that one should ignore such wrongs. Pardon provides a way of dealing with those wrongs.

The Wimbum people who believe that they have been hurt by *tfu* seek adjudication for public rituals. Such rituals will not mean very much if they do not establish possibilities for the pardon and restoration of the guilty party in the community. I have referred to the case of Shey Riba, who was accused of giving youths the flesh of someone who was allegedly killed by *tfu* people. The youths then would acquire similar *tfu* capabilities, and kill their own relatives, and share the flesh with Shey Riba and his *tfu* friends. This was resolved when the community ordered the youths to pay Shey Riba with fowls at a public ceremony. Shey Riba also was given pardon and was reinstated into the community. When he died, he was in good standing with the Catholic Church and the *nwarong* society. Both groups celebrated his death.

One could argue that if it is true that people have employed *tfu* in a negative way, then pardon may deprive the wounded party of justice. My emphasis on pardon does not ignore the fact that when people establish guilt and extend pardon, they often also ask the guilty person to pay some restitution. Such discipline should not destroy the notion of pardon itself but should aim at restoring the individual. Ultimately it is this capacity to pardon that will open the way into the future.

Levinas's bold proposal for a phenomenology of eros, which defines the ethical act as responsible desire expressed toward the feminine as a distinct representation of alterity and exteriority, has drawn mixed reactions. Simone De Beauvoir argues that Levinas does not depart from tradition because the male is subject and the female is Other through his characterization of the erotic relationship (De Beauvoir 1971, xvi). "When he writes that the woman is mystery, he implies that she is mystery for man. Thus, his description which is intended to be objective is in fact an assertion of masculine privilege" (Ibid.).[45]

Luce Irigaray (1991) offers a similar but much more substantive critique of Levinas's phenomenology of eros. Irigaray argues that the feminine appears in the work of Levinas as the reverse side of man's aspiration and is apprehended from the man's perspective (Ibid., 109). Irigaray contends that even in fecundity, Levinas makes use of the feminine for his own becoming, because in order to return to himself, Levinas needs a son. Thus sex as alterity eludes Levinas, for two reasons. First, "he knows nothing of communion in pleasure . . . [since] distance is always maintained with Other in the experience of love" (Ibid., 110–111). Second, Levinas "substitutes the son for the feminine" (Ibid., 111). This, according to Irigaray, falls short of alterity and a genuine recognition of the Other, because there is no particular Other, and where there is it is the son. Alterity takes place within paternity. Furthermore, Levinas's vocabulary is problematic. He employs a hermeneutical, metaphysical, and theological tone in his work, but he does not always resolve the issues raised by the employment of such language and frequently falls back into the "masculine subject" (Ibid., 113). Thus Levinas clings to patriarchal love and leaves the feminine in "pseudoanimality" without a face of her own. Such an account, according to Irigaray, falls radically short of ethics.[46]

I concede that the language and model of love that Levinas employs could be perceived as male oriented, but I think that Irigaray ignores the intent and spirit of Levinas's phenomenology of eros as a model for intersubjective interactions. I now respond to Irigaray's critique to provide a balanced account of Levinas and indicate why I prefer Levinas's phenomenology of eros as a basis for developing a theology of community relations.

First, I agree with Irigaray and with other interpreters of Levinas that his language is complex because he brings together terms and ideas such as the feminine, eros, voluptuousity, fecundity, paternity, and dwelling with bewildering and challenging novelty. [47] Ricoeur believes that Levinas uses "hyperbole, to the point of paroxysm."[48] While I cannot defend Levinas by simply saying that he is practicing rigorous philosophy, I find comfort in the fact that Levinas's excesses provoke a rethinking of some of the issues that he addresses, so that we do not lose sight of the ethical. However, what appeals to me is the direction in which he takes the language he employs from the philosophical tradition. Levinas highlights difference and calls for the elimination of control and domination as a basis for intersubjective relations. The need for clarity is not an indication that he has failed in achieving this goal.

I agree with Tina Chanter that Levinas's gender-specific language seems contradictory, because Levinas seems to claim that the woman does not have to be present for the dimension he calls feminine (Chanter 1991, 132ff). It seems that what we have in Levinas's account is a principle, not a genuine human and the feminine as a distinct quality (Ibid., 133). There is certainly that dimension in Levinas. Cohen, who has analyzed the metaphorical use of the notion of feminine in the Levinas corpus, argues that one can push the idea that the feminine is a principle in Levinas (Cohen, 195ff). However, regardless of how one looks at it, Levinas's account highlights radical difference, and these questions tend to ignore that Levinas's phenomenology prioritizes a human being who is different and should not be totalized.[49] In the Wimbum context, such a difference may be just what is needed to counter the cultural beliefs that put women at the bottom.

A sympathetic reading of Levinas, however, should not minimize questions that confront any philosophical or theological inquiry. Does Levinas essentialize women when he explores the structure of difference through the feminine? (Chanter 1991, 143). This is not the case. Derrida argues that in thinking difference through a woman, Levinas evokes a reversal that puts the woman "against him in the place of the wholly Other as *arche*" (Derrida 1991, 44).[50] I am convinced that in spite of Levinas's sometimes ambiguous language, what is revolutionary is that the feminine, whether "idealized or personalized," challenges manipulation and commands responsibility toward the Other. Attempting to think such difference is the genius and risk that Levinas takes in his interpretation of eros.[51]

Irigaray also charges that Levinas "substitutes the son for the feminine." Irigaray has said emphatically, "The son should not be the place where the father confers being or existence on himself, the place where he finds the resources to return to himself in relation to this Same as and Other than himself constituted by the son" (Irigaray 1991, 111). If that is what Levinas has done with the notion of fecundity, then this critique is in order. However, this misses the point that Levinas makes regarding the relationship in paternity. It is not meant to subvert the feminine but rather to highlight the notion that the Otherness of the father is not completely obliterated in the face of another human being, even one's child. Although a child is the extension of the parent, that child nevertheless is a person who is independent and distinct from the parent. One would argue that this would hold true of the mother-daughter relationship, and that such a position would not be a subversion of masculinity.

The metaphor that Levinas uses is not intended to put the masculine above the feminine. These metaphors challenge masculine pride and virility and invite one to care for the neighbor. [52] Wendy Farley writes about the kind of beauty that invites obligation in a way that is relevant here.

Another being recognized as beautiful is no longer a drab object, an empty utility, a pretty thing for my enjoyment, a threat, a nothing, a trinket to be possessed. It need not be transformed into my rapture, my enlightenment, my salvation, enjoyment, interpretation, apprehension, or idea. It [She] stands pristine and lovely, having nothing to do with me[53] (Farley 1996, 81).

Catherine Chalier describes what happens as a *kenosis* of the One before the Other.[54] Levinas sees the maternal as the idea of substitution, and the good beyond Being. For Levinas, the biblical figure of the feminine is Rebecca, who sets the criterion of choice to be *mitzvah* or hospitality. She is chosen because she ignores class and demonstrates feelings for the Other by offering water. She is thus chosen because of the responsibility she demonstrates toward the Other. Rebecca reaches out to the one that is waiting in a disruption that brings peace to the Other. This is the meaning of the feminine in the human being that Levinas is advocating (Chalier 1991, 127).

While defending Levinas, I do not want to ignore the implications of Irigaray's questions on paternity, because Wimbum society is largely a patriarchal one, and the son is in many ways the mirror of the father. I have wondered many times if the allegation that people give away kin to *tfu* is done so easily because kinship structures could be manipulated into the kind of controlling relationship that Irigaray is concerned about. Parents and even uncles expect children to provide all of their needs because they believe that their life continues in their children. As radical as Levinas's thought is, ethics requires that such continuation should not erase distinctions, and with Levinas, that those distinctions spell difference, and invite respect rather than control through *tfu*.

Levinas and Tillich are not the only ones who recover the erotic for theological and philosophical discourse, but they present a compelling case.[55] There is a growing appreciation of the erotic as a resource for theological and philosophical thinking that is counter to certain Christian understandings of eros. The turn taken by feminist and womanist writers to the theme of eros comprises a rejection of the patriarchal, manipulative, and dualistic understanding of eros. Audre Lorde, in her poetic imagination, interprets eros as a life force that encompasses the wholeness of being in spiritual, social, psychological, and physical dimensions (Lorde 1984, 53–57). In reaction to the predominant male vision of Christ, Nakashima Brock has proposed a Christology of erotic power, a Christa-community in which the forces of *eros* are brought to govern relationships in a community (Brock 1991). Similarly, Judith Plaskow analyzes the bonds of community through erotic vision and proposes a theology of sexuality (Plaskow 1990, 171–177). Carter Heyward regards eros as a holistic movement of sensuality that binds people together in right relationships. "Our eroticism is the deepest stirring of our relationality, our experience of being connected to others" (Heyward 1987, 55). Eros is the capacity for transpersonal relationships that allows people to focus on the here and now in a new interconnectedness (Ibid., 90).[56]

In appropriating Levinas's argument on eros for a new kind of philosophical and theological praxis, I am tracing his ethical philosophy to the heart of his proposal, which calls for a desire that will establish relationships of respect among people. Theologians and philosophers have to engage in a multivocal discourse that will allow further reflection on the way in which particular communities understand and respond to the erotic. Theologians cannot do their work in isolation. They have to draw from the resources of their community to articulate the need for a desire that we have seen in Levinas.

Robert Pool's postmodernist ethnography, which has the very telling title "There Must Have Been Something," now published as *Dialogue and the Interpretation of Illness*, raises the question of traditionalism and theism (Pool 1994, 205–212). Pool is not seeking to provide any answers to issues that deal with interpreting illness and *tfu*. The opposition he sets between traditionalism and theism implies that there are differences of perspective on these and many other issues. The "traditionalist" in Wimbum society, according to Pool, is one who does not believe in any god or gods, except, as the case may be, the gods of the land. There is no doubt that in the conflicting interpretation of God, or gods, there is a tacit recognition that there are many in the Wimbum society who do not interpret the world in light of the God of agape. Many of these people have a perspective, and in many cases, it is their perspective that is decisive when it comes to ethical and moral questions. A philosophical and theological appropriation of Levinas's vision of eros interpreted as insatiable desire that does not totalize offers an opportunity to engage in a humanistic enterprise that might join together philosophers and theologians in a forceful way to carry on the analysis and critique of *tfu*. Entering the conversation at this level, philosophers and theologians can rightly call for a more humane treatment of the Other and those who are accused of practicing negative *tfu*.

Conclusion

I have analyzed Wimbum *tfu* as part of a complex set of terms addressing meaning making and existential problems, including dealing with misfortune. We have discovered through this analysis that *tfu* is a very dynamic concept. The Wimbum people have borrowed new terms from other parts of Cameroon to express activities that resemble what they consider the negative aspects of *tfu*. We also have examined the concept of *tfu* as a postmodern problematic, stressing that it can be regarded as power, gender, economic, and religious discourse.

I have borrowed from Bernstein to argue that we can move beyond the debate on rationality and do contextual ethics. I call such an enterprise "critical contextualism." It is contextual because we can draw from Wimbum ideas to discuss dimensions of individuality. It is critical because concepts that are used should be subjected to scrutiny. While we have not looked at the entire range of issues involved in *tfu*, it has become clear that the dimensions of individuality present in Wimbum society call for an understanding of personhood that permits us to borrow from Levinas's argument of the Other as a basis for ethics.

I have argued that ethics in the tradition of Levinas should prioritize the personal. I make no claims that Levinas is the only source for a critical discourse on *tfu* matters. Furthermore, I do not claim that only Western philosophical categories can be used to settle these questions. I have drawn from Levinas because his philosophical revisions address human concerns that can be expressed and echoed across cultures. The inviolability and distinctiveness of the individual Levinas articulates is very appealing, especially when one considers the totality of *tfu*. Furthermore, employing metaphysical desire as a philosophical and theological motif holds promise for a critical engagement with issues raised by the discourse and alleged practice of *tfu*. My analysis and critique is far from comprehensive or complete. I do not think I have even started to answer some of the crucial questions I have on *tfu*.

I reflect on these things as one who was born and grew up among the Wimbum people before moving to the United States. I continue to ask questions about the central claims of *tfu*. As I think about this, I realize, after spending several years to obtain my doctorate, that there are many things I do not understand, even in my narrow field of philosophy of religion. Why should I bother with the fact that I cannot understand what *tfu* is but can only describe it because I depend on others? The things I do not understand, as much as I am baffled by *tfu*, do not confuse me. Furthermore, for the many things that I do not know in philosophy, religion, theology, anthropology, and politics, I make a concerted effort to know in the sense that I attempt to master those fields. I have spent a lot of time trying to understand *tfu* and to make sure that I have a good grasp of the issues involved, yet I do not find myself wanting to possess it or practice it, as I would like to do with other areas of knowledge. The discourse and practice of my colleagues in the science department do not threaten or pose a problem for me as much as *tfu* discourse does. If anything, I find much comfort in scientific activity. Does this mean that I can concur with Charles Taylor that science has finally carried the day? This is not the issue. I simply mean that in many ways I am more open to scientific discourse than I am to *tfu* discourse. Indeed, I can become part of the scientific discursive "family" in a way that I cannot with *tfu*. This is a rather long way of saying that I have not solved all questions on *tfu* through this critique. If anything, I expect some scholars to ask better questions than I have asked in this book. As I conclude this inquiry, I want to emphasize several points.

WIMBUM MORAL CONCEPTS OUGHT TO BE RECOGNIZED

Wimbum people pay a lot of attention to *tfu*, and for that reason scholars should continue to study their ideas as they attempt to provide a deeper understanding of the Wimbum society, particularly moral discourse among the Wimbum people. Members of the Wimbum community who are clergy have shown interest in the subject of *tfu*. All one can hope for at this time is that an open dialogue will continue as people seek to understand the dynamics of the Wimbum society and its evolving relationship with *tfu*.

THIS CALLS FOR CRITICAL APPROPRIATION AND ENGAGEMENT

I appropriate Wimbum ideas through a method I call "critical contextualism." I refer to the fact that Wimbum ideas have to be subjected to scrutiny as members of that society and interested scholars continue to probe these issues. Wimbum writers who analyze these issues "from the inside," such as Mburu, Tanto, Mbunwe-Samba, and I, must not romanticize Wimbum thought. This is a danger that can be avoided by adopting critical contextual discourse that questions Wimbum beliefs and practices while granting their validity and richness as a form of moral discourse.

Further work needs to be done to employ local religious ideas in this critical process. Wimbum moral ideas ought to be utilized where contextually beneficial. *Tfu* discourse takes place within a "moral space," where people claim that others deliberately employ power not available to all to hurt other members of the community. People who can warn others of these practices are always held in high regard, because as moral exemplars, they disclose negative plans and activities. Accusations and denials are moral claims that also should be subjected to scrutiny. When people accuse an individual of negative *tfu*, they make a moral claim about what is appropriate or acceptable. These claims rest on the dignity of another person and the violation of that dignity. They attribute negative, hurtful behavior to occult powers. These claims cannot be taken at face value. I am not sure what it will take to validate these claims in ways that are democratic, that is, use of criteria that is open and available to all. Regardless of how it is done, all accusations should be subjected to a critical examination to ensure that someone is not tainting the moral standing of another person by false claims. By the same logic, it ought to be stated that when a person has been accused and he or she denies it, such a denial itself constitutes a moral claim. This counterclaim is not only a claim of innocence but also an attempt to disassociate from the violations a person is charged with. If these claims were not true, I would argue that the dignity of the person who has been accused falsely has been violated.[1]

Elaborate rituals in Wimbum society, as well as explicit moral claims, should always be examined critically for their moral standing. Different rituals make moral claims, because the people who participate in them want to accomplish several things, including rituals to seek protection, to make a confession, to atone for an offense, or to conform to what one is told to do. One particular incident that was brought to my attention when I returned to Cameroon for a short time in the spring of 1995 involved an individual's participation in a ritual due to family expectations. I heard that a certain schoolteacher was asked to buy a goat to give to his maternal uncles so that they could forgive him for a grudge. It was claimed that he was sick because his maternal uncles had a problem with him. This teacher was not accused of using *tfu*. It was alleged that he had attended a meeting, during which there ensued a negative discussion about his maternal uncles. His maternal uncles thought this was as bad as taking part in *tfu* practices against them. He continued to maintain his innocence but had to comply to receive emotional well-being, although he was not healed of his illness. Such pressure and practices need to be called into question.

Disciplinary measures taken against people constitute moral claims. People accused of practicing *tfu* may be asked to give a goat or fowl, or some other punishment may be administered, depending on the severity of the case. Sometimes these offerings are prepared and eaten by the entire community as part of a reconciliation meal. Some accused people often choose to pay the penalty, even though they would in general continue to insist that they are innocent. All of these fines constitute moral claims. While paying a fine may be appropriate in some cases, other forms of punishment ought to be subjected to criticism to see if the punishment is not cruel and unusual. I am thinking particularly of the practice of exiling people from their homes, which has been used recently with impunity in the Wimbum land. The very ambiguities of *tfu* itself call for consideration when punishment is given, and it seems to me that exile is certainly cruel and unusual punishment.

My comments are provisional and serve as a springboard for further investigation as people continue to search for ethical solutions to what remains an unclear, thorny realm of discourse. Scholars of Wimbum as well as outsiders who are interested in the subject matter should continue to ponder these issues. Genuine attempts to understand the religious world of the Wimbum people could yield some fruitful results in the quest for an ethical stance on *tfu*. I have by no means solved Wimbum *tfu* crises, but seeing *tfu* as an intersubjective engagement and employing Levinas's call to respect the Other open the door for a new discourse on *tfu*, especially its negative uses.

Notes

PREFACE

1. I am indebted for this point to Robert Bernasconi for his essay "African Philosophy's Challenge to Continental Philosophy." Bernasconi writes: "The Eurocentric view of philosophy is still largely intact, both in the institutional presentation of philosophy and in the declarations of some of western philosophy's finest minds. Take Levinas, for example. In spite of the pluralism that his thought celebrates, Emmanuel Levinas was quite explicit that he was not willing to look beyond the Bible and the Greeks as models of excellence: 'I always say—but in private—that the Greeks and the Bible are all that is serious in humanity. Everything else is dancing'" (Bernasconi 1997, 185).

2. Levinas subordinates knowledge to the spontaneous activity of justice, which happens in a similar way as obligation happens for John Caputo (Caputo 1993).

3. Patricia Werhane points out that justice is part of being a human, and being equals justice (Werhane 1995, 66).

4. Levinas argues that there exists above the complex structures of interpersonal relationship a desire that welcomes the Other who questions the subject's right to power as arbitrary and violent freedom (Levinas 1969, 84).

5. This is not his real name.

6. This inquiry into the question of "being" was opened by Parmenides and pursued with dazzling profundity in Heidegger's hermeneutic ontology. In raising the question of Otherness, which has always been subjected to the reflective horizon of being, the self-conscious, the rational self, or the doubting subject, Levinas returns to an important philosophical issue.

7. Morality takes place, or as Caputo argues in *Against Ethics*, happens, in the very concreteness of daily life (Caputo 1993). Furrow argues that such a perspective reminds us that "friendships, family, relationships, religions and national heritage, economic status, and of course the slights,

133

traumas, accomplishments and joys of everyday life guide us in our complex judgments about morality" (Furrow 1995, xiii).

8. This comment is from the philosopher and Levinas scholar Edith Wyschogrod in personal communication.

9. Furthermore, in grafting, he retrieves themes such as the erotic and transforms them into a nontotalizing desire with far-reaching implications for gender discourse.

10. The irony, as some have pointed out, is that MacIntyre himself is deeply rooted in some of the principles that come from the Enlightenment. Edith Wyschogrod points out that, "[MacIntyre] attacks modern liberalism while at the same time profiting from its disinterested stance. Despite his strong preference for Thomism, MacIntyre refuses to station himself within that or any other tradition, he remains conceptually disaffiliated" (Wyschogrod 1988, 136).

11. Stephen Luckes has pointed out in a review that "MacIntyre's solution to this typically modern problem [i.e., the difficulty of resolving ethical disputes] is to extol the virtues of pre-modern societies . . . MacIntyre loads the dice throughout . . . He is consistently charitable towards Plato, Aristotle, Augustine, Aquinas and Hutchinson but unrelentingly hostile, above all to Hume and to modern liberalism generally. Thus Aristotle's justification of slavery and his exclusion of women from citizenship are plausibly claimed to be excisable from his thought while leaving his central argument intact; yet Hume is described as 'articulating the principles of the dominant English social and cultural order, an order itself deeply inhospitable to philosophy'" (Lukes 1988, 35).

12. Jeffery Stout argues in favor of overcoming the dichotomy between communitarians and liberals, yet he draws on MacIntyre's insights without endorsing his historicism and lament on the fragmentation of society (Stout 1988). Stout offers a non-theory based "social criticism" that probes and searches for values, as Stout puts it, with both eyes open, so that one could reconstruct virtues in a positive direction. Echoing the strategy that has been employed by postmodernists, Wyschogrod has moved away from theory and focused on the narrative of the lives of saints. Wyschogrod argues that we know from Heidegger that theory can be a manipulative tool, and for that reason the *point d'appui* of postmodernist ethics should be located in the question of the "Other," because in the Other, we are dealing not with a mere "conceptual anchorage" but with a human being who is also very much alive as "a living force" (Wyschogrod 1990, xxvi).

13. "Tempels" is a reference to Placides Tempels, author of Bantu Philosophy.

14. Emmanuel Eze, in a response to our papers at the African Studies Association in Chicago in 1998, pointed out that there is some similarity

between the anthropologist's quest for knowledge about sorcery and the sorcerer's quest "to uncover another world. In my view, both sorcery and anthropology are, disciplinarily and existentially, affairs of hunt, escape, and 'border-crossing.' The metaphors of escape, longing, and [re]search—though derived by Devisch from sorcery—evoke adequately what anthropology has gone to Africa and elsewhere to do since its inception, and its history may well be viewed as a documentation of these 'fantastic adventures'."

15. Maxwell Owusu's essay, "Ethnography of Africa: The Usefulness of the Useless," questioned the validity of anthropological knowledge created by field workers who lacked the language competency and so often depended on informants (Owusu 1997, 705).

16. Meyer Fortes once stated this notion of the construction of reality very clearly when he pointed out that writing ethnography is a specific task. "It is not merely a question of putting his observations on record. Writing an anthropological monograph is itself an instrument of research and perhaps the most significant instrument of research in the anthropologist's armory. It involves breaking up the vivid kaleidoscopic reality of human action, thought, and emotion which lives in the anthropologist's notebooks and memory, and creating out of the pieces a coherent representation of a society, in terms of the general principles of organization and motivation that regulate it. It is a task that cannot be done without the help of theory" (Fortes 1945, vii).

17. Fabian's two works, *Time and the Other* and *Time and the Work of Anthropology*, are fascinating approaches to the issues and practice of reflexivity in representation (Fabian 1983, 1991; MaGrane 1989). Wyatt MacGaffey's illuminating essay on ideology and belief in African study clearly highlights multivocality and interdisciplinary styles that have structured the construction of any kind of ideology and belief (MacGaffey 1981). Paul Rabinow has pointed out that in this process anthropologists have turned to the texts of other anthropologists to analyze their representational strategies as well as politics (Rabinow 1986). Fardon says that one characteristic of this movement is that the practitioners of postmodern anthropology engage in "a production of texts by means of texts, rather than by means of fieldwork" (Fardon 1990, 5). According to Fardon, the quest for justice has resulted in a situation where ethnographers themselves have become Other. He suggests that if this textualization is going to be constructive, we will have to wait a long time for the healing to come.

18. Writing about the construction of reality, Dell Hymes had this to say about Clifford Geertz's narrative skills: "Through his narrative skill, he is able to convey a sense (mediated by his personal involvement) of the quality and texture of Balinese fascination with cock fighting. Evidence of the fascination is important. It supports taking the activity as a key to something essential about the Balinese, it helps us understand the analytic statements. A film might help too, but it would need something verbal from Geertz to teach us what we should learn from it. The narrative part

of Geertz's article in effect points, as the narrator of a film might do, and in the absence of a film, shows. It does so through texture and proportion" (Hymes, 1978, 16).

19. Jackson notes that the intersubjective is ambiguous space, in several respects. It is a site for constructive, destructive, and reconstructive relation; it is a place where the ideational and personal commingle in human relationships; at the intersubjective level, regardless of the inequalities among people, each is "existentially dependent" on the other. Jackson argues that there are several forms to intersubjectivity, because it may appear as dyadic but is shaped by the conscious and unconscious. The intersubjective space reflects the instability of human consciousness and one can explore its ambiguity as a problem of knowledge (Jackson 1998, 8–10).

20. Owusu points out that Kenneth Hale emphasizes the importance of knowing the local language. "The linguist depends upon native speakers of the language he studies. It is a prevailing fact about anthropological linguistics . . . that the linguist and the native speaker are not the same individual . . . I question whether significant advances beyond the present state of knowledge of the world's languages can be made if important sectors of linguistics continue to be dominated by scholars who are not native speakers of the languages they study" (Quoted in Owusu 720).

21. In both the *Nicomachean Ethics* and *Eudiamonian Ethics*, Aristotle clearly states that actions which are voluntary are subject to sanction 1109b31 and *NE* 3.1-5. "A responsible (proper candidate for praise and blame) for doing x if and only A does x voluntarily."

22. In a recent discussion of Professor Oruka's Sage Philosophy, Bruce Janz broadens our understanding of critique with several questions about what it means to engage in a critique (Janz 1998, 64). Does critique mean finding fault and expressing disagreement? Is critique used in its Kantian form, which means "finding the scope and limits of something" (Ibid.). Does it have something to do with explaining a misunderstanding? Janz points out that Professor Oruka "tends to identify critique by establishing a communal or individual belief or practice, and then looking for divergence from it" (Ibid., 65). But more than that, he points out that there is creativity in Oruka's work because he attempts to go beyond the boundaries of communal understanding. However, he also points out that Oruka seems to take critique as a universal moment in philosophy, even though Wittgenstein started that such a universality is merely an illusion. "One cannot assume that the nature of critique is universal, if critique itself is tied to a particular contingent philosophical system" (Ibid.).

23. This is a play on the titles of two works by Cameroonian theologian Jean-Marc Ela, *African Cry*, Maryknoll, N.Y.: Orbis Books, 1986; *My Faith As an African*, Maryknoll, N.Y.: Orbis Books, 1988.

CHAPTER 1

1. This area is also known as the Bamenda Grassfields because Bamenda has served as the chief town of this area. In addition, it corresponds to the administrative unit known as the Northwest Province (see Pool 1994, 27). I refer to the area as the Northwest Province, except where necessary to use the word "Grassfields." The most recent studies of the Northwest Province, which also are key sources for my survey, are those of Paul Nkwi and Jean P. Warnier (Nkwi and Warnier 1982; Nkwi 1987). Earlier studies of the Northwest Province include monographs published during the colonial period and post–independence anthropological monographs (see Kaberry 1952; Jeffreys 1962; Chilver 1966; Chilver and Kaberry 1967).

2. Five other groups also occupy the Donga-Mantung plateau, the Yamba to the northeast, the Mfumte to the north, the Mbembe Misaje to the northwest, and the Mbaw to the east.

3. The Wimbum of the Donga-Mantung Division are different from the group of people in the southwestern part of Chad, as well as those of the Western Province of Cameroon.

4. Peter Probst and Brigitte Bühler (1990) suggest that the Wimbum have borrowed the Nso term *kibai* for reasons of prestige. I suspect that the idea of prestige employed here is rooted in an understanding that the Wimbum borrowed the term from the Nso people to benefit from the power of a larger group governed by one of the "paramount" *fons*. Such an understanding, however, misses much of the complexity involved in the languages of the Northwest Province.

5. It would take an entirely different book to spell out the complicated nature of their relationship. The conclusion I draw is that the similarities in titles do not stem from the fact that the Nso have a more prestigious office and title, as Probst and Bühler suggest; it has nothing to do with whether the Nso are superior to the Wimbum. The commonalties between language groups indicate the fact that they share vocabulary and reflect the settlement patterns, as well as diplomatic and economic relationships that have developed over the years.

6. I should point out that a claim made by Robert Pool in his dissertation, now published as *Dialogue and the Interpretation of Illness,* is problematic. Pool claims, "The *Fon* of Ndu, head of the Wiya Clan, is the most influential and impressive of the Wimbum *fons* and is, for this reason, seen by some as the leader of all the Wimbum" (Pool 1989, 6). Unfortunately, it is not immediately clear in what sense "the *Fon* of Ndu . . . is the most influential and most impressive." Although I have no reason to doubt that, as an individual, the head of the Wiya Clan is well respected and liked, as was his predecessor *Fon* William Nformi, nevertheless, neither

he or his predecessor has been viewed by people as the head of the Wimbum people. The *Fon* of Ndu is the head of the Wiya Clan and is affectionately called by most Wimbum people *Tarr Wiya,* the father/head of Wiya.

7. In further notes on "The Origin of the Warr Clan, Wimbum Area Council Donga-Mantung Division, West Cameroon," *Abbia* 26, 2 (1973): 103–105, Mafiamba reports that the *Fon* of Chup affirmed the Kimi origin of the Warr people. The *Fon* reportedly told Mafiamba that there were four founding fathers who settled at Mbirbaw: Chup, Ntumbaw, Sop (Nsop), and Mbot. According to this view, Mbot was the youngest of the brothers and the others left because of disagreements with Mbot. Chup went away and had Kungi, Mbissa, and Mbah. Ntumbaw had Saa, Sunjaw, and Bum. Sop had Esu, Kochi (Noni), and Dumbo, while Mbot, who remained at Mbirbaw, had Njap, Wat, Nkambe, and Tabesop in (Nso). These children would later move away from their fathers and form the towns of the Warr Clan that bear those names.

8. It is not clear whether the Luh were originally part of the Wiyah group in Kimi and separated during the period of migration, or if they were just an independent group that settled in the Nso area.

9. *Ndap* literally means house, but when used in this way, it means the family of *Fai* and the family of Ndzi.

10. With the exception of Moses Tansi and Usumanu Nfor, the names in this paragraph are actual family names. I have used real names when discussing noncontroversial matters.

11. Probst refers to the case of *Fai* Ndzingong, who socialized in the market too much and was disciplined by the authorities, thus one of the challenges posed by modernity is that the *fais,* who are expected to keep their authority, are forced to violate seclusion in order to acquire the means by which to maintain their power. Probst correctly observes that what is happening in Wimbum land needs to be evaluated by seriously considering the reality of money, power, and authority in the "modern" state.

12. Peter Geschiere argues that in the case of the Maka of Southeastern Cameroon, the intellectuals also play an important role as power brokers between their respective villages and the national government (Geschiere 1982, 301).

13. Although these views were later modified when Dr. Dunger wrote his doctoral dissertation, they were premature observations by a missionary who otherwise was a very astute, sympathetic observer of the Cameroon situation and the North American Baptist endeavor in Cameroon.

14. In *Divinity and Experience,* Godfrey Lienhardt noted that divinities, or what he called "powers," also are the representations that the Dinkas call upon in their interaction with their physical and social environment. Lienhardt argues that even a foreigner could have direct knowledge of these powers (Lienhardt 1990, 147).

15. Nkwi and Warnier translate this as the "god of country" (*op. cit.,* 164).

16. While Pool's postmodernist anthropology rightly gives a voice to his informants, such a conclusion leaves the reader wondering to what extent Wyatt MacGaffey's comment is still true regarding the practice of anthropology, even theology: "We deem it essential to preserve a difference between us, an elite [this elite now, in the case in question, would include some local informants and those of us who write from inside] no matter how small, who see the world as it really is, and them, who see only through a glass, darkly" (MacGaffey 1978, 110).

17. This work was revised in 2000. For other works on religion see David Lan's *Guns and Rain* (1985); and J. Matthew Schoffeleers's, *River of Blood* (1992). Madison: University of Wisconsin Press, 1992; See also Terence Ranger's essay, "Religious Movements and Politics in Sub-Saharan Africa," in *African Studies Review* Vol. 29, No. 2 (1986): 1-69 and Richard Werbner's *Ritual Passage, Sacred Journey* (1989).

18. I should distinguish this from the singular *nshep,* which refers to a masked figure from any of the regulatory societies. I also should distinguish this from the word *mshep* itself, which simply means medicine.

19. Nkwi and Warnier refer to the annual *Fon*'s hunting expedition at Ntumbaw, when all of the males who were eligible to go were expected to bring their spears and hunting weapons to the palace and to place them at *Mbidi Nkon,* for a special blessing (Nkwi and Wannier 1982).

20. This is a prayer used at one of the occasions recorded by Jeffreys: "Nyu help us in our hunting so that when we see game we may kill it and return rejoicing. My spear when I throw you go straight striking kill the animal" (quoted in Nkwi and Warnier 1982, 164).

21. Kwast quotes missionary Gebauer's now-famous comment among the Baptists in Cameroon, in which Gebauer indicated that the Cameroonians were the pioneers. "They leveled the ground for missions and missionaries who followed up their trails in 1928 and 1929. The glory of having brought the gospel to tribes unknown belongs to Mamadu, an African of Africans" (Kwast 1971, 117).

22. Sanneh indicates that the material condition of the Africans at the time of missionary penetration did not matter. The material condition of the churches of the West, which went out to do missionary work, was marginal. Sanneh does not ignore the impact of Western missionary bureaucracy or the fact that it is a multimillion-dollar venture. What Sanneh states clearly is that in carrying out the missionary task of proclaiming, "The *Missio Dei,* the western missionary, is merely heeding a call whose echo has long reverberated throughout the edifice of African religiosity" (Sanneh 1983, 247). Sanneh is interested in African religious impact on the spread of Christianity in West Africa but, to a certain extent, what he

says reflects Robin Horton's thesis that Christianity and Islam were merely the catalyst for change that would have taken place in Africa anyway. When that change took place, it did not mean that indigenous African religions were abandoned. According to Horton, Christianity offered Africans another means of controlling and dealing with human experience and cosmic reality (Horton 1971, 85-108).

23. *Sarki Hausawa* is the term for the Hausa Chief, and *Ardo* is the Fulani term for chief.

24. In the 1950s and most of the 1960s, it was an important market in the region, following the market of Ndu and Nkambe. It was normal for traders to come from all over the Northwest Province, to attend the Ndu market on *Sing,* to attend the Ntumbaw market the next day, *Lih,* and then to proceed to Nkambe the following day, *Nkapye.* The Binka market, which meets on the same day as Ntumbaw, was also important, but Ntumbaw had established a long reputation, dating back to the days of early trading between the people of the Northwest Province of Cameroon and the northeastern and southeastern regions of Nigeria. Traders traveled on foot, using donkeys to carry their goods, and many went as far as Enugu, Benin, and Onitcha, in the southeastern region and in central Nigeria. Some even went as far as Kano and Sokoto in northern Nigeria. Ntumbaw was an important stop, and most of the Hausa and Fulani traders would eventually settle in Ntumbaw, making it one of the largest concentrations of Hausas and Fulanis in the Northwest Province. There was a quarter head at Ntumbaw who was short in stature. Since he was well known by these traders, and since Ntumbaw had become such an important stop, many people knew the town simply as *Njikajerri,* meaning "the short Nji." The fame enjoyed by Ntumbaw has now declined.

25. There is an interesting version of this that relates to Christianity. When the Baptists first settled at Ndu, the *Fon* of Ndu gave them land on which to build. In giving them the land, the *Fon* also performed the ritual that established the "mission compound," by planting a fig tree. According to the customs of the Wimbum people, this fig tree represents the "mission compound," the location of the Cameroon Baptist Theological Seminary. The fig tree has grown and provides shade when the sun is hot. In 1970, a chapel was built right next to it. Excavation was done carefully around it to keep the tree intact. I earned my income for the summer holidays working with the construction crew. I am sure that if you were to ask a missionary, he or she would tell you that it would be wrong to pull down that tree. They had to preserve it because, from an aesthetic perspective, it adds to the beauty of the area, but as most people in Ndu would tell you, if that tree was cut down, that would been the end of the "mission compound." In this case, aesthetic qualities helped avoid what could have become a very difficult problem, but in the case of Ntumbaw, some people claimed that their market had declined because it had literally been cut down.

CHAPTER 2

1. Although I use hermeneutics in the general sense as interpretation, my project also includes not only understanding but appropriating to the extent that I seek to understand the material in order to draw some ethical implications from such an understanding. Recently, Johaness Fabian, whose early work is grounded in hermeneutics and the social sciences, has argued that the notion of an interpretation of history in the case of the history of the Democratic Republic of the Congo assumes that there is some standard by which one is measuring the data. He prefers the notion of confrontation as an epistemological model. One could argue that what I am attempting is a type of confrontation, not only with the data on *tfu* but with perspectives that shy away from considering the ethical implications of the discourse on *tfu* (see Fabian 1996, 297ff).

2. Leny Lagerwerf (1985) presents documentation for this claim and provides an extensive bibliography that reflects a theological perspective. (See also Kerkhofs, 1980.)

3. Alan Macfarlane and others have offered definitions and theories of witchcraft. While these definitions attempt to state what witchcraft is, they pose problems such as the very idea of the translatability of terms and concepts from one language and context to another (see Macfarlane 1982).

4. The force of Crick's claim is that different societies should be seen as "moral spaces" in which the terms employed are a mirror of specific activities. What this calls for is an in-depth analysis of the terms employed in those cultures. It is only when that is done that "the mark of our comprehension would be a decreasingly frequent employment of the term" (Crick 1970, 346).

5. Although I do not pursue the structural-functionalist interpretation of Evans-Pritchard's work, I stress that it remains the *Locus Classicus* because of the broad themes of "witchcraft" discussed, the aporias of his overall project, and the invitation it gave to a multidisciplinary conversation on this aspect of African studies. Victor Turner's reaction to the distinction that Evans-Pritchard made between witchcraft and magic also is familiar and will not be pursued in this discussion. Crick's claim that most of the functionalist and structuralist schools have failed to introduce anything strikingly new after Evans-Pritchard is a bit sweeping. However, I focus on studies that are more recent, because these tend to deal with the dynamism of witchcraft in the wake of modernist and postmodernist interpretations.

6. See Barrie Reynolds, *Magic, Divination, and Witchcraft among the Barotse of Northern Rhodesia*, Berkeley: University of California Press, 1963. See also Jean Masamba Ma Mpolo's dissertation, "Psychotherapeutic Dynamics in African Bewitched Patients: Toward a Multi-Dimensional Therapy

in Social Psychiatry," Ph.D. diss., the School of Theology at Claremont, 1975.

7. The work of Cyprian Fisiy, Peter Geschiere, Miriam Goheen, E. Ardener, Ralph Austen, Eric de Rosny, Michael Rawlands, and Jean Pierre Warnier has provided new insights into "witchcraft" discourse and practice in other areas of Cameroon. The insights I have gained from these studies will be evident throughout this discussion.

8. Lawrence O'Keefe (1982) argues that there is a clear interrelationship between religion and magic. Other scholars who have addressed religious concerns in their study of witchcraft include Wyatt MacGaffey, who has discussed *Kindoki* among the BaKongo as an institutional phenomenon that the prophetic movements of that region have attempted to address (MacGaffey 1977, 177–93). Stanley Tambiah, Jean Comaroff, and John Comaroff also demonstrate in some of their works that witchcraft is a form of religious discourse. Although I will not engage in the discussion of magic in this work, it might be helpful to note that the claim that witchcraft is a religious discourse can be further illustrated when one looks at the relationship between religion and magic. I am mindful of the distinction that Evans-Pritchard made between these two realms of knowledge, but because they both claim paranormal power, their relationships to religion, though not always complementary, show some family resemblance.

9. Peter Geschiere, Cyprian Fisiy, Miriam Goheen, Dickson Eyoh, Robert Pool, Edwin Aderner, Tatah Mbuy, Daniel K. Musa, and Ralph Austen highlight some socioeconomic issues in witchcraft in Cameroon. Diane Ciekawy's study of witchcraft in the Kilifu District of Kenya demonstrates that the eradication process was incorporated into the political process and manipulated by different people for their own purposes (Ciekawy 1992). Even when "witchcraft" cases were brought before the court, there was an indication that the process was used as revenge or a weapon for "a larger political conflict" (Ibid., 82). Gender issues in witchcraft have been discussed by Masamba Ma Mpolo, who has studied *Kindoki* in the Democratic Republic of Congo from a psychotherapeutic perspective. Mark Auslander also has addressed gender issues in his study of Ngoni witch-finding (Auslander 1993, 167).

10. Witchcraft also has been addressed philosophically by Stanley Tambiah, Peter Winch, Robin Horton, Barry Hallen, and J. Sodipo. To the extent that it is part of the discourse on Africa, the methodological critiques in philosophy offered by V. Y. Mudimbe, Anthony Appiah, Dismas Masolo, and Kwasi Weridu have pointed to different ways of addressing the philosophical dimensions of it. It is within this general area that my attempt at what Mudimbe has called a *prise de parole* will be located. I argue that when considered from the religious, "meaning-making" perspectives, as well as from a sociopolitical viewpoint, witchcraft practice is ethically problematic. I employ philosophical ethics to highlight these

problems and suggest some theological insights that can be used to address these ethical problems.

11. See Robert Tanto, "Witchcraft among the Wimbum of Tabeken," Bambui, Cameroon: Regional Major Seminary, 1976; J. M. Mburu, "Witchcraft among the Wimbum," unpublished B.A. thesis in philosophy, Bambui, Cameroon: Regional Major Seminary, 1979; J. Njingti, "Witchcraft among the Wimbum," unpublished B.A. thesis in philosophy, Bambui, Cameroon, Regional Major Seminary, 1979, Mbunwe-Samba, *Witchcraft, Magic, and Divination: A Personal Testimony,* Bamenda, Cameroon: Archives Edition, 1989.

12. See M. D. W. Jeffreys, "The Wiyah Tribe," (Parts I and II), *African Studies* 21 (1962): vols. 1–2, 83–104, and 21 (vols. 3–4) 174-222. Also see Peter Probst and B. Bühler, "Patterns of Control on Medicine, Politics, and Social Change among the Wimbum, Cameroon Grassfields," *Anthropos* 85 (1990): 478–495.

13. Emmanuel Eze has indicated to me the ambiguity of carrying out an exposition of the phenomenon commonly called "witchcraft" that the Wimbum call *tfu*. The ambiguity here is that I attempt an interpretation of what most people claim is secret knowledge. The question is, can one grasp it? Eze, in personal communication, points out that I grasp it as a discourse of power, gender, ongoing problems in the postcolony, religion, and ethics. How can I do this? It is important to stress that I do not possess *tfu*. What I attempt is an analysis of the activities associated with those terms and the impact on personal and communal relations. One can interpret all of that. What remains difficult to understand, as I claim later on, is what exactly constitutes such power. This is something known only to people who claim to have it. Furthermore, how that power is used is not known. This is where a difference between *tfu* and magic stands out. With magic, one can employ material substance, but *tfu* does not depend on this at all. Eze also pointed out that I use expressions that give the impression that there may be no *tfu* at all. This is a difficult question to answer, and I do not attempt such an answer in this exposition. My assumption is that it is possible that such knowledge exists, but in the event that it does not exist, I argue that the discourse on *tfu* still causes results in unethical practices among the Wimbum calling for this kind of analysis.

14. The spelling of these words is mine, and I have based them solely on the way that they are pronounced. They do not necessarily reflect the orthography being developed in Cameroon by Wycliff Bible Translators in collaboration with the Ministry of Higher Education.

15. This is not his real name.

16. The expression *Nkwi* is used by the Wimbum people when designating a particular *Fon*. One also could say *Nkfu* Ntumbaw, but *Nkwi* Ntumbaw is what the Wimbum people normally use when referring specifically to the *Fon* of a specific town.

17. See Peter Probst's discussion of "Hexerie, medicin und Titel: Über Legitimät und Autorität," in *Schrift, Staat und Symbolisches Kapital bei den Wimbum: Ein Ethnographischer Bericht aus dem Grasland von Kamerun,* Münster: LIT Verlag, 1992.

18. The *Nwarong* society is an important closed association in most of the Northwest Province of Cameroon. It also is called *Kwifon.* The society is an important indication of the independence of a kingdom and is an important regulatory society because the different masked figures of this society are used for law enforcement.

19. Peter Geschiere argues that the Maka indicate that people use the force *djambe* because they believe it is a source of power (Geschiere 1997, 104).

20. Some of the older people among the Wimbum claim that such post-mortem exams were done in the past. Jeffreys claims that the practice was put to an end by the colonial administration (Jeffreys 1962).

21. Thomas notes that, according to Evans-Pritchard, the witch uses powers through the occult and does not have any rites, spells, or potions. Evans-Pritchard distinguished this kind of activity from sorcery, which he indicated was carried out using magic, spells, and sometimes formulas. Thomas rightly indicates that Evans-Pritchard may have been influenced in making such a distinction (a distinction that Victor Turner challenged) by traditional English usage surrounding "witchcraft" discourse. Therefore, it is clear that although some features may have a certain resemblance, a one-to-one correspondence cannot be maintained.

22. At the Baptist school in Ntumbaw, a member of the teaching staff was accused of handing out human flesh to children. The uproar over this matter forced the Baptist school manager to transfer this teacher to the Mbembe Misaje area, part of the same school district within the Cameroon Baptist Convention. In the period 1976–1977, when this school was run by the government, another teacher, who had been there when it was a Baptist school, also was accused of giving human flesh to schoolchildren.

23. In the conversation that Pool reports, Francis, one of the participants, asked if some can give a fowl. " 'A fowl,' " Tangwa shouted indignantly as he leaned forward. 'Is a fowl a man? If I give you a man are you only going to give me a fowl in return? So if you bring a fowl and they refuse what are you going to do? I am only telling you how I see it. I would refuse to take the fowl and tell you to bring a man' " (Pool 1994, 151–152).

24. The terms generally used are *tfu yibi* and *tfu yebu.* I have added a third category, *tfu jarr,* because it communicates what is implied in *Limbum,* although it has not been conceptualized in that way. (See Probst and Bühler 1990, 449; Mbunwe-Samba 1989, 10ff; Pool 1994, 148).

25. In the essay, Marwick also discusses the vandalism of graves. I will not address this issue here. Although some people view cannibalistic

rituals as no longer being performed, there is still a belief in this practice. Mbunwe-Samba writes about the allegations, still being made among the Wimbum today, that the flesh of a prominent politician from Tabenken, Mr. J. T. Ndze, who died thirty years ago, is still being traded today. In the early 1970s there were rumors spread in the town of Ntumbaw and among the Wimbum people that some were trading in human skulls. These people reportedly vandalized graves and cut off the heads of people buried in the graves.

26. Janzen adds, "African traditional medicine has been criticized by western missionaries and colonials as superstition that victimizes individuals ostensibly to benefit the social group. But it could be equally well argued that western medicine focuses on the individual patient and leaves the social context of his illness in pathological chaos."

27. When I was pastor at Etoug-Ebe Baptist Church in Yaounde, a university student from the Wimbum area died. It was suspected that his death was caused by relatives who envied his educational attainments and feared that his new status would enable him to succeed his father as the ruler of their town.

28. Unpublished paper, "Sorcery Discourses, Knowledge and the Ambivalence of Power: Access to a Second Pair of Eyes" (Fisiy 1994).

29. See also Lucy Mair's discussion of confessions (Mair 1960, 165, 167, 171).

30. In the urban areas, the annual boom time for the "traditional doctors" started in April, because civil servants sought consultation to clear their paths for their desired governmental appointments, which usually were made from the end of May through August. Massive shake-ups in the system, in the form of transfers, promotions, and demotions, were enacted through presidential decrees. These decrees usually reorganized entire governmental departments, starting with the Secretary General and continuing down to the Chief of Services. The way in which the French text of the decrees was written made for captivating news bulletins. When read, it was as if the entire country tuned in to hear the news director at the time, Joseph Marcel Ndi, say things such as "Charges d'Etudes, Monsieur James Nfor, en remplacement de Monsieur Elias Tanko, appellée á d'autre functions." If the previous occupant of that post was transferred the text would read, "En remplacement de Monsieur Elias Tanko, muter." If the previous occupant had been removed, the text read, "En remplacement de Monsieur Elias Tanko, relève des ses function." This way of handling the Civil Service not only created a chaotic, tense atmosphere in the country during the summer months but enabled the rise of a booming industry for "traditional doctors" who claimed they could improve the fortunes of the civil servants. These "traditional doctors," based their claims on their possession of what I have described as *tfu yebu*.

31. This is the singular, *nga seng* is the plural.

32. He also had a reputation as one who possessed *bfiu*—the benign form of *tfu,* mentioned above. Because he had these powers, it was claimed that he could immerse himself in a lake near his compound and remain in it for a long time. Part of his practice involved using large pythons. The claim was that when a patient came to him, Njong would incarnate himself as a python. This python would then wrap itself around the fracture. When the python left the room, Njong would tie the fracture with bands and sticks to hold it in place. After several weeks, the fracture would have healed completely.

33. During the "traditional doctor" craze, one of his sons, Daniel Tawe, became a licensed traditional doctor and was actually addressed as Dr. Tawe. Dr. Tawe made a fortune and bought himself a car. He had a thriving practice in Douala, the Seaport City and economic capital of Cameroon. The irony is that, although his Father, Pa Yeri, did not advertise and joined neither a national association nor its local chapter, Pa Yeri was far more popular than Dr. Tawe. Dr. Tawe usually referred his most difficult cases to Pa Yeri. I am distinguishing between father and son to highlight the effects of the commodification of what some still consider among the Wimbum to be sacred practice. This commodification has been brought about by the rise of the political economy and the growing urban capital that have invented new ways of making the logic of *tfu* and medicine work for the benefit of the new elite. My point here is that people such as Pa Yeri were able to do what they did because it was and is believed among the Wimbum that Pa Yeri had the ability to "see" things. When I was a pastor at Ntumbaw, he always complained to me that he did not like some of the men who were deacons in the church because they practiced *tfu.* He could not understand how people who were good deacons in the church could at the same time practice *tfu.* He also said that it was not up to him to deal with them; his role was just to treat illness.

34. Alfred Bongabi reportedly confessed that he and several others had gone out and brought strong winds to destroy Rev. Ndzi's house.

35. In his critique of the practice of providing overseas medical treatment to senior civil servants, Jean-Marc Ela says that this is a treatment that the majority of poor people never receive (Ela 1988, 67ff).

36. Dickson Eyoh discusses *Nyongo* in the context of recent political liberalization and the resultant struggle for power in Cameroon. His rich essay provides insights into the workings of the structures of power and manipulation in the contemporary state of Cameroon.

37. For a detailed discussion of these forms of "sorcery" and "witchcraft" in other places in Cameroon, the works of Ardener (1970), Austen (1993), De Rosny (1981, 1992), Eyoh (1998), Fisiy (1990), Geschiere (1991), Probst (1992), Probst and Bühler (1990), and Rawlands and Warnier (1988) provide helpful historical context and analysis.

38. When I was pastor of the Etoug-Ebe Baptist Church in Yaounde, the capital of Cameroon, we had our own monthly contribution. I was required to do a Bible study at each monthly meeting, which was held in different homes. In places such as Ntumbaw, many of these meetings are likely to take place at one location, even though the monthly contribution goes to different people.

39. This interview was recorded in March 1994 at *Fai* Kuh's compound in Ntumbaw. When the people decided to depose the former *Fon* in 1972, *Fai* Kuh, acting as the leader of the town, and "king makers," provided sanctuary for the new *Fon* who was installed. For several years, his compound was also the de facto palace. The newly installed *Fon* ruled from there for several years before temporary quarters were erected just outside of the permanent palace.

40. See two other essays in the same publication that address this issue: Auslander (1993, 167–192) and Schmoll (1993, 193–220).

41. In 1999, there were several cases in the Wimbum area where women were accused of practicing *tfu*. Several women were exiled from the town of Ndu and Ntumbaw. One woman was reportedly beaten to death, and one died later. Many suspected that she died because she had been beaten so severely by the *nwarong* that was sent to exile her.

42. Locals use this expression to indicate that when government officers went on tour, people were expected to provide them with gifts, which included chickens, and in some cases, cattle.

43. For works that discuss economic issues, see Ardener (1970), Ciekawy (1992), Austen (1993), and Apter (1993a). Gender issues in "witchcraft" have been discussed by Masamba Ma Mpolo, who has studied *Kindoki* in the Democratic Republic of the Congo from a psychotherapeutic perspective. Mark Auslander also has addressed gender issues in his study of Ngoni witch finding (Auslander 1993, 167).

44. The Baptist, Catholic, and Presbyterian denominations run schools and clinics in the area that offer employment to some members of the public. The Baptists also have a secondary school and a theological seminary in Ndu that offer valuable employment to the area. There is a government high school in Nkambe and a government hospital. The commercial centers are in Ndu and Nkambe. The markets of these two towns are well attended, and usually one can find traders at these markets from away as far as Foumban and Baffousam in the Western Province. Perhaps one phenomenon among the Wimbum that should be mentioned is the exodus of schoolteachers into Nigeria from Cameroon. In the 1970s the Voluntary Agencies, the Baptist, Catholic, and Presbyterian denominations that run many schools in the area, laid off many teachers. What complicated the situation was that in the mid-1960s, the Voluntary Agencies, in preparation for dealing with the crisis of a shortage of teachers for

the primary schools, changed the "gate-keeping" system of teacher training, in which teachers were trained stage by stage. The first stage involved the training of a Category "C" teacher—a level just one year beyond primary school, or acquired through experience. After that level, the teacher was trained at the Elementary Teacher Training Center for three years to obtain the Teacher Grade III Certificate. The next two stages were for higher elementary schools, in which teachers were trained for two more years and obtained the Teacher Grade II Certificate followed by the Teacher Grade I Certificate. The changes that were made involved instituting one system in which candidates for teaching were admitted into teacher training schools, went for five years, and received the Grade II certificate upon completion. Within a short period, the country was flooded with too many Grade II teachers, and there was a shortage of jobs. Further, when the Voluntary Agencies had financial trouble, they laid off many of their teachers. In the Wimbum area, where a majority of the people are Baptist, almost every town had too many Grade II teachers, who were idle and needed something to do. A partial remedy for this situation appeared when Nigeria decided that its oil boom could be used to facilitate universal free primary education. To implement such a policy, more teachers were needed. Therefore, many of the Grade II teachers from the Wimbum area, and from many other places in Anglophone Cameroon, found gainful employment in Nigeria. The majority of the people in the Wimbum area went to Gongola and the Bornu States of Nigeria.

45. The economic impact of the marketing cooperative system among the Wimbum, as well as in other parts of Cameroon, has been obvious. For the most part, these organizations have been responsible for marketing all of the produce and bringing in the fertilizers and tools farmers need for their work. As important as their role in Wimbum society is, this organization also has been the most criticized. For instance, it has been alleged that when a person joins the cooperative as a junior staff member, in just a matter of months, or at least in a few years, he or she becomes very wealthy. The person may not have a farm of his or her own, but the belief is that there is enough corruption in the system for a worker to enrich himself or herself very quickly. The leaders are constantly accused of bribery. They have the most disposable cash, and in local towns such as Ndu, which has a surprisingly active nightlife for a small community, the people who work for the cooperatives can be seen every evening drinking expensive beer and socializing with the "choice ladies" of the area. Many of these people are accused of "keeping" the women, meaning that they "patronize" them and keep them as their exclusive concubines. The cooperative employees also drive good vehicles.

46. People have coined a phrase out of "cooperative" (in pidgin English "cooperate and *tief*") to mean that the members of the union cooperate with each other to loot the coffers of the union or to cheat the farmers. *Tief* is the pidgin word for steal.

47. See Thomas (1982) and O'Keefe (1982).

48. See Hastings' (1976) discussion on the strategies employed by the indigenous Churches to fight these beliefs.

49. *Bkinto* is the plural form of *Winto,* the wife of a *Fon*; *Wibah* is the wife of a *Fai.*

CHAPTER 3

1. Two works on the subject that have received wide attention are *Rationality*, edited by Bryan Wilson (1970), and *Rationality and Relativism*, edited by Martin Hollis and Steven Lukes (1986). For discussions by African philosophers, see Wiredu (1980); Masolo (1994); and Bourdillon (1990).

2. I use the expression "early Rorty" to demarcate positions that he stated early in his career from those more recent remarks that amount to a denial of the possibility of African philosophy. See Desai (1994) and the response by Hallen (1995).

3. Lukes argues that in the social sciences, scientific data is not just brute facts, but something "meaningful for subjects whose . . . understandings of their meanings are constitutive of them, essential to their being realities they are" (Hollis and Lukes 1986, 302). Lukes argues that scientific activity is interpretive, such a perspective that brings out truth in any given inquiry. This calls for openness in the process, which establishes justification for a position as well as an assurance that the available data is not distorted (Ibid., 304, 305). Lukes agrees with Edward Said, that "the student must feel he or she is answerable to and in uncoercive contact with the culture or people being studied" (Said 1981, 155; Hollis and Lukes 1986, 305).

4. Italics are mine.

5. Robin Horton has contributed to the debate in his numerous publications on African and Western thought. See also Tambiah (1990).

6. It is important to point out that I do not raise the issue of rationality here in the hope that understanding *tfu* or witchcraft will provide a key to understanding Wimbum beliefs and *Weltanschauung*. Ghanaian philosopher Kwasi Wiredu has rightly pointed out that, "Those who are tempted to see in such a thing as witchcraft the key to specifically African thought . . . ought to be reminded that there are numbers of white men in London today who proudly proclaim themselves to be witches" (Wiredu 1980, 42). Wiredu's pragmatic position has made him argue vigorously that Africans should abandon witchcraft beliefs and take science seriously if they are going to develop economically. At present, I endorse

his argument that witchcraft should not be seen as the key to African philosophy.

7. Dismas Masolo indicates that other writers who have attempted similar projects include Fabian Eboussi-Boulaga, Marcien Towa, and Paulin Hountondji (Masolo 1994, 147). Masolo rightly points out that in "excavating" Africa in Western discourse, these thinkers, who are critical of ethnophilosophy, attempt in different ways to articulate the criteria for philosophy. Eboussi-Boulaga characterizes Placide Tempel's ethnophilosophy and the philosophies of his African interpreters, such as Vincent Mulago and Alexis Kagame, as a philosophy of domination (Eboussi-Boulaga 1984, 148). Towa is critical of both ethnophilosophy and Senghor's *Négritude*, describing such perspectives as another form of servitude to Western domination (Towa 1991, 164). Hountondji criticizes ethnophilosophy and vigorously argues that philosophy is philosophy and that it does not matter who does it (Hountondji 1976). He argues that African philosophy is philosophical reflection by Africans. This African self-reflection has distinct Francophone and Anglophone strands to it, according to Masolo.

8. See also Jean Comaroff's argument about the development of a capitalist economy among the Tshidi people in the apartheid State of South Africa (Comaroff 1985; Comaroff and Comaroff 1991).

9. Fabian's work, *Time and the Other: How Anthropology Makes Its Object* (1983), is a tightly argued one that offers a critique of the practice of anthropology along similar lines. See also McGrane, *Beyond Anthropology: Society and the Other* (1989).

10. Masolo has commented, "Mudimbe builds his structuralist phenomenology of African knowledge on a meticulous combination of the position of Michel Foucault and Claude Levi-Strauss. What Mudimbe says of the invention of Africa as a product of western discourse is an illustration of the power of knowledge" (Masolo 1994, 180).

11. In recent African anthropology, Fabian calls this approach a reflexive one, and both volumes of *Time and the Other* are written with a reflexivity that constantly challenges and evaluates epistemological positions of the anthropologist.

12. I should point out that one should take the resemblance that Ricoeur talks about in the specific context in which Mudimbe is appropriating it—the dichotomization in Western discourse that results in a distortion of Africa and of African culture. I make this distinction because of my endorsement of the Levinasian perspective that seeks to establish a radical Other by advocating a distinction between the Same and the Other, which according to Levinas permits ethics to take place. See Ricoeur (1984, 25).

13. The original quotation by Mveng is in his essay, "Récents développements de la théologie Africaine," *Bulletin of African Theology* 5 (1983): 9.

14. The work of W. E. Abraham, O. Bimwenyi, H. Djait, F. Eboussi-Boulaga, A. P. E. Elungu, P. J. Hountondji, E. Mveng, A. M. Ngindu, T. Obenga, T. Okere, J. O. Sodipo, I. Sow, M. Towa, and K. Wiredu all contributes to this approach. Mudimbe argues that what is distinctive about this group of scholars is their high level of training and the fact that most of them are priests and theologians (Mudimbe 1988, 40).

15. By "progressive" I am simply alluding to the fact that even though Evans-Pritchard was very much a part of the *episteme* of the Same, he gave a new meaning to fieldwork and social anthropology, especially in his studies on witchcraft in the Azande society.

16. This is a view with which Alasdair MacIntyre, who also was part of the conversation on understanding different societies, would agree. As MacIntyre puts it, every tradition "is embedded in some particular set of utterances and actions and thereby in all particularities of some specific language and culture" (MacIntyre 1988, 371).

17. In his discussion of the *Benge* practice, Evans-Pritchard notes that it belongs to the Zande network of beliefs. For instance, what appears to an outsider as the failure of the oracle could be explained in several ways. If it does not work, it is possible that the *Benge* is bad. Failure also could be attributed to the uncleanliness of the one who practices it. In some cases, people say that a more powerful witchcraft is counteracting it. This happens in Ntumbaw among the Wimbum, who believe that some people have such powerful witchcraft that nothing will stand in their way and no diviner will be able to detect or forestall their activities. If consistent results from the application of the *Benge* were later broken, the above explanations would still be employed to explain the "abnormality." Winch reviews this process to argue that witchcraft practices are not a scientific hypothesis and cannot be examined from a scientific viewpoint. For that reason, it is wrong to say that the scientific view is right and the Zande view is wrong.

18. Winch clearly indicates that since MacIntyre is using standards of society other than that of the Azande, it is wrong to criticize Azande notions of magic if the standards of rationality had to meet the litmus test set in a different context. MacIntyre has criticized James Frazer for imposing his views on others. In his interpretation of Azande culture, however, MacIntyre missteps in the same fashion. Winch points out that even Evans-Pritchard is clear about the problems of comparing the magical with the technical and highlights the ambiguity in this relation: "Since it is we who want to understand the Zande category, it appears that the onus is on us to extend our understanding so as to make room for the Zande category, rather than to insist on seeing it in terms of our own ready-made distinction between science and non-science" (Winch 1970, 101).

19. MacIntyre has pointed out that, "Objective rationality is therefore to be found not in rule following but in rule transcending, in knowing how

and when to put rules and principles to work and when not to" (quoted by Bernstein 1988, 57, from an original typescript of the essay, "Epistemological Crises, Dramatic Narrative, and the Philosophy of Science," which was later published in an abridged form in *Monist* 60 (1977): 435–472.)

20. Bernstein's discussion in *Beyond Objectivism and Relativism* (1988) is interesting, because he has broadened it to take into account some of the reactions to Kuhn's thesis. For example, Feyerabend, on his part, has followed the Kuhnian path by deploring fixity, stability, or what he called "puritanical seriousness." For Feyerabend, "A society that is based on a set of well-defined and restrictive rules so that being a 'man' becomes synonymous with obeying these rules, forces the dissenter into a no-man's land of no rules at all and thus robs him of his reason and his humanity" (quoted by Bernstein 1988, 63; original in Feyerabend, *Against Method: Outline of an Anarchistic Theory of Knowledge*, London: NLB, 1975, 218–219).

Lakotas has argued for openness of options but places this openness within a research program so that it does not appear to be a chaotic situation in which there are no guiding principles. Rorty thinks "it is an illusion to think that there is a permanent set of ahistorical standards of rationality which the philosopher or epistemologist can discover and which will unambiguously tell us who is rational and who is not" (Rorty 1980, 316–317).

Bernstein takes issue with some Rortian formulations, such as "accident of history," and Bernstein points out that the use of such language merely muddies the waters. In his analysis of the movement toward a more open approach to rationality, Bernstein points out that in a way this move is not a very recent one. To demonstrate that this debate has a long history, Bernstein traces it back to the pragmatic tradition in general, specifically to the contribution of Charles Peirce, who argued that there are multiple strands and different evidence that can be presented to support a scientific theory. It is this multiplicity that made Peirce emphasize the need for a scientific community of inquirers, in which the validity of each argument can be examined. A different viewpoint has been advanced by Popper, who attacks what he understands to be Kuhn's relativism. Popper argues that objective knowledge cannot be reduced to subjective knowledge. Furthermore, he criticizes Kuhn's "normal science," arguing that it will lead to dogmatism and hinder novelty and change. He wants to defend the rational growth of knowledge.

21. Such a movement, according to Bernstein, historically emerges in four dialectical stages. First, scientists attempt to ground scientific knowledge under a single term, thus making that term the primary epistemological unit. At the second stage, shifts occur that push the term to propositions, statements, and sentences, forming an epistemological unit. Here the emphasis is on the search for cognitive meaning. In the third period, scientists attempt to delineate conceptual schemes. Historically, we are now at the fourth stage, and researchers recognize that rationality in

scientific inquiry demands differing theories, conflicting paradigms, and different research programs, and that genuine attempts should be made to take all traditions seriously. Bernstein argues that MacIntyre's view that tradition is a narrative argument ought to compel us to consider seriously the notion of communities of inquirers where issues of rationality can be discussed and all options examined (Bernstein 1988, 77). Charles Peirce called for an analysis that considers norms as regulative, critical tools. Kuhn's idea of a community of scientists provides the locus in which competing paradigms are advanced, thus making scientific progress possible.

22. To give depth to the idea of incommensurability, Bernstein brings to our attention some related ideas, such as incompatibility. This is simply a situation where there is a logical contradiction or an idea that does not necessarily follow in another context. Kuhn attacks full-scale derivation— for instance, claiming that one can derive Newtonian dynamism from Einstein's theories. Here, incompatibility is not only a matter of time and space but is embedded in the theories themselves. This does not mean that reinterpretation of older theories cannot yield approximation. If there are any approximations in the theories of Newton and Einstein, they are just approximations, and one could not say that Einstein's theories derive directly from Newtonian physics. Perhaps a better way of looking at the relationship, according to Bernstein, is to see derivability somewhat like Hegel's *Aufhebung*, in which the old is appropriated but transcended. When seen from this Hegelian process, the old, scientific tradition is maintained, but there is a recognition that it has been transcended and that something new is in place.

23. Feyerabend extends the discussion on incommensurability into the social disciplines, and according to Bernstein, this move is clearly an opening rather than a closure. Bernstein calls this an inversion. By this he simply means that we can understand incommensurable paradigms and differing forms of life without imposing the categories taken from our own language games. Thus what we have here is a position that views incommensurability as a representation of the multiple forms and approaches available in research and discussion. What is not described is a representation of relativism, where scientists and researchers are compartmentalized in their own epistemological and foundational grids.

24. I am convinced that what Geertz describes can be seen in the anthropological work of Victor Turner, Wyatt MacGaffey, Thomas Biedelman, Johaness Fabian, Jean and John Comaroff, John Middleton, Allen Roberts, Andrew Apter, Wim Van Binsbergern, Matthew Schoffeleers, Rosalind Hackett, Richard Werbner, Ivan Karp, Michael Jackson, Terence Ranger, Eric De Rosney, Dickson Eyoh, Peter Geschirie, Miriam Goheen, Mark De Lancey, Achille Mbembe, Euginia Shanklin, James Fernandez, B. Jules Rosette, Robert Pool, Peter Probst, Cyprian Fisiy, Sheila Walker, and Diane Cikawey. This is just a short list of some of the Africanists whose work

touches upon the insights of Geertz. Winch has talked not only about representing alien cultures correctly but also about learning from them. He wants to point out, as we have seen already, that we go astray when we impose alien standards on a different society in the process of learning from that society.

25. Quoted in Bernstein (1988, 96).

26. What we learn from a different society is how it and by extension, we, can make sense of human life. Winch has been taken to task by Jarvie—a student of Popper, who accuses Winch of propagating the "myth of the framework." Bernstein is right in suggesting that this is a misreading of Winch, whose question is not whether comparison is possible but what kind of comparison will be done. Winch clearly argues that it is wrong to compare magic to Western science. One might say that even Evans-Pritchard said as much. Winch is not, however, claiming that there is a commonality between Western science and African thought. Bernstein rightly points out that Winch is arguing that there should be an openness to different possibilities of rationality. The only limitation then should be the formal requirement of consistency; but here again, Winch would say that what one considers consistent should be determined in a wider context rather than by some fixed principles. When this happens, one would be cautious in identifying so-called contradictions in Zande thought—and here one would add contradictions in much of the discourse and literature on African witchcraft.

27. Alison Wylie indicates that, although Bernstein uses secondary accounts of practice effectively, his move to philosophical hermeneutics means that he abandons the inquiry on how "practitioners proceed 'on the frontiers of inquiry' when they must mediate deep cultural and theoretical pluralism" (Wylie 1989, 1–18). I have found Wylie's essay very informative and a good demonstration of the kind of scholarship that Bernstein himself does, namely, the ability to build on contributions from others while at the same time taking the conversation in a different direction.

28. Bernstein notes that Habermas, in his famous review of *Wahrheit und Methode,* agrees with Gadamer that understanding should not be separated from "action oriented self-understanding" (Habermas 1977, 351). Habermas argues that speech acts should be analyzed and clarified, implying that one can make some validity claims. What is important here is that claims for validity should be contextual and should not be considered fixed but rather open and negotiable. Bernstein argues that Habermas's position can be related to the Azande and, I would add, the Ntumbaw and Wimbum *tfu* beliefs. What this means is that even though the researcher brings some knowledge, Habermas's thesis requires that the Zande speech acts be evaluated and analyzed on Zandean terms. Furthermore, by underscoring historicity, Habermas wants to bring together "performative participation" and Intersubjective understanding in an objective way. James Fernandez (1982) has attempted such an analysis of speech and religious

performances in Gabon, and he has made us understand the world of *Bwiti* religion.

Bernstein argues that Habermas's universalism is one that emerges from his own horizon. Habermas imports a cognitive, practical discourse into his theoretical discourse with a "transcendental" and "pragmatic voice." The transcendental refers to the technical, practical, and emancipatory aspects of Habermas's theory.

"The goal of coming to an understanding (*Verständigung*) is to bring about an agreement (*Einverständnis*) that terminates in the intersubjective mutuality of reciprocal understanding, shared knowledge, mutual trust, and accord with one another. Agreement is based on recognition of the corresponding validity claims of comprehensibility, truth, truthfulness and rightness." (Habermas in Bernstein 1983, 185) Habermas criticizes neo-Aristotelianism, because its focus on Aristotle's ethics and politics mirrors Aristotelian biology as well as the Greek *Polis,* so that one ought to only appropriate it critically. Furthermore, Habermas sees neo-Aristotelianism as neo-conservatism, which is attempting to anchor its ideological position in the Aristotelian framework.

Habermas notes that these attempts to return to some pristine past have been brought about by the "problematic of our times," exemplified by postmodernist dissatisfaction with what MacIntyre calls the "Enlightenment project." This dissatisfaction, however, is coupled with, and has been made difficult by, problems raised by scientism, positivism, and preference for instrumental reason. According to Bernstein, Habermas wants us to retrieve the past without doing away with the rigor of scientific knowledge. We should do this by employing critical standards for praxis and a rational justification of those standards. Bernstein rightly points out that despite Habermas's claim that he has made the break from Kant, Habermas still wants a solid foundation for ethics. Bernstein argues that a fruitful reading of Habermas should pursue the moral and political intentions of our actions through which Habermas calls attention to the interpretive dialectics of praxis (Bernstein 1988, 183, 186, 189, 190).

29. Bernstein points out that Rorty questions Habermas's attempt to ground ethics and praxis in communicative acts because such an approach gives credibility to a positivistic view that legitimate and illegitimate meaning can be determined, thus perpetuating the false notion that philosophy is a fundamental discipline (Bernstein 1988, 198). Rorty also is critical of what he sees as Gadamer's "weak textualism," which seeks the comforts of a consensus, even if the consensus is *Bildung* (see also Rorty 1980). Rorty proposes a pragmatism that inculcates Socratic virtues such as a willingness to listen to others, which does not presuppose any foundations and does not attempt to build any metaphysical structure. Rather, Rorty offers a way of coping with life, hoping that genuine dialogue involving all disciplines will "renew a sense of community" (Rorty 1980). This will be a community in which people can cling together against darkness,

not merely because they believe that they have the right way of doing things. The moral task one faces is to be open to human conversation.

30. Bernstein notes that Arendt uses the notion *Vita Activa* to call for a new sense of praxis in which individuals and communities can seek to bring about freedom and liberation by acting ethically in a public place such as the *Polis* (Bernstein 1988, 208). Bernstein points out that Arendt's distinctions can be confusing. For example, in Arendt's distinction between social liberation and freedom, she is forgetful that, in many of the cases she cites, social liberation provided the base or testing ground for modern political action. Arendt also distinguishes between the social and political. This distinction for Bernstein tends to promote the view that there are so-called experts who have the inside track on solving political and social problems. Furthermore, Arendt distinguishes between truth and opinion, arguing that opinions should be tested in the community and should not be the imposition of a single individual's views but should instead reflect the views of the entire community. Thus to do praxis is to do justice in particular communities.

31. I should point out that Ricoeur also has given a new reading to Hegel's *Sittlichkeit*. Ricoeur maintains that *Sittlichkeit* should be seen no longer as a third agency on a different plane from ethics but rather should "designate one of the places in which practical wisdom is exercised, namely, the hierarchy of institutional mediations through which practical wisdom must pass if justice is truly to deserve the name of fairness" (Ricoeur 1992, 250). I do not intend to show that Ricoeur and Bernstein are engaged in the same project, although one could argue that Ricoeur would be sympathetic to the spirit of Bernstein's proposals. It is important to note that both Bernstein and Ricoeur point to the need for a community. For Bernstein, such a community makes it possible to return to the practice of *phronesis*, as Gadamer has argued. Ricoeur addresses the issues of conflict arbitration and states clearly that, "The arbitration of the conflict between the spheres of justice will then have to be placed under the Hegelian category of *Sittlichkeit* rather than under the Aristotelian category of *Phronesis*" (Ricoeur 1992, 253). Ricoeur also argues that reading Hegel in this way makes the opposition between Hegel's *Sittlichkeit* and Kant's *Moralität* useless.

32. Stanley Deetz (1985), in a review of Bernstein's work, indicates that from the various thinkers Bernstein analyzes, three core "compatabilities" can be documented—I add a fourth. First, Deetz observes that the various thinkers Bernstein has discussed point effectively to the view that foundationalism is passé. Second, all of them argue that there are competing arguments out there, some better than others, but there is no way of saying in advance that a particular argument is the right or only way of establishing validity. Third, according to Bernstein, these thinkers suggest that by admitting that there are several options, one is not irretrievably committed to the notion that everything goes. Finally, I add that

Bernstein feels that these thinkers are emphatic that, with the vast incommensurability we face, new doors are opened. It is this "openness of
language and communication," challenging us with the validity of different
forms of life, to which I return in my closing remarks.

33. He faults Winch for attributing a different meaning for the word
"irrational" in the religious context. Witches in Europe were charged with
maleficence. What was crucial, however, was not only its practice but the
idea that the people who did this derived their power from the devil.
According to Williamson, this is the distinction that Winch misses, and in
so doing, he fails to realize that what was unorthodox was the practice of
those in power who persecuted alleged witches. Accordingly, Winch misses
the class wars.

CHAPTER 4

1. Kwame A. Appiah argues that every culture has its folk wisdom
that could be the basis for critical philosophy, while at the same time a
distinction between the two also can be maintained (Appiah 1992). Appiah
argues that, "There is . . . in every culture a folk philosophy, and implicit
in that folk philosophy are all (or many) of the concepts that academic
philosophers have made central to their study in the West. Of course there
might not be in every society people who have pursued a systematic critical conceptual inquiry, but at least in every culture there is work for a
philosopher, should one come along, to do" (Ibid., 87).

2. It is clear that Appiah is every bit as much at home at Harvard
as he is in his father's house. This is a play on the title of Appiah's
excellent work *In My Father's House* (1992).

3. As Kwame Gyekye has pointed out, Menkiti's position was a further analysis of Mbiti's basic claim that, in Africa, the community comes
before the individual (Gyekye 1992, 101ff). Mbiti's original claim was that
in Africa, the understanding is "I am because we are, and since we are,
therefore I am." For Menkiti, this expression laid out, as Gyekye has
rightly observed, the ontological primacy of the community and the dependence of the individual on the community (Ibid., 103). Furthermore, in his
analysis, Menkiti maintained that the community defines personhood. He
makes an even stronger claim that personhood is a good that is acquired,
not simply given, by being born into a family and community (Gyekye
1992, 103; Menkiti 1994, 173).

4. "The possibility of re-evaluation means, surely, that the person
cannot be absolved by the communal or cultural apparatus, but can to
some extent wriggle himself [herself] out of it, distance himself from it,
and thus be in a position to take another look at it; it means, also, that
the communal structure cannot foreclose the meaningfulness and reality of

the quality of self-assertiveness which the person can demonstrate in his actions" (Gyekye 1997, 112).

5. A further argument for strengthening individual rights that takes personhood seriously can be made by highlighting the communitarian component of the Western liberal tradition. This is what Jack Donnelly (1990) has done in "Human Rights and Western Liberalism." Donnelly points out that in Locke's *Second Treatise,* individual self-preservation is coupled with the duty to preserve all humankind (Donnelly 1990, 37). According to Locke, the proper understanding of political society holds that individuals "and all the rest of [humanity] are one community." God created human community by putting the person "under strong obligations of necessity, convenience, and inclination to drive him [her] into society, as well as fitted him [her] with understanding and language to continue and enjoy it" (Ibid., 38; see also John Locke, *Two Treatise of Government,* ed. Peter Laslett, 2d ed., Cambridge: Cambridge University Press, 1967, s. 77, 1–5).

6. My interpretation is similar to a more elegant approach undertaken by B. Hallen and J. Sodipo (1986) in their study of the Yoruba world.

7. The plural is *bi.*

8. Although these injunctions sound very much like they are taken from Hebrew, they are Wimbum.

9. Levinas's original text makes important distinctions between *autre, Autre* and *Autrui,* which often is translated in English as "other" and the "Other." I have used "Other" to refer to a concrete human other and sometimes employed the designation "Otherness" to refer to the notion of difference.

10. I have discussed Levinas's relationship to the philosophical tradition in the dissertation on which this manuscript is based ("African Witchcraft and Otherness," Ph.d. dissertation, University of Denver and the Iliff School of Theology, Denver 1995).

11. I have found, among others, the works of Edith Wyschogrod, Adrian Peperzak, John Caputo, Robert Bernasconi, Robert Manning, Alphonso Lingis, Tina Chanter, and Richard Cohen fruitful in my interpretation of Levinas. See also Wyschogrod (1974); most of Wyschogrod's writings on Levinas and philosophical ethics; Cohen (1994). Both of John Caputo's works, *Radical Hermeneutics* (1987) and *Against Ethics* (1983) are provocative ones that articulate a vision of ethics that I find consistent with the postmodern spirit of Levinas, even though Caputo insists on calling his approach openness to obligations.

12. His program then is aimed at what Peperzak refers to as post-Platonic and post-Heideggerian metaphysics, which replaces the horizon of Being (Peperzak 1993, 131).

13. Heidegger's critique of technology is well known. The point that Levinas is making is that Heidegger's position on the tyranny of technology ignores the fact that this very position privileges the ego and that the ego has led to the domination of technology in human lives, which Heidegger himself decries.

14. One source that Levinas draws from is Descartes's third *Meditation* (Levinas 1969, 48ff). Descartes posits the idea of a transcendent being initially discovered in his own consciousness. He indicates that since this idea could not have been put there by his finite consciousness, then there must be a being transcendent of the thinking "I."

15. The target of attack is Heidegger's *Vorhandenheit* (present-at-hand) and *Zuhandenheit* (ready-to-hand). Levinas believes that Heidegger's critique of *Zuhandenheit* does not go far enough. According to Levinas, Dasein's relation to things conceived through *Zuhandenheit* should be seen as the emphasis of Dasein on its own nourishment.

16. Discourse is the basis of relations with the Other. Levinas argues that this relationship is crystallized in separation and discourse. Infinity produces a relationship with a distinct individual who resists integration into the same. Integration into the same is achieved through the totality of the historical process in which birth and death are moments of a universal time in which interiority does not count (Levinas 1969, 55). Separation gives new meaning to birth and death. Separation and exteriority is not solipsism but a distinction from the universal human. This is not a transhistorical Other that breaks into history, but an individual who rejects thematization and grasping and appears as a naked face who speaks, commands, and obligates the Same to responsibility. The question is, why does Levinas posit such a radical separation?

Separation is the condition for the possibility of truth, which is rooted in being but found "in a relation not because one is defined by something Other than oneself, but because in a certain sense one lacks nothing" (Levinas 1969, 61). The quest for truth, according to Levinas, is always a relationship with the Other in desire. This requires what Levinas calls a conversion to exteriority and infinity, which brings a revelation that occasions a desire for the face of the Other. The Other who is revealed speaks in a language that teaches, calls, and commands. In this manifestation, truth and language are categories of infinity. Desire is born when the already content "I" finds enjoyment in the desire for the truth and justice that lie beyond being (Ibid., 63). Levinas later deals with desire under the phenomenology of *Eros*, but at this point he detaches it from Platonic trappings by portraying desire as a movement toward the stranger, a movement Levinas calls "justice." Justice here means recognizing and acting responsibly in the face of the Other.

Levinas overturns ontology, rejecting reason as an "I" who carries on a monologue. What is new here is the view that language and discourse bring ethics. Language is the manifesting of transcendence and strangeness of the Other that make freedom possible for being and the Other. In other words, strangeness guarantees autonomy and opens critical dialogue in which a manifestation occurs. The Other's epiphany questions my "joyous possession of the world" (Ibid., 76).

17. Levinas points out that the "I" has always chosen what to do. The philosophical tradition demonstrates that the "I" has chosen to enter a totality; one needs only to look at the systems of Hegel and Spinoza to see this. This path has reduced the Other. Existents are reduced to an idea. Levinas recasts knowing as a concrete welcoming of the Other, thus opening the door for language. The language of discourse and speaking will lead to a break from totality and make way for a new beginning (Levinas 1969, 88).

At this point, Levinas reiterates his belief that metaphysics is not solitary cogitation, as in Descartes. It is not the "know thyself," of Socrates or the resulting bad faith of Sartre; it is a human activity of dependence that maintains its independence in a face-to-face relation. In his or her critical posture, the individual puts himself or herself into question. The miracle that takes place here is the recognition that the individual is a created being and a moral being.

18. Levinas points out that truth presupposes justice, which he calls to his readers' attention in several short theses. The first thesis portrays anarchy, the spectacle of a silent world in which, nevertheless, the speech of the Other exists as a signification declining interpretation. Levinas points out, however, that if there is a principle to look for, it is the expression of the Other. In this situation of anarchy, the world is given "in the language of the Other." In a potent critique of Descartes, Levinas asserts that in doubt and negation of the Same, it is not the "I" that is the source of affirmation. "It is not 'I,' it is the Other that can say 'yes.' From him [her] comes affirmation; he [she] is at the commencement of experience" (Levinas 1969, 93).

19. This does not imply anarchy and a disregard for institutions of justice. Levinas's notion of a third party is part of his argument for society. Society carries out its process of justice in a linguistic system, but as John Llewelyn points out, these are always addressed to persons, and this process transforms the "said" to "saying" (Llewelyn 1995, 140). "Justice would be primary violence without this repeated reconversion of the said into saying, without the tie to fraternity, without the manifold of claims and symmetrical counterclaims being folded back to the symmetry of the face to face (Ibid., 140–141).

20. Jill Robbins develops the notion of trace in Levinas to map out the different nuances of the invitation to responsibility ("Tracing Responsibility in Levinas's Ethical Thought," pp. 173–184, in *Ethics As First Philosophy: The Significance of Emmanuel Levinas for Philosophy, Literature, and Religion*, ed. Adriaan T. Peperzak, New York and London: Routledge, 1995).

21. Miriam Goheen (1993b) discusses this notion of a double pair of eyes and the responsibility that it entails among the Nso, neighbors of the Wimbum people.

22. Bénézet Bujo argues that, in some cases, the relatives of an individual make it difficult because they not only overstay their welcome but put excessive demands on their well-to-do relatives, which causes the relatives that have the means to ignore their immediate family of wife and children (Bujo 1990/1998, 102).

23. Simon Critchley has rightly observed that the transition here is not that of time but instead remains in the Levinasian conception of discourse where the response to the face of the Other is a "response to the prophetic word that makes the community a commonality . . . the community has a double structure; it is a commonality among equals which is at the same time based on the inegalitarian moment of the ethical relation" (Critchley 1992, 227).

24. Levinas does not discuss how these laws are made. We do not have a discussion of a particular kind of society such as the Greek *Polis* It is certainly not a community similar to Hegel's society, which provides the basis of *Sittlichkeit*. The laws are certainly not a guarantee of justice, such as Kant's kingdom of ends. Levinas simply argues that the presence of the third person calls for justice.

CHAPTER 5

1. Theologians who seek to be relevant to the contemporary needs of Africa, listed by Mudimbe, include: Tshibangu and Bimwenyi from The Democratic Republic of Congo and Cameroonian theologians Hegba, Ela, and Eboussi-Boulaga.

2. The models of missionary discourse that Mudimbe cites as representative of missionary discourse proclaimed with authority and exclusivity the rejection of any dialogue with the local people, including Giovanni Romano (who worked in the Congo from 1645); Nigerian Bishop Samuel Ajayi Crowther; and the founder of Bantu philosophy, Placide Tempels, 1933–1962.

3. Eboussi-Boulaga (1984) articulates five features of missionary language. First, missionaries used a language of derision to refer to the divinities in African religions as "pagan gods." Second, they employed the language of "refutation and systematic reduction" to sideline the importance of African realities. Third, they used the language of demonstration and presented their faith as the only coherent historical process. In doing so, the virtues of Christianity were transformed through a systematic presentation of biblical categories as the logic of civilization now intended to sacrilize the missionaries' "cultural model over African models."

Missionaries to Africa demonstrated "truths to be believed . . . command-
ments to be observed . . . [emphasis on] work and property" (Ibid., 38–39).
Fourth, they used the language of orthodoxy to stipulate their particular
faith as the only true one. And, finally, they used the language of conformity, demanding adherence to the message and norms that they proclaimed
without regard to other religions (Ibid., 51; see also 30ff).

4. Beti criticizes missionary Christianity because its doctrines brought
humiliation to Africans. African followers who succeeded in this new
Christian-influenced world became as materialistic and individualistic as
the missionaries (Bjornson 1991, 99).

5. T. O. Beidelman's critique focuses on the work of the Church
Missionary Society among the Ukaguru in East Africa.

6. For example, most of the women in the Ntumbaw and Njirong
areas who were members of the *toh* society were forced to abandon their
membership because the church did not think that Christians should
participate in performances that included masking.

7. Tshibangu, in his essay "The Task of African Theologians," argues
that theologians should undertake an analysis of theological concepts that
can be drawn from traditional religion (*African Theology en Route*, eds.
Kofi Appiah-Kubi and Sergio Torres, Maryknoll, N.Y.: Orbis Books, 1979,
77). Mudimbe also cites Modupe Oduyoye's *The Vocabulary of Yoruba
Religious Discourse* (1971) as a good example of this approach. Oduyoye
examines the notion of the representation of divinity among the Yoruba, as
well as the categories of sin and repentance, pardon and absolution, and
prayer. He also reflects on the mystical and metaphysical understanding
of time, the beginnings of humanity, and issues of life and death.

8. Theologians and clerics offering critiques of apartheid include: Bishop
Desmond Tutu, Allan Boesak, Beyers Naude, Denise Ackermann, Manas
Buthelezi, Simon Mamiala, T. Mofokeng, Itumeleng Mosala, M. B. G.
Motlhabi, Barney Pityana, Buti Tlhigale, Charles Villa Vicencio, John De
Gruchy, Jonathan Draper, Gerald West and J. Cochrane. However, this is
not intended to be an exhaustive list of African theologians since the 1960s
whose theological reflections have been critical of the apartheid system.

9. "Moreover, one might also conceive the intellectual signs of Otherness not as a project for the foundation of a new science, but rather as
a mode of reexamining the journeys of human knowledge in a world of
competing propositions and choices. . . . Concretely from the background of
colonial politics of conversion, this mode seems imperative" (Mudimbe 1988,
79). Mudimbe agrees with the following quotation from Robin Horton:
"The kind of comparative conceptual analysis that the 'philosopher of'
traditional thought could offer would do much to help the contemporary
intellectual in his struggle to think through the relationship between his
two super compartments (that is, tradition and modernity). It would be
supremely relevant to such questions as: Should there be a global stand in

favor of traditional thought patterns and against modern patterns? Or should there be a global commitment to the running down of the traditional in order to make way for the modern? Or again, should traditional thought patterns be encouraged to coexist with modern? And if so, in what manner? Or yet again is traditional thought a many-stranded thing, whose various strands must be disentangled and their appropriate relations to modernity considered one by one?" (Horton in Mudimbe 1988, 79–80; Horton 1976a, 71).

10. Josiah Young also spells out major themes and issues of Pan-African theology in his recent work (see Young 1992).

11. It should be said that the date of this publication makes it indeed an early work in the field of African theology, coming as it did on the eve of the crumbling of the colonial edifice in most African countries.

12. Critiques of négritude have been written by Soyinka, Irele, and Marcien Towa.

13. I should stress here that what characterizes the work of the new critics in Africa, for example, Jean-Marc Ela, is that, while their critique of the colonial project is uncompromising, their critique of the present situation, for which they lay on the responsibility of contemporary political structures run by Africans, is equally strong.

14. See Tsenay Serequeberhan's *The Hermeneutics of African Philosophy: The Essential Readings,* New York: Routledge, 1994.

15. See Mudimbe (1988) for a list of other practitioners of hermeneutics.

16. Another theologian who engages in hermeneutics is N. Tshiamalenga. His "ontological hermeneutics" is indebted to the tradition of Tempels and Kagame. Nkombe, on the other hand, pursues a "psychosocially oriented hermeneutics," integrating phenomenological perspectives (Mudimbe 1988, 174). For a treatment of theological hermeneutics, see Paul Ricoeur, *Essays on Biblical Interpretation,* edited with an introduction by Lewis S. Mudge, Philadelphia: Fortress Press, 1985; and *Interpretation Theory: Discourse and the Surplus of Meaning,* Fort Worth, Tex.: Texas Christian University Press, 1976; see also Thiselton 1980, 1992; Klemm 1986; Jeanrond 1991; Smith 1991.

17. While I am sympathetic to Tracy's proposal because of the pluralism that such a methodological alternative opens, there are other proposals such as Raschke's *Theological Thinking* (1988), Kaufman's *In the Face of Mystery* (1993), Ogden's *On Theology* (1986), and Ebeling's *The Study of Theology* (1978), that do not argue specifically for the hermeneutical approach. Raschke, for example, argues that theological thinking has to take seriously science, hermeneutics, and scripture. From science, he argues that a new metaphysics can emerge that will lead to thought and piety. In hermeneutics, the theologian should bring depth to his or her work in order to remain in dialogue with the culture. Regarding scripture, Raschke

calls for seeing the text of scripture as a finite inscription that is charged with the infinite. He wants to rehabilitate theological thinking through this path, because if approached through these three trajectories, theological thinking will become the "unthought thought of thought" (Raschke 1988, 137).

18. Tracy argues that some, such as Tertullian, choose confrontation between society, the academy, and the church. Contemporary scholars such as Schubert Ogden and Langdon Gilkey take the path of critical transformation. Tracy also indicates that others, such as Elliot and Danielou, have hoped for identity with the most extreme form of identity represented by Ritschl's cultural Christianity. Another fruitful interrelationship between these public disciplines makes a demand on theologians to proceed with a definite ethical position. In fundamental theology, this requires honest, critical inquiry in accordance with proper academic standards; systematic theology involves a "creative fidelity" to the tradition of the theologian; and practical theology a responsible commitment and involvement in theological praxis (Tracy 1988, 57).

19. The examples Tracy gives are existentialist, liberal, and political approaches to the New Testament, where differences are suspended in order to develop a hermeneutics that can clarify arguments.

20. Tracy argues that to use hermeneutics in the interpretation of religion, the interpreter should choose the object of interpretation such as a "text, symbol, myth, ritual, person, event, or doctrine" (Tracy 1988, 50). What governs the conversation is the subject matter of the text, not the interpreter. The text seen as work, in Ricoeur's sense of the word, should be regarded as a text that unveils a world and possibilities for being-in-the-world (Ibid., 51). Itumeleng Mosala's materialist approach to texts in *Biblical Hermeneutics and Black Theology in South Africa* (1989), calls for a greater understanding of the forces involved in textual production.

21. See also Alan Boesak's critique of the Reformed tradition in *Black and Reformed: Apartheid, Liberation, and the Calvinist Tradition*, Johannesburg: Skotaville, 1984.

22. Some of the missionaries have worked constantly to discourage the search for theological training by Cameroonians by promoting an antagonistic atmosphere between Cameroonian intellectuals and the church. For example a prominent Baptist educator had difficulties with some members of the mission. This educator received training in Nigeria, Switzerland, and the United States, where he finally received his doctorate. However, when he returned home, he was perceived as a threat rather than as an asset.

23. See Gifford (1998).

24. In other parts of Africa, the early history of theological and leadership development is filled with images of missionary power, especially through the drive for bureaucratic control. Such control was intended to

produce leaders whom churches could show off as products of Africanization. There have been some remarkable accomplishments, but sometimes they have contributed to a distantness of the individual from the culture and from African identity. A good example from the turn of the century is the case of the protégé of the White Fathers, Stefano Kaoze of Democratic Republic of Congo (Roberts 1989, 193–214). He was singled out because of his brilliance, was given good training, and was ordained into the priesthood. European colonials working in the Congo at the time were apprehensive, however, about kneeling in front of this African priest. Kaoze went on to make contributions to the understanding of Africans in his work *La Psychologie des Bantu*. He also published lexicons, grammar texts, and history books. However, Roberts points out that "Kaoze was rudely separated from his family and his peers, and learned a western philosophy at the seminary which assisted him in stepping outside of his culture to describe it as an ethnographer" (Roberts 1989, 206). In the end, Kaoze could not be called one of his own.

25. I am thinking especially of the anthropologists who I have already mentioned in Chapter 3.

26. Surber (1994) also argues that for Levinas, one can only know God through "the ethical command." Carrying our responsibility toward the Other is obeying the command of God. "Levinas insists that God actually begins to come to us in the idea, begins to come to a certain meaning, through ethics, through the reality of the ethical command to protect and be responsible for the Other" (Surber 1994, 294–317).

27. Surber states that, like Kant, Levinas would regard any theology that does not presuppose the ethical relation with a human Other as onto-theology that should be seen as atheism (Surber 1994, 312). Levinas's thought bears some semblance to Kant's position in *Religion within the Limits of Reason Alone* (1960), where Kant grants the legitimacy of theological discourse but also indicates that it should lead to ethical discourse. "Kant's attempt to sanction a sort of 'post-critical' religious discourse as a 'symbolics' of a fundamentally ethical view of the world mediating human finitude and infinity is echoed by Levinas in *Totality and Infinity*." Surber concludes accurately that theology from a Levinasian perspective is a task that constructs and systematizes the "Saids of a more fundamental religious 'Saying' which binds us to the infinity presented in the face of the Other" (Surber 1994, 312).

28. See also Cohen (1986, 23).

29. The complete translation of 1953 reversed the original title of the work, which was *Eros and Agape*.

30. Barth is critical of Nygren's dichotomy between eros and agape, describing such a dichotomy as manichean in tendency (Barth 1961, 741–747). Martin D'arcy remarked that such a separation between the two loves would lead to the withering of agape (D'arcy 1962, 96).

31. Nygren presented a historical account of the attempt to reconcile eros and agape by Augustine into *Caritas*. His argument was that this reconciliation never worked, and that the Reformation destroyed this synthesis. In a critical review of the work, Frederick Grant wrote: "To make Plato's dramatic exposition of the meaning of *eros* for different men and in different circumstances, the formal statement of the Hellenistic conception of love, and to describe it as a wholly self-regarding, acquisitive, egocentric emotion, is simply to ignore the real conception of that motive as it is displayed in the heroic figures which dominated Greek drama, art, sculpture, and poetry for a thousand years, including the Hellenistic age and far beyond. The theologian's determination to compress everything into a formula or a definition, to find a suitable foil against which to set the Christian teaching, at all costs to show the superiority of Christianity to paganism, and of St. Paul to the rest of early Christianity (including the gospel of our Lord)—this is what has led to the strange theological exposition of the *Symposium*" (Grant 1955, 67 ff.).

32. Other thinkers such as Helmut Thielicke and C. S. Lewis, while recognizing the importance of eros, continue to do injustice to eros by placing it in a lesser role than agape. They focus on the sexual dimensions of eros at the expense of all of its richness (Lewis, 1960; Thielicke 1964).

33. See Irwin's rich discussion of Tillich's response to Nygren's work (Irwin 1991, 22 ff, 44ff).

34. Irwin has demonstrated the strengths as well as the *aporias* of Tillich's position on eros. He argues that the faces of the erotic in Tillich encompass several themes, including powers of existence, philosophical reflection, knowledge, morality, community life, religion, the world, and a connection to the transcendent being (see ch. 3, Irwin 1991).

35. Heyward writes, "The liberal deity, in some anthropomorphic sense, may 'love,' us; but it is likely to tax our understandings of what actual loving involves. A God above God (or an essential God-man) remains eternally unaffected by the clamor and clutter of human struggle, including the passions, problems, and confusions of human sexuality" (Heyward 1987, 67).

36. For another critique of ontology see Elias Bongmba, "The Priority of the Other: Ethics in Africa, Perspectives from Bonhoeffer and Levinas" In *Bonhoeffer for a New Day*. ed. John de Gruchy. Grand Rapids: William Eerdmann, 1997, 190–208.

37. Richard Cohen observes that Levinas drew on the concept of decency to articulate "a place for the sympathy and pairing that he has rejected as ultimately constitutive of the inter-subjective relationship" (Cohen 1994, 83). According to Cohen, regardless of what we might see as a slip into Husserlian intentionality or Heideggerian identity, Levinas went on to articulate a relationship with the Other that is in sharp contrast to sameness.

38. See Levinas's fourth lecture in *Time and the Other* (1987, 80 ff).

39. Alphonso, Lingis has noted, in his introduction to *Collected Philosophical Papers*, that by selecting the second area of alterity as eroticism, Levinas has chosen to traverse ground that neither Husserl nor Heidegger attempted. Sartre and Merleau-Ponty have analyzed erotic behavior, but Lingis rightly points out that their analysis deals with erotic behavior as a function of its sense and intentionality.

40. Levinas uses the future here to overturn certain Heideggerian notions of temporality, because for Levinas, the future does not present anxiety due to the imminent death of Dasein, but it does open up possibilities. As Wyschogrod argues in a different way in *Saints and Postmodernism* (1990), the in-between time offers opportunities for ethical actions.

41. Alphonso Lingis writes, again in his introduction to *Collected Philosophical Papers*, that what Levinas intends to portray is a: "None teleological action, play, search, addressed to some one who can face, but whose face is clouded with ardor and trouble, before whom speech becomes equivocation, nonsense, laughter, the erotic movement is a movement not of presentification but of approach, closeness with the irreducibly alien, contact with an alterity that does not appeal but incites, does not contest but provokes"(Levinas 1987, xvi).

42. The problematic representation of female bodies raised by some art historians is well known, and I will not pursue it here.

43. Wyschogrod notes that, "The feminine transcends erotic anticipation for she retreats into a future where she cannot be followed, she is both known and unknown" (Wyschogrod 1974, 118).

44. Wyschogrod argues that Levinas's erotic journey is not trapped in what she calls a "hopeless impasse of subjectivity . . . but a redemptive engagement in history," whereby erotic love opens up a transcendence and transformation of self-love in the birth of a child" (Wyschogrod 1974, 120).

45. Peperzak writes, "If pardoned, [one's] deed can become part of a 'history' that is better than a series of innocent events" (Peperzak 1993, 200).

46. In his discussion of this subject, Cohen points out that while the issue that De Beauvoir raises is important, Levinas's position is not that simple, "because for Levinas the Other has a priority over the subject" (note 69 on page 85 of *Time and the Other*).

47. Irigaray also takes Levinas to task for his notion of the fecundity of caress. Under Levinasian formulations, in the fecundity of caress, the woman appears only as the object of love and caress. Irigaray argues that the woman also can be the subject in love. If the woman is to be subject and lover, the two genealogies have to be divinized. It is Irigaray's conclusion

that Levinas has employed traditional metaphysics and the law of God to articulate a position that treats the woman as less than a genuine Other.

48. David Klemm (1989) argues that Levinas's use of language involves shifts between philosophy, religion, and the prophetic.

49. See Ricoeur, (1992).

50. If the feminine is a principle, can it be employed in a non-heterosexual relationship? The mistake here is that in raising the question of non-heterosexual relationships one is pushing Levinas into areas in which he has not directed his reflections. Levinas is aware of this possibility, even though he has not developed it. In terms of the masculine, writing in a new preface for *Time and the Other*, Levinas indicates: "The notion of transcendent alterity—one that opens time—is at first sought starting with an alterity—content—that is, starting with femininity. Femininity—and one would have to see in what sense this can be said of masculinity or of virility, that is, of the difference between the sexes in general—appeared to me as a difference contrasting strongly with other differences, not merely as a quality different from all others, but as the very quality of difference" (Levinas 1987, 36).

51. Derrida writes, "For in the end the derivation of femininity is not a simple movement in the . . . text. The feminine is also described there as a figure of the wholly other. And then, we have recognized that his work is one of the first and rare ones, in this history of philosophy to which it does not simply belong, not to feign effacing the sexual mark of his signature: hence, he would be the last one surprised by the fact that the other (of the whole system of his saying of the other) happens to be woman, and commands him from that place. Also, it is not a matter of reversing places and putting woman against him in the place of the wholly other as *arche*. If what I say remains false, falsifying, faulty, it is also to the extent that dissymmetry (I speak from my place as woman, and supposing that she be definable) can also reverse the perspectives, while leaving the schema intact" (Derrida 1991, 44).

52. Levinas, as Manning (1993) points out, is "interpreting other than Heidegger." Levinas's point is that when the Other is thought of within the ontology of being, a genuine Other does not really stand out, because the intentionality and autonomy of being, with all of its organizational structuring, defines the Other on its own terms.

53. Wyschogrod has stated that Levinas's project is not intended to be another patriarchal rearrangement of relations between male and female by making one sex human and the other less than human. "His effort is directed not to reducing the human status of women, but separating the feminine element from the humanity of the woman in order to bring to light the meaning of the erotic" (Wyschogrod 1974, 120). Wyschogrod further notes that, according to Levinas, the woman can be the interlocutor,

the teacher, but in this feminine role, she also can be elusive, disingenuous, seductive, and dangerous. "The failure is not hers but belongs to the infra-ethical status of the erotic itself" (Ibid.).

54. Farley raises serious questions about the notion of self-abnegation in the subject, arguing that Levinas fails to distinguish between "violent egocentrism and appropriate or innocuous self-affirmation." She argues that this results from Levinas's isolation of the moment of responsibility from the concreteness of existence. Furthermore, Levinas, Farley believes, presents an aggressive "self-immolation" through a constant attitude that examines everything one does to see if it is contaminated with the poison of self-interest. Such an approach can have an opposite effect (Farley 1996, 94). The context in which Farley raises these questions is pertinent, especially the self-abnegation of women, which may actually have the opposite effect, that one can be taken advantage of. The question of self-affirmation is one that I cannot address here, but I will note that although Levinas is not interested in quid pro quo relationships, he is also very clear that the self also is an Other to another person.

55. Catherine Chalier draws from Levinas's remarks on Judaism and the feminine and points out that what Levinas proposes here is a femininity that welcomes, questions, compels, and restricts the intentionality that conquers (Chalier 1991, 119ff).

56. Alexander Irwin rightly points out that feminist and womanist scholars who address this subject have not been necessarily influenced by Tillich (Irwin 1991, 123). Irwin provides a full-length discussion of Tillich's understanding of eros, and new perspectives from feminist thinkers that advance as well as serve as correctives for Tillich's project.

57. Irwin argues that eros for feminist and womanist scholars is an opening into a life of joy (Irwin 1991, 128). They see eros as an opening to knowledge. This is not knowledge that ignores passion or disregards the subjective; it is knowing in the inner and outer layers of the self, a knowing that Brock says is multilayered, multilateral and intertwined (Brock 1991, 37). The erotic for these writers is relational. The emphasis is on an interrelationship that is not totalizing. The erotic relationship does not seek to obliterate differences, but draws power from these differences (Irwin 1991, 131).

CONCLUSION

1. In Ntumbaw, even some members of the royal family have been accused of negative *tfu*. In the past one, a Wimbum *fon* was accused of disrupting the royal family, because he killed all potential successors to the throne. One of the *fais* of Ntumbaw was accused of practicing *tfu* and was urged to desist or to face outright expulsion from the town.

Appendix: Different Levels of *Tfu* Knowledge

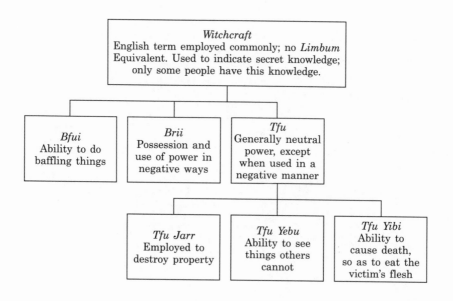

Witchcraft
English term employed commonly; no *Limbum* Equivalent. Used to indicate secret knowledge; only some people have this knowledge.

Bfui
Ability to do baffling things

Brii
Possession and use of power in negative ways

Tfu
Generally neutral power, except when used in a negative manner

Tfu Jarr
Employed to destroy property

Tfu Yebu
Ability to see things others cannot

Tfu Yibi
Ability to cause death, so as to eat the victim's flesh

Glossary

I have used my own spellings for the *Limbum* words and for some of the Nso, Hausa, and Fulani terms. I have followed the pronunciation common among the Wimbum people who inhabit the central region of the Wimbum area. For example, I have spelled medicine *mshep*. This is the way that someone in Ndu and Ntumbaw would pronounce it. The people in Tabenken and Nkambe would pronounce it slightly different, similar to *mchep*.

Ardo	The head of the Fulani community (Fulani term).
Bfui	The ability to do things that will baffle other people.
Brii	The possession and deployment of secret powers for negative purposes. The person who has this power is called *Nrii*. The expression is usually used in a lighthearted manner between friends when someone does something that seems extraordinary.
Dzini	To avoid contact with someone because of disagreements (*Bzini* plural).
Fo Nkfu	The annual hunting expedition for the *Fon*, undertaken by the eligible males of Ntumbaw.
Fon	The head of a town or village. The Wimbum also call the *Fon Nkfu*. In normal usage, the title *Nkwi Ntumbaw* would mean the *Fon* of Ntumbaw.
Kibai	The title for the quarter head. The same person is popularly called *Fai*. Among the Wimbum, various expressions can be employed to refer to the one who holds this office, such as *Talla Nwe* or *Tar Nte*. The plural form is *Bkibia*.
Kupe	A new form of witchcraft introduced among the Wimbum people from the southern part of Cameroon.

173

It is believed that those who practice this offer up their relatives for money.

Li   This word alone means "language." It is the prefix for the word *Limbum*, which means the language of the Mbum people. Sometimes this term is used to refer to the eighth day of the week, which is also the market day for the Ntumbaw and Binka people.

Limbum   The language spoken by the Wimbum people.

Mankfu   The female counterpart of the *Fai*, who is installed at the time of the installation of a *Fai*.

Mbidi Nkon   The place in Ntumbaw where hunters brought their spears to be blessed before the annual hunting season.

Mmir Nkfu   A figurative expression that refers to the *Fon*'s ability to know what is going on.

Mshep   This word means two things. First, it means medicines, and it can be used to refer to herbal and local medicines as well as Western medicines. It also means the ritual protection undertaken to ward off danger to an individual or to an entire community. The Wimbum people refer to the ritual process in this case as *kupse mshep*.

Ndap   House. When employed with reference to specific people, it means family.

Ndap Ngong   Literally, the "house of the country." This is the shrine where religious practices are undertaken in the town of Ntumbaw.

Ndurma   Refers to one's uncles, literally, "the brothers of one's mother."

Nfu   The traditional warrior society of the Northwest Province.

Ngambe   A pidgin English expression meaning the practice of divination.

Nganga   Diviner.

Ngwa   Gatherings where financial contributions are made, either on a weekly or a monthly basis.

Njicang	The *Limbum* word for the place where *tfu* gatherings take place. Some people believe that it is a specific place, others interpret the term as a generic name for all such places.
Nkfu	The *Limbum* title for the head of a town or village, sometimes referred to in the literature as "Chief."
Nkfusi	A term used to refer to a dead person. (The plural is *Bkfusi*.)
Nshep	The singular of *mshep*. When used in the singular, it refers to a masked figure from the palace.
Nsingong	A closed society with a restrictive membership that circles the town to place protective medicines that people believe can cause the death of *tfu* people who are out to hurt people.
Nta Tfu	A place or location where practitioners of *tfu* gather to trade, exchange, or "take" things.
Ntoo	The palace of the *Fon*, which usually is the center of religious and social activities for the town.
Nusi	The ritual process through which twins are given certain medications or "treated" so that they cannot do harm to their parents. *Nusi* itself means to give someone something to drink. The ritual includes preparing a medicine and mixing it with wine, which is then given to the twins—hence the term *nusi*.
Nwarong	The regulatory closed society found in many of the towns across the Grassfields of Cameroon. It also is called *Kwifon*.
Nwe Jaja	A person who does not have *tfu* knowledge or powers.
Nwe Nkup	A healer who treats fractures.
Nwe Nshep	A diviner who practices the craft of warding off danger from a community.
Nwe Rbvu	A term used to refer to a person who has *tfu* powers.
Nwe Tfu	A person who possesses witch knowledge. (*Nga Tfu* is the plural.)

Nwie Yamba   A term for god. The Yamba people live on the north-eastern part of the Donga Mantung Plateau.

Nya nwe   Human flesh that is reportedly consumed by *tfu* people.

Nyir   The spirit of a dead person. It is believed that such spirits come back to bother members of the community.

Nyongo   A new form of *tfu* introduced among the Wimbum people from the southern part of Cameroon. It is believed that those who practice this type of *tfu* offer their relatives for money.

Nyu   The *Limbum* word for God. (The plural form is *mnyu*.)

Nyu Kop   The god of the forest. The word *Nyu* means god, and *kop* means forest.

Nyu Lah   The god of the compound.

Nyu Mmkfu   The god of the farm.

Nyu Roh   The god of water.

Rkwi   Death.

Rkwi bipsi shu   Literally, a shocking death that leaves the bereaved with no appetite to eat.

Rla   A community or quarter under the leadership of a *Fai*.

Sa Fo   To have a sense of dignity and self-worth.

Sarki   The head of a Hausa community (Hausa term).

Seng   The *Limbum* expression for the practice of divination.

Tambeya   The Hausa term for asking. It is used to refer to the practice of consulting a diviner or a wise person regarding one's fortunes.

Tangsi   Ritual offerings or sacrifice.

Tawong   In Ntumbaw, this is the *Fai* responsible for the religious affairs of the town. This position in Ntumbaw is usually held by a member of the *Fon*'s immediate family. In the history of Ntumbaw, two previous holders of this title have succeeded the *Fon* upon his death. The female counterpart of this position is *Yewong*, however, she does not succeed the *Fon* in the event of a vacancy.

Tfu This is the *Limbum* term that has come to have negative connotations. It also is the word many people now use for "witchcraft." While it is difficult to define, there are three characteristics of *tfu*. There is *tfu yebu*, which refers to the ability to "see" what witches are doing, *tfu yibi* refers to the practice of killing other people and consuming their flesh; and *tfu jarr* is a term that I have created to describe the belief that others have the power to inflict severe damage on people and their property. I have characterized it as secret, effective knowledge that can be used intentionally for the benefit of the practitioner or at the expense of the victim.

Tfunji Darkness.

Tseri A shrine located at the entrance of the palace in Ntumbaw.

Virim The Nso word for the *Limbum* word *Nrii*.

Wibah The wife of a *Fai*. (The plural is *bkibah*.)

Winto The wife of a *Fon*. (The plural is *bkinto*.)

Ya The Queen mother, who is installed at the same time as the *Fon*.

Yu Nyor To have a proud attitude.

Selected Bibliography

Abble, A. et al. *Des Prêtres Noirs S'interrogent*. Paris: Présence Africaine, 1956.

Adeney, Miriam A. "What Is 'Natural' About Witchcraft and Sorcery?" *Missiology* 2: 3 (1974): 377–395.

Altorki, S.; C.F. El-Solh. Eds. *Arab women in the field: Studying Your own Society*. New York: Syracuse University Press, 1988.

Anderson, Vernon A. "Witchcraft in Africa: A Missionary Problem." Ph.d. diss., The Southern Baptist Theological Seminary, 1942.

Anyambod, Emmanuel A. "Functional African Christology in Community and Social Life Based on a Study of 1 Cor. 10:1–11.1." Th.d. diss., Boston University School of Theology, 1993.

Appiah, Kwame A. *In My Father's House: Africa in the Philosophy of Culture*. New York: Oxford University Press, 1992.

Appiah-Kubi, Kofi, and Sergio Torres, eds. *African Theology En Route*. Maryknoll, N.Y.: Orbis Books, 1979.

Apter, Andrew. "Atinga Revisited: Yoruba Witchcraft and the Cocoa Economy, 1950–1951," in Jean Comaroff and John Comaroff, eds., *Modernity and its Malcontents: Ritual and Power in Postcolonial Africa*. Chicago: University of Chicago Press, 1993a, pp. 89–128.

———. *Black Critics and Kings: The Hermeneutics of Power in Yoruba Society*. Chicago: University of Chicago Press, 1993b.

Ardener, Edwin. "Witchcraft, Economics, and the Continuity of Belief." In Mary Douglas, ed., *Witchcraft Confessions and Accusations*. London: Tavistock Publications, 1970, 141–160.

Arendt, Hannah. *The Human Condition*. Chicago: The University of Chicago Press, 1958.

———. "Love and Saint Augustine." Dissertation. Washington, D. C.: The Collection of the Manuscript Division, Library of Congress, 1929.

Arens, E., and Ivan Karp, eds. *Creativity of Power: Cosmology and Action in African Societies.* Washington, D.C.: Smithsonian Institution Press, 1989.

Arens, W. *The Man Eating Myths: Anthropology and Anthropophagy.* New York: Oxford University Press, 1979.

Asal, Talal, ed. *Anthropology and the Colonial Encounter.* New York: Humanities Press, 1973.

Atterton, Peter. "Levinas and the Language of Peace: A Response to Derrida." *Philosophy Today* (1992): 59–70.

Auslander, Mark. " 'Open the Wombs!': The Symbolic Politics of Modern Ngoni Witchfinding." In Jean Comaroff and John Comaroff, eds., *Modernity and Its Malcontents: Ritual and Power in Postcolonial Africa.* Chicago: The University of Chicago Press, 1993, 167–192.

Austen, Ralph A. "The Moral Economy of Witchcraft: An Essay in Comparative History." In Jean Comaroff and John Comaroff, eds., *Modernity and Its Malcontents: Ritual and Power in Postcolonial Africa.* Chicago: The University of Chicago Press, 1993, 89–110.

Avis, Paul. *Eros and the Sacred.* London: SPCK, 1989.

Bâ, Mariama. *Une si longue lettre.* 1979. Dakar: Les Nouvelles Editions Africaines, 1986.

———. *So Long a Letter.* Trans. Modupé Bodé-Thomas. 1981. London: Heinemann, 1989.

Barley, N. *Adventures in a Mud Hut.* New York: The Vanguard Press, 1984.

Barth, Karl. *Church Dogmatics* IV/2. Trans. Geoffrey W. Bromiley. Edinburgh: T & T Clark, 1961.

Bayart, Jean F. *The State in Africa: The Politics of the Belly.* London: Longmans, 1992.

Beidelman, Thomas O. *Colonial Evangelism: A Socio-Historical Study of an East African Mission at the Grassroots.* Bloomington: Indiana University Press, 1982.

———. *The Moral Imagination in Kaguru Modes of Thought.* Washington, D.C.: Smithsonian Institution Press, 1993.

———. "Towards More Open Theoretical Interpretations." In Mary Douglas, ed., *Witchcraft Confessions and Accusations.* London: Tavistock Publications, 1970, 351–356.

Beidelman, T. O., ed. *The Translation of Culture.* London: Tavistock Publications, 1971.

Berglund, Axel-ivor. *Zulu Thought-Patterns and Symbolism.* London: C. Hurst and Co., 1976.

Bernasconi, Robert. "African Philosophy's Challenge to Continental Philosophy." In Emmanuel Chukwudi Eze, ed., *Postcolonial African Philosophy: A Critical Reader*. London: Blackwell Publishers, 1997, 183–196.

Bernasconi, Robert, and Simon Critchley. *Re-reading Levinas*. Bloomington and Indianapolis: Indiana University Press, 1991.

Bernasconi, Robert, and David Wood, eds. *The Provocation of Levinas: Rethinking the Other*. London: Routledge, 1988.

Bernstein, Richard J. *Beyond Objectivism and Relativism: Science, Hermeneutics, and Praxis*. Philadelphia: University of Pennsylvania Press, 1988.

———. *Philosophical Profiles*. Philadelphia: University of Pennsylvania Press, 1986.

Beti, Mongo. *Le Pauvre Christ de Bomba*. Paris: Présence Africaine, 1956.

———. *Le Roi Miraculé. Chronique des Essazam*. Paris: Corrêa, Buchet/ Chastel, 1958.

Betti, Emilio. *Die Hermeneutik als Allgemaine Methode der Geisteswissenschaften*. Tübingen: J. C. B. Mohr, 1962.

Bjornson, Richard. *The African Quest for Freedom and Identity: Cameroonian Writing and the National Experience*. Bloomington: Indiana University Press, 1991.

Bleicher, Josef. *Contemporary Hermeneutics: Hermeneutics As Method, Philosophy, and Critique*. London: Routledge and Kegan Paul, 1980.

Bockie, Simon. *Death and the Invisible Powers: The World of Kongo Belief*. Bloomington: Indiana University Press, 1993.

Bongmba, Elias K. "African Witchcraft and Otherness." Phd diss., The University of Denver and the Iliff School of Theology, 1995.

———. "Beyond the Rationality Debate to Contextual Ethics." In *African Philosophy*, Vol. 12: 2, 1990: 125–148.

———. "Eros as Theological Response to *tfu*." In *Journal of Theology for Southern Africa*, 106, April 2000, 17–34.

———. "The Priority of the Other in Ethics: Ethics in Africa, Perspectives from Bonhoeffer and Levinas." In *Bonhoeffer for a New Day: Theology in a Time of Transition*, ed. John de Gruchy, Grand Rapids: William B. Eerdmans, 1997, 190–208.

———. "Toward a Hermensutic of Wimbum *tfu*." In *African Studies Review*, Vol. 41 no. 3, December 1998, 165–191.

Boniwets, Isaac. *Real Magic: An Introductory Treatise on the Basic Principles of Basic Magic*. York Beach, Maine: Weiser, 1989.

Bosch, David J. "The Problem of Evil in Africa: A Survey of African Views on Witchcraft and of the Response of the Christian Church." In P. de Villiers, ed., *Like a Roaring Lion*. Pretoria: C. B. Powell Book Center, 1987, 38–62.

Boulaga, Eboussi F. *Christianity without Fetishes: An African Critique and Recapture of Christianity*. Trans. Robert Barr. Maryknoll, N.Y.: Orbis Books, 1984.

Bourdillon, M. *Religion and Society: A Text for Africa*. Gweru, Harare: Mambo Press, 1990.

Brock, Rita N. *Journeys by Heart: The Christology of Erotic Power*. New York: Crossroads Publishing Company, 1991.

Briggs, Sheila. "Sexual Justice and the Righteousness of God." In Linda Hurcombe, ed., *Sex and God: Some Varieties of Women's Religious Experience*. New York: Routledge and Kegan Paul, 1987, 274ff.

Bujo, Bénézet. *African Christian Morality: At the Age of Inculturation*. Nairobi, Kenya: Paulines Publications of Africa, 1990/1998.

———. *African Theology in Its Social Context*. Trans. John O'Donohue. Maryknoll, N.Y.: Orbis Books, 1992.

Burnham, Philip, *The Politics of Cultural Difference in Northern Cameroon*. Washington D.C.: Smithsonian Institution Press, 1996.

Caplan, P. "Engendering Knowledge: The Politics of Ethnography," *Anthropology Today* 4, 5: 8–12, 14–17, 1988.

Caputo, John. *Against Theory: Contributions to the Poetics of Obligation with Constant Reference to Deconstruction*. Bloomington and Indianapolis: Indiana University Press, 1993.

———. *Radical Hermeneutics: Reception, Deconstruction, and the Hermeneutic Project*. Bloomington and Indianapolis: Indiana University Press, 1987.

Chalier, Catherine. "Ethics and the Feminine." In Robert Bernasconi and Simon Critchley, eds., *Re-reading Levinas*. Bloomington: Indiana University Press, 1991, pp. 119–129.

Chanter, Tina. "Antigone's Dilemma." In Robert Bernasconi and Simon Critchley, eds., *Re-reading Levinas*. Bloomington: Indiana University Press, 1991, 130–146.

Chanter, Tina, and Robert Bernasconi. "The Face of the Other: A Review of the Work of Emmanuel Levinas." *Religious Studies Review* 16 (1990): 227–232.

Chilver, E. M., "Native Administration in the West-Central Cameroons." In K. Robinson and M. Midden, eds., *Essays in Imperial Government*. Oxford: B. Blackwell, 1963, 89–139.

Chilver, E. M., and P. M. Kaberry. *Traditional Bamenda: The Pre-Colonial History and Ethnography of the Bamenda Grassfields*. Buea: Government Printing Press, 1967.

———. *Zintgraff's Explorations in Bamenda, Adamawa, and the Benue Lands, 1889–1892*. Buea: Ministry of Education and Social Welfare, 1966.

Ciekawy, Diane M. "Witchcraft Eradication As Political Process in Kilifi District, Kenya, 1955–1988." Ph.d. diss., Columbia University, 1992.

Clifford, James, and George E. Marcus. *Writing Culture: The Poetics and Politics of Ethnography*. Berkeley: University of California Press, 1986.

Cohen, Richard. *Elevations: The Height of the Good in Rosenweig and Levinas*. Chicago: The University of Chicago Press, 1994.

———. ed. *Face to Face with Levinas*. Albany, N.Y.: State University of New York Press, 1986.

Comaroff, Jean. *Body of Power, Spirit of Resistance: The Culture and History of a South African People*. Chicago: The University of Chicago Press, 1985.

———. "Healing and the Cultural Order: The Case of the Barolong boo Ratchidi of Southern Africa." *American Ethnologist* 7:4: 637–657.

———. "Healing and Cultural Transformation: The Tswana of Southern Africa." *Social Science and Medicine* 15: B (1981): 367–378.

Comaroff, Jean, and John Comaroff, eds. *Modernity and Its Malcontents: Ritual and Power in Postcolonial Africa*. Chicago: The University of Chicago Press, 1993.

———. *Of Revelation and Revolution: Christianity, Colonialism, and Consciousness in South Africa*. Chicago: The University of Chicago Press, 1991.

Cooper, John. "Aristotle on Friendship." In Amelia Oksenberg Rorty, ed., *Essays on Aristotle's Ethics*. Berkeley: University of California Press, 1980, 301–340.

Crapanzano, Vincent. "The Life History in Anthropological Fieldwork." *Anthropology and Humanism Quarterly* 2 (2–3): 3–11.

Crick, Malcolm. "Recasting Witchcraft." in Max Marwick, ed., *Witchcraft and Sorcery*. London: Penguin Books, 1970, 343–364.

Critchley, Simon. *The Ethics of Deconstruction: Derrida and Levinas*. Oxford: Blackwell, 1992.

Dallery, Arleen B., and Charles Scott, eds. *The Question of the Other: Essays in Contemporary Continental Philosophy*. Albany: State University of New York Press, 1989.

Dallmayr, Fred R., and Thomas A. MacCarthy, eds. *Understanding and Social Inquiry*. Notre Dame, Ind.: University of Notre Dame Press, 1977.

Daneel, Marthinus L. "Communication and Liberation in African Independent Churches." *Missionalia* 11 (August 1983): 57–93.

D'arcy, Martin C. *The Mind and Heart of Love, Lion, and Unicorn: A Study in Eros and Agape.* London: Faber and Faber, 1954.

De Beauvoir, Simone. *The Second Sex.* Trans. and ed. by H. M. Parshley. New York: Alfred A. Knopf, 1971.

De Boer, Theo. "Theology and Philosophy of Religion according to Levinas." In *Ethics as First Philosophy: The Significance of Emmanuel Levinas for Philosophy, Literature, and Religion.* Ed. Adriaan Peperzak, New York: Routledge, 1995.

Debrunner, H. *Witchcraft in Ghana: A Study of the Belief in the Destructive Witches and its Effect on the Akan Tribes.* Kumasi, Ghana: Presbyterian Book Depot, 1959.

Deetz, Stanley. "Review of *Beyond Objectivism and Relativism.*" *Quarterly Journal of Speech* 71 (1985): 138.

De Gruchy, John W. *Christianity and Democracy: A Theology for a Just World Order.* Cape Town: David Phillips, 1995.

———. *Liberating Reformed Dogmatics: A South African Contribution to an Ecumenical Debate.* Grand Rapids: William B. Eerdmans Publishing Company, 1991.

De Heusch, Luc. *The Drunken King or the Origin of the State.* Bloomington: Indiana University Press, 1982.

Derrida, Jacques. "At This Very Moment, in This Work Here I Am." Trans. Ruben Berezdivin. In Robert Bernasconi and Simon Critchley, eds., *Rereading Levinas.* Bloomington: Indiana University Press, 1991, 11–48.

———. "Violence and Metaphysics: An Essay on the Thought of Emmanuel Levinas." In *Writing and Difference*, trans. Alan Bass. Chicago: The University of Chicago Press, 1978, 79–153.

Desai, Gurav. "Stories of Difference: A Conversation with Richard Rorty." *Sapina Bulletin,* Vol. V. No. 2/3 (July–December 1994): 23–45.

Descartes, Rene. "Meditations on First Philosophy." In *The Philosophical Works of Descartes.* Trans. Eli. S. Heildane. Cambridge: GRT Ross, 1969.

Devisch, Renaat. "Perspectives on Divination in Contemporary Sub Saharan Africa." In Wim van Binsbergen and Matthew Schoffeleers, eds.,*Theoretical Explorations in African Religion.* London: KPI, Ltd., 1985, 50–83.

Devisch, Rene. *Weaving the Threads of Life: The Khita Gyn-Eco-Logical Healing Cult among the Yaka.* Chicago: The University of Chicago Press, 1993.

Diamond, Stanley. *In Search of the Primitive: A Critique of Civilization.* New York: E. P. Dutton, 1974.

Dillion-Malone, Clive. "Witchcraft Beliefs As a Pastoral Problem." *AFER* 29 (1987): 36–45.

Donnelly, Jack. "Human Rights and Western Liberalism." in Abduliahi Ahmed an-Nai'im and Francis Deng, eds., *Human Rights in Africa: Cross-Cultural Perspectives.* Washington, D.C.: The Brookings Institution, 1990, 31–55.

Douglas, Mary. *Natural Symbols: Explorations in Cosmology.* London: Cresset Press, 1970a.

———. *Witchcraft Confessions and Accusations.* London: Tavistock Publications, 1970b.

———. *Implicit Meanings.* London: Routledge and Kegan Paul, 1975.

Driessen, Henk. *The Politics of Ethnographic Reading and Writing: Confrontations of Western and Indigenous Views.* Fort Lauderdale, FL: Verlag Breitenbach Publishers, 1993.

Dunger, George. "Beliefs and Customs Among the Cameroon Tribes and their Significance in Christianizing Life in all its Aspects." Masters Thesis, Hartford Seminary Foundation, 1949.

Duval, Raymond. "Exode et Altrit." *Revue des Science Philosophiques et Theologiques* 59 (April 1975): 217–241.

Ebeling, Gerhard. *The Study of Theology.* Trans. Duane Priebe. Philadelphia: Fortress Press, 1978.

Eboussi-Boulaga, Fabian. *Christianisme sans Fetiche: Revelation et Domination.* Paris: Presence Africaine, 1981.

———. *Christianity without Fetishes: An African Critique and Recapture of Christianity.* Trans. Robert Barr. Maryknoll, N.Y.: Orbis Books, 1984.

Ela, Jean-Marc. *African Cry.* Translated by Robert Barr. Maryknoll, N.Y.: Orbis Books, 1986.

———. *My Faith As an African.* Trans. John Pairman and Susan Perry. Maryknoll, N.Y.: Orbis Books, 1988.

Erivo, Samuel U. "Adrian Hasting's Views on Witchcraft Challenged." *AFER* 22 (June 1980): 176–178.

———. "Christian Attitudes to Witchcraft." *AFER* XVll: 1 (1975): 23–31.

Etube, Peter N. "The Role of Traditional Medicine: The Educated Cameroonian Perspective." Ph.d. diss., Saint Louis University, 1989.

Evans-Pritchard, E. E. *Nuer Religion.* London: Oxford University Press, 1956.

——. *Theories of Primitive Religion*. Oxford: Clarendon Press, 1980.

——. "Witchcraft." *Africa* 8 (4) 1935: 417–422.

——. *Witchcraft, Oracles, and Magic among the Azande*. Oxford: Clarendon Press, 1937.

Eyoh, Dickson. "Through the Prism of a Local Tragedy: Political Liberalisation, Regionalism, and Elite Struggles for Power in Cameroon." *Africa* 68: 3 (1998): 338–359.

Eze, Emmanuel. *Postcolonial African Philosophy: A Critical Reader*. London: Blackwell Publishers, 1997.

Fabian, Johaness. *Power and Performance: Ethnographic Explorations through Proverbial Wisdom and Theater in Shaba Zaire*. Madison: University of Wisconsin Press, 1990.

——. *Remembering the Present: Painting and Popular History in Zaire*. University of California Press, 1996.

——. *Time and the Other: How Anthropology Makes Its Object*. New York: Columbia University Press, 1983.

——. *Time and the Work of Anthropology: Critical Essays, 1971–1991*. Philadelphia: Harwood Academic Publishers, 1991.

Fardon, Richard. *Localizing Strategies: Regional Traditions of Ethnographic Writing*. Edinburg, Scotland: Scottish Academic Press, 1990.

——. "Sisters, Wives, Wards, and Daughters: A Transformational Analysis of the Political Organization of the Tiv and Neighbors." *Africa* (Int. African Inst.) 54: 4 (1984): 2–21; 55:1 (1985): 77–91.

Farley, Wendy. *Eros for the Other: Retaining Truth in a Pluralistic World*. University Park: Pennsylvania State University Press, 1996.

Fernandez, James. *Bitwi: The Religious Imagination in Africa*. Princeton, N.J.: Princeton University Press, 1982.

——. "The Idea and Symbol of the Savior in a Gabon Syncretistic Cult: Basic Factors in the Mythology of Messianism." *International Review of Mission* 53 (1964): 281–289.

Feuerbach, Ludwig. *The Essence of Christianity*. Trans. G. Eliot. New York: Harper & Row, 1957.

Fields, K. E. "Charismatic Religion As Popular Protest: The Ordinary and the Extraordinary in Social Movements." *Theory and Society* 11 (1982): 321–361.

Fisiy, C. F. "Palm Tree Justice in Bertoua Court of Appeal: The Witchcraft Cases." *Proceedings of the African Studies Center*. Leiden: African Studies Center, 1990.

———. "Sorcery Discourses, Knowledge and the Ambivalence of Power: Access to a Second Pair of Eyes." Unpublished paper, 1994a.

———. "Power and the Quest for Recognition: Pseudo-Traditional Titles among the New Elite of Nso, Northwest Province Cameroon." Paper presented at the African Studies Association, Toronto, Canada, 1994b.

Fisiy, C. F., and P. Geschiere. "Judges and Witches, or How is the State to Deal with Witchcraft? Examples from Southeastern Cameroon." *Cahiers d'Etudes Africaines* 118 (1990): 135–156.

———. "Socellerie et accumulation." In *Les iteneraire de l'accumulation au Cameroon*, eds. Peter Geschiere and Piet Konnings, 99–131. Paris: Karthala, 1993.

———. "Sorcery, Witchcraft, and Accumulation-Regional Variation in South West Cameroon." *Critique of Anthropology* 11: 3 (1991): 251–278.

Floyd, Wayne W. *Theology and the Dialectics of Otherness.* Lanham, Md.: University Press of America, 1988.

———. "To Welcome the Other: Totality and Theory in Levinas and Ardono." *Philosophy and Theology*, Vol. IV, No 2 (1989): 145–170.

Forde, Daryll, ed. *African Worlds: Studies in the Cosmological Ideas and Social Values of African Peoples.* London: Oxford University Press, 1991.

Fortes, Meyer. *The Dynamics of Clanship among the Tallensi.* London: Oxford University Press, 1945.

———. *Oedipus and Job in West African Religion.* Cambridge: Cambridge University Press, 1959.

———. *Religion, Morality, and the Person: Essays on Tallensi Religion.* Ed. with an introduction by Jack Goody. Cambridge: Cambridge University Press, 1987.

Fortes, M. G. D. *African Systems of Thought.* Oxford: Oxford University Press, 1965.

Foucault, Michel. *Power/Knowledge: Selected Interviews and Other Writings.* Ed. and trans. Colin Gordon et al. New York: Pantheon Books, 1972.

Furrow, Dwight. *Against Theory: Continental and Analytic Challenges in Moral Philosophy.* New York: Routledge, 1995.

Gadamer, Hans-Georg. *Truth and Method.* Trans. Joel Weinshiemer and Donald Marshall. New York: Crossroads, 1989.

Ganly, John C. "Witchcraft Beliefs As a Pastoral Problem." *AFER* 29 (O 1987): 315–316.

Gebauer, Paul. *Spider Divination in the Cameroons.* Milwaukee: America Press, 1964.

Geertz, Clifford. "From the Native's Point of View: On the Nature of Anthropological Understanding." In Rabinow and Sullivan, eds., *Interpretive Social Science*. Berkeley: University of Califorina Press, 1973, 225–242.

―――. *The Interpretation of Cultures*. New York: Basic Books, 1973.

Geschiere, P. *The Modernity of Witchcraft: Politics and the Occult in Postcolonial Africa*. Trans. Peter Geschiere and Janet Roitman. Charlottesville and London: University of Virginia Press, 1997.

―――. "The Transfer of Knowledge and the Discourse on Occult Forces— The State and New Witchcraft Trials in Eastern Cameroon." Paper presented at African Studies Association, St. Louis, November, 1991.

―――. *Village Communities and the State: Changing Relations among the Maka of Southeastern Cameroon*. London: Routledge and Kegan Paul, 1982.

Gifford, Paul. *African Christianity: Its Public Role*. Bloomington and Indianapolis: Indiana University Press, 1998.

Gilles, Eva. "Introduction" in *Witchcraft, Oracles, and Magic among the Azande* by E. E. Evans-Pritchard, abridged edition. Oxford: Clarendon Press, 1976.

Gluckman, Max. *Custom and Conflict*. Oxford: Basil Blackwell, 1970.

Goheen, M. "Gender and Accumulation in Nso." In P. Geschiere and P. Konings, eds., *Les Iteneraires de l'accumulation au Cameroun/Pathways to Accumulation in Cameroon*. Paris: Karthala/Leiden: African Studies Center, 1993a, 241–272.

―――. *Men Own the Fields, Women Own the Crops—Gender and Power in the Cameroon Highlands*. Madison: University of Wisconsin Press, 1993b.

Goody, Jack. *The Expansive Moment: The Rise of Social Anthropology in Britain and Africa, 1918–1970*. Cambridge, N.Y.: Cambridge University Press, 1995.

Gottlieb, Alma. *Under the Kapok Tree: Identity and Difference in Beng Thought*. Bloomington and Indianapolis: Indiana University Press, 1992.

Goud, J. F. "Uber Definition und Infinition: Probleme Bei Der Interpretation Des Denkens Des Emmanuel Levinas." *Nederlands Theologisch Tijdschrift* 36: 2 (1982): 126–144.

Grant, Frederick C. "Review of *Agape and Eros*." *Anglican Theological Review* 37 (January 1955): 67–73.

Gray, John. *Ashe, Traditional Religion, and Healing in Sub-Saharan Africa and the Diaspora: A Classified International Bibliography*. New York: Greenwood Press, 1989.

Griaulle, Marcel. *Conversations with Ogotemmeli: An Introduction to Dogon Religious Ideas*. London: Oxford University Press, 1965.

Grottanelli, Vinigi L. *The Python Killer: Stories of Nzema Life*. Chicago: The University of Chicago Press, 1988.

Gwei, Solomon N. "History of the British Baptist Mission in Cameroon with Beginnings in Fernando Po, 1841–1886." B.D. thesis, Baptist Theological Seminary, Ruchlikon-Zurich, Switzerland, 1966.

Gyekye, Kwame. "Person and Community in Akan Thought." In *Person and Community*, edited by Kwasi Wiredu and Kwame Gyekye. Washington, D.C.: Council for Research in Values and Philosophy, 1992.

————. *Tradition and Modernity: Philosophical Reflections on the African Experience*. New York: Oxford University Press, 1997.

Haar, Gerrie Ter. *The Spirit of Africa: The Healing Ministry of Archbishop Milingo of Zambia*. Trenton, N.J.: Africa World Press, 1992.

Habermas, Jürgen. "A Review of Gadamer's *Truth and Method*." In Dallmayr and McCarthy, eds., *Understanding and Social Inquiry*. Notre Dame, Ind.: University of Notre Dame, 1977, 335–363.

Hackett, Rosalind I. J. *Religion in Calabar: The Religious Life and History of a Nigerian Town*. Berlin: Mouton de Gruyer, 1989.

Hallen, Barry. "Phenomenology and the Exposition of African Traditional Thought." *Second Order* 5 (1976): 45–65.

————. "Philosophy Does Not Translate: Richard Rorty and Multiculturalism." *SAPINA*, Vol. VIII, No. 3 (July–December 1995): 1–43.

————. "Robin Horton on Critical Philosophy and Traditional Thought." *Second Order* 6 (1977): 81–92.

Hallen, Barry, and J. Sodipo. *Knowledge, Belief and Witchcraft: Analytical Experiments in African Philosophy*. London: Ethnographica, 1986.

Hammersley, Martyn, and Paul Atkinson. *Ethnography Principles in Practice*. London: Tavistock, 1983.

Hart, W. A. "The Philosopher's Interest in African Thought: A Synopsis." *Second Order* 1 (1972): 43–52.

Hastings, Adrian. *African Catholicism: Essays in Discovery*. Philadelphia: Trinity Press International/SCM Press, 1989.

————. *African Christianity*. New York: Seabury Press, 1976.

————. "On African Theology." *Scottish Journal of Theology* 3 (1984): 359–374.

Heald, Suzette. "Witches and Thieves: Deviant Motivations in Gisu Society." *Man* 21: 1 65–78.

Hebga, M. et un groupe de Chercheurs. *Croyance et Guerison.* Yaounde, editions CLE, 1973.

――. *Sorcellerie at Priere de Deliverance.* Paris: Presence Africaine, 1982.

Hegel, G. W. F. "Self Consciousness." In *Phenomenology of Mind.* Trans. J. M. Balie. New York: Harper & Row, 1967, 216–267.

Heidegger, Martin. *Identity and Difference.* Trans. and with an introduction by Joan Stambaugh. New York: Harper & Row, 1969.

Heyward, Carter. *Touching Our Strength: The Erotic As Power and the Love of God.* San Francisco: Harper & Row, 1987.

――. *When Boundaries Betray Us: Beyond Illusions of What Is Ethical in Therapy and Life.* San Francisco: Harper Collins, 1993.

Hillman, Eugene. *Toward African Christianity.* New York: Paulist Press, 1993.

Hoch-Smith, Judith. "Radical Female Sexuality: The Witch and the Prostitute (Study of Yuroba Theater)." In J. Hoch-Smith, ed., *Women in Ritual and Symbolic Roles.* New York: Plenum Press, 1978, 245–267.

Hollis, Martin, and Steven Lukes, eds. *Rationality and Relativism.* Cambridge: MIT Press, 1986.

Hood, Robert. *Must God Remain Greek: Afro-Cultures and God-Talk.* Minneapolis: Fortress Press, 1990.

Hopkins, Joseph M. "Theological Students and Witchcraft." *Journal of Religion in Africa* XI: 1 (1980): 56–66.

Horton Robin. "African conversion." *Africa* 41, 2 (1971): 85–108.

――. "Levy-Bruhl among the Scientist: A Reply to Mr. Skorupski." *Second Order* 2 (1973a): 14–30.

――. "Paradox and Explanation: A Reply to Mr. Skorupski, Part II." *Philosophy and Social Science* 3 (1973b): 289–312.

――. *Patterns of Thought in Africa and the West.* Cambridge: Cambridge University Press, 1993.

――. "Traditional Thought and the Emerging African Philosophy Department: A Comment on the Current Debate." *Second Order* 6 (1977): 64–80.

――. "Understanding Traditional African Religion: A Reply to Professor Beattie." *Second Order* 5 (1976): 3–29.

Hountondji, Paulin. *African Philosophy: Myth and Reality.* Bloomington: Indiana University Press, 1976.

Hubert, L. Drefus, and Paul Rabinow. *Michel Foucault: Beyond Structuralism and Hermeneutics.* Chicago: The University of Chicago Press, 1982.

Husserl, Edmund. *Ideas Pertaining to a Pure Phenomenology and to a Phenomenological Philosophy, First Book*. Trans. F. Kersten, The Hague: Martinus Nijhoff, 1982.

———. *Logical Investigations*. Trans. J. N. Findlay. New York: Humanities Press, 1970.

Hymes Dell, ed. *Reinventing Anthropology*. New York: Random House, 1969.

———. "What is Ethnography? Sociolinguistic Paper 45, Austin, TX: Southwest Educational Development Laboratory, 1978.

Idoniboye, D. E. "The Idea of an African Philosophy: The Concept of 'Spirit' in African Metaphysics." *Second Order* 2 (1973): 83–89.

Idowu, Bolaji. *African Traditional Religion: A Definition*. Maryknoll, N.Y.: Orbis Books, 1973.

Irigaray, Luce. "Questions to Levinas on the Divinity of Love." In Robert Bernasconi and Simon Critchley, eds., *Re-reading Levinas*. Bloomington: Indiana University Press, 1991, 109ff.

Irwin, Alexander. *Eros towards the World: Paul Tillich and the Theology of the Erotic*. Minneapolis: Fortress Press, 1991.

Jackson, Michael. "The Man Who Could Turn into an Elephant: Shape-Shifting among the Kuranko of Sierra Leone." In M. Jackson and I. Karp, eds., *Personhood and Agency: The Experience of Self and Other in African Cultures*. Washington, D.C.: Smithsonian Institution Press, 1990, 59–78.

———. *Minima Ethnographica: Intersubjectivity and the Anthropological Project*. Chicago: The University of Chicago Press, 1998.

———. *Paths toward a Clearing: Radical Empiricism and Ethnographic Inquiry*. Bloomington and Indianapolis: Indiana University Press, 1989.

Jackson, Michael, and Ivan Karp, eds. *Personhood and Agency: The Experience of Self and Other in African Cultures*. Washington, D.C.: Smithsonian Institution Press, 1990.

Jacobsen, Forde F. *Theories of Sickness and Misfortune among the Handandowa Beja of the Sudan: Narratives As Points of Entry into Beja Cultural Knowledge*. London: Kegan and Paul International, 1998.

Jacobson-Widding, Anita. "The Shadow As an Expression of Individuality in Congolese Conceptions of Personhood." In M. Jackson and I Karp, eds., *Personhood and Agency: The Experience of Self and Other in African Cultures*. Washington, D.C.: Smithsonian Institution Press, 1990, 31–58.

Jahoda, Gustav. "Magic, Witchcraft, and Literacy: Beliefs and Attitudes among West Africans (Ghana)." *Lumen Vitae* 15 (1960): 315–324.

Janz, Bruce. "Thinking Wisdom: The Hermeneutical Basis of Sage Philosophy." *African Philosophy*, Vol. 11 No. 1 June 1998: 57–72.

Janzen, John. *The Quest for Therapy in Lower Zaire.* Berkeley: University of California Press, 1978.

Jeanrond, Werner G. *Theological Hermeneutics: Development and Significance.* New York: Crossroad, 1991.

Jeffreys, M. D. W. "The Wiya Tribe." *African Studies* 21 (1962): 83–104.

Jules-Rosette, Bennetta, ed. *The New Religions of Africa.* Norwood, N.J.: Ablex Publishing, 1979.

Jungel, Eberhard. *God As the Mystery of the World: On the Foundation of the Theology of the Crucified One in the Dispute between Theism and Atheism.* Trans. Darrel Gruder. Grand Rapids, Mich.: William B. Eerdmans, 1983.

Kaberry, Phyllis M. "Witchcraft of the Sun." In Mary Douglas and Phyllis Kaberry, eds., *Man in Africa.* Garden City, N.Y.: Anchor Books, 1971, 177–197.

————.*Women of the Grassfields: A Study of the Economic Position of Women in Bamenda, British Cameroons.* London: Her Majesty's Stationery Office, 1952.

Kant, Immanuel. *Critique of Practical Reason.* Trans. Lewis White Beck. Indianapolis: Bobs-Merril Co., 1956.

————. *The Metaphysics of Morals.* Trans. Mary Gregor. Cambridge: Cambridge University Press, 1991.

————. *Religion within the Limits of Reason Alone.* Trans. Theodore Greene and Hoyt Hudson. New York: Harper & Row, 1960.

Kapenzi, Geoffrey Z. "Shona and Navaho." *Missiology* 2: 4 (1974): 489–495.

Karp, Ivan, and Charles Bird, eds. *Explorations in African Systems of Thought.* Bloomington: Indiana University Press, 1980.

Kato, Byang. *Theological Pitfalls in Africa.* Nairobi: Evangel Publishing House, 1975.

Kaufman, Gordon D. *In the Face of Mystery: A Constructive Theology.* Cambridge: Harvard University Press, 1993.

Keifert, Patrick R. "The Other: Hospitality to the Stranger, Levinas, and Multicultural Mission." *Dialog* 30: 1 (1991): 36–43.

Kerkhofs, Jon, ed. "Who Is Who in African Witchcraft." *Pro Mundi Vita: Dossiers* (February 1980): 1–41.

Kiev, Ari. *Magic, Faith, and Healing.* New York: The Free Press, 1964.

Kimmerle, Heinz, ed. *I, We, and Body.* Atlantic Highlands: Gruner, 1989.

Kirwen, Michael C. *The Missionary and the Diviner: Contending Theologies of Christian and African Religions.* Maryknoll, N.Y.: Orbis Books, 1987.

Klemm, David E. *Hermeneutical Inquiry,* Vol. I and II. Atlanta: Scholar's Press, 1986.

———. "Levinas's Phenomenology of the Other and Language As the Other of Phenomenology." *Man and World* 22 (1989): 403–426.

Kluckhohn, Clyde. *Navaho Witchcraft: Papers of the Peabody Museum* 22: 2. Cambridge: Harvard University Press, 1944.

Kuhn, Thomas. *The Structure of Scientific Revolutions.* Chicago: The University of Chicago Press, 1962, 1970.

Küing, Hans, and David Tracy, eds. *Paradigm Change in Theology.* Trans. Margaret Kohl. New York: Crossroads, 1989.

Kuper, Adam. *Anthropology and Anthropologist: The Modern British School.* London: Routledge and Kegan Paul, rev. ed., 1983.

Kurzweil, Edith. *The Age of Structuralism: Levi-Strauss to Foucault.* New York: Columbia University Press, 1980.

Kwame, Gyekye. *An Essay on African Philosophical Thought.* New York: Cambridge University Press, 1979.

Kwast, Lloyd E. *The Discipling of West Cameroon: A Study of Baptist Growth.* Grand Rapids, Mich.: William B. Eerdmans, 1971.

Lagerwerf, Leny. "Witchcraft, Sorcery, and Spirit Possession: Pastoral Responses in Africa." *Exchange* 14 (1985): 1–62.

Lan, David. *Guns and Rain: Guerrillas and Spirit Mediums in Zimbabwe.* London: James Currey, 1985.

Lear, Jonathan. "Moral Objectivity." In S. Brown, ed., *Objectivity and Cultural Divergence.* New York: Cambridge University Press, 1984, 135–170.

Lefvre, Charles. "Autrui et Dieu: La Pense d'Emmanuel Levinas, Question aux Chretians." *Melanges de Science Religieuse* 37 (1980): 255–273.

Levack, Brian P., ed. *Anthropological Studies of Witchcraft, Magic, and Religion.* Hamden, Conn.: Garland, 1993.

Levinas, Emmanuel. "Beyond Intentionality." In A. Montefiore, ed., *Philosophy in France Today.* Trans. Kathleen McLaughlin. Cambridge: Cambridge University Press, 1983, 100–115.

———. *Collected Philosophical Papers of Emmanuel Levinas.* Trans. Alphonso Lingis. Dordrecht: Martinus Nijhoff, 1987.

———. *Difficile Liberte.* Paris: Albin Michel, 1963.

———. *Difficult Freedom: Essays in Judaism.* Trans. Sean Hand. Baltimore: Johns Hopkins University Press, 1990.

————. *Discovering Existence with Husserl*. Trans. Richard Cohen. Bloomington: Indiana University Press, 1988.

————. "Ethics of the Infinite." In R. Kearney, ed., *Dialogues with Contemporary Continental Thinkers*. Manchester: Manchester University Press, 1984, 47–69.

————. *Ethics and Infinity: Conversations with Philippe Nemo*. Trans. Richard A. Coven. Pittsburgh: Duquesne University Press, 1985.

————. *The Levinas Reader*. Ed. Sean Hand. Oxford: Basil Blackwell, 1989.

————. "On the Trail of the Other." Trans. Daniel J. Hoy. *Philosophy Today* 10: 1 (1966): 34–46.

————. *Otherwise Than Being: Or Beyond Essence*. The Hague: Martinus Nijhoff, 1981.

————. *The Theory of Intuition in Husserl's Phenomenology*. Trans. Andre Orianne. Evanston, Ill.: Northwestern University Press, 1973.

————. *Time and the Other*. Trans. Richard Cohen. Pittsburgh: Duquesne University Press, 1987.

————. *Totality and Infinity: An Essay on Exteriority*. Trans. Alphonso Lingis. Pittsburgh: Duquesne University Press, 1969.

Levi-Strauss, Claude. *The Savage Mind*. Chicago: The University of Chicago Press, 1962.

Levy-Bruhl, Lucien. *The Soul of the Primitive*. Trans. Lilian A. Claire. Chicago: Henry Regnery, 1966.

Lewis, C. S. *The Four Loves*. San Diego: Harcourt, Brace, Jovanovich, 1960.

Lienhardt, G. *Divinity and Experience*. London: Clarendon Press, 1961.

Lienhardt, P. *The Medicine Man*. London: Oxford University Press, 1968.

Lingis, Alphonso. *The Community of Those Who Have Nothing in Common*. Bloomington and Indianapolis: Indiana University Press, 1994.

————. "Emmanuel Levinas and the Intentional Analysis of the Libido." *Philosophy in Context* 8 (1978): 60–69.

————. *Excesses: Eros and Culture*. Albany: State University of New York Press, 1983.

Little, Kenneth. *West African Urbanization: A Study of Voluntary Associations in Social Change*. Cambridge: Cambridge University Press, 1965.

Llewelyn, John. *Emmanuel Levinas: The Genealogy of Ethics*. London: Routledge, 1995.

Lorde, Audre. *Sister Outsider and Speeches by Audre Lorde*. Trumansburg, N.Y.: The Crossing Press, 1984.

Lowe, Walter. *Theology and Difference: The Wound of Reason.* Bloomington and Indianapolis: Indiana University Press, 1993.

Luckes, Stephen. "Review of *Whose Justice? Which Rationality.*" In *New Statesman and Society,* Vol. 1, No. 11 (August 1988): 35–36.

Lyotard, Jean-Francois. *The Postmodern Condition.* Manchester, 1984.

———. *The Postmodern Condition Explained.* Trans. Julian Pefanis *et al.,* Minneapolis: University of Minnesota Press, 1992.

MacFarlane, Alan. "Definitions of Witchcraft." In Max Marwick, ed., *Witchcraft and Sorcery.* London: Penguin Books, 1982, 44–48.

———. "Murray's Theory: Exposition and Comment." In Max Marwick, ed., *Witchcraft and Sorcery.* London: Penguin Books, 1982, 233–235.

MacGaffey, Wyatt. "African History, Anthropology, and the Rationality of Natives." *History in Africa* 5 (1978): 101–20.

———. "Cultural Roots of Kongo Prophetism." *History of Religions* 17: 2 (1977): 177–193.

———. "Ideology and Belief." *African Studies Review* 24: 2–3 (1981): 227–274.

———. *Modern Kongo Prophets: Religion in a Plural Society.* Bloomington: Indiana University Press, 1983.

MacIntyre, Alasdair. *After Virtue.* Notre Dame, Ind.: University of Notre Dame Press, 1981.

———. *Three Rival Versions of Moral Inquiry.* Notre Dame, Ind.: University of Notre Dame Press, 1990.

———. *Whose Justice? Which Rationality?* Notre Dame, Ind.: University of Notre Dame Press, 1988.

Macmurray, John. *Persons in Relation.* New York: Harper & Row, 1961.

Mafiamba, P. "Notes on the Polyglot Populations of Nkambe." *Abbia* 21 (1969): 59–90.

Mair, Lucy. *Witchcraft.* New York: McGraw-Hill, 1960.

Makinde, Akin M. *African Philosophy, Culture, and Traditional Medicine.* Athens, Ohio: Ohio University Center for International Studies, 1988.

Malinowski, Branislaw. *Magic, Science, and Religion.* New York: Doubleday Anchor Books, 1954.

Mangoh, Jones Tanko Kort. "The Wimbum of the North-West Province of Cameroon: c 1700–1961." B.A. hons. thesis, University of Ilorin, Nigeria, June 1986.

Manning, Robert J. S. *Interpreting Otherwise than Heidegger: Emmanuel Levinas's Ethics as First Philosophy* Pittsburgh, PA: Dusquesne University Press, 1993.

Marcus, Geroge E., and Michael M. J. Fischer, eds. *Anthropology As Cultural Critique.* Chicago: The University of Chicago Press, 1986.

Martey, Emmanuel. *African Theology: Inculturation and Liberation.* Maryknoll, N.Y.: Orbis Books, 1993.

Marwick, Max. "The Sociology of Sorcery in a Central African Tribe," *African Studies* 22: 1 (1963): 1–21.

———. *Sorcery in Its Social Setting: A Study of the Northern Rhodesia Cewa.* Manchester: Manchester University Press, 1965.

Marwick, Max, ed. *Witchcraft and Sorcery: Selected Readings.* London: Penguin Books, 1970.

Masamba Ma Mpolo, Jean. *La Liberation des Envoutes.* Yaounde: Editions Cle, 1976.

———. "Psychotherapeutic Dynamics in African Bewitched Patients: Towards a Multi-Dimensional Therapy in Social Psychiatry." Th.d. diss., the School of Theology at Claremont, 1975.

Masamba Ma Mpolo, Jean, and Daisy Nwachuku, eds. *Pastoral Care and Counseling in Africa Today.* Frankfurt am Main: Peter Lang, 1991.

Masamba Ma Mpolo, Jean, and Wilhelmina Kalu, eds. *The Risks of Growth: Counseling and Pastoral Theology in the African Context.* Geneva: World Council of Churches, 1985.

Masolo, D. A. *African Philosophy in Search of Identity.* Bloomington and Indianapolis: Indiana University Press, 1994.

Masters, R. E. L. *Eros and Evil: The Sexual Psychopathology of Witchcraft.* New York: The Julian Press, 1962.

Mbembe, Achille. "Provisional Notes on the Postcolony." *Africa* 62: 1 (1992): 3–38.

Mbiti, John. *Introduction to African Religion.* London: Heinemann Books, 1991.

Mbunwe-Samba, P. *Witchcraft, Magic, and Divination: A Personal Testimony.* Bamenda, Cameroon: Archives Edition, 1989.

Mburu, John. "Witchcraft among the Wimbum." Unpublished B.A. thesis in philosophy, Bambui Regional Major Seminary, Bambui, Cameroon, 1979.

Mbuva, James Muli. "Witchcraft among the Akamba and Africa Inland Church." M.A. thesis, Fuller Theological Seminary, 1993.

Mbuy, Tatah H. *African Traditional Religion As Anonymous Christianity: The Case of the Tikars of the Bamenda Grassfields.* Bamenda, Cameroon: Unique Printers, 1994.

———. *Understanding Witchcraft Problems in the Life of an African: Case Studies from Cameroon.* Owerri, Imo State Nigeria: High Speed Printers, 1992.

McGrane, Bernard. *Beyond Anthropology: Society and the Other.* New York: Columbia University Press, 1989.

Meeker, Michael E. *The Pastoral Son and the Spirit of Patriarchy: Religion, Society, and Person among East African Stock Keepers.* Madison: University of Wisconsin Press, 1989.

Menkiti, Ifeanyi A. "Person and Community in African Traditional Thought." In Richard Wright, ed., *African Philosophy: An Introduction.* Lanham, Md.: University Press of America, 1984, 171–182.

Meynell, Hugo. "Witchcraft and Professor Winch." *Heythrop Journal* 13 (1972): 162–172.

Middleton, John, ed. *Magic, Witchcraft, and Curing.* Garden City, N.Y.: The Natural History Press, 1967.

Middleton, John, and E. H. Winter, eds. *Witchcraft and Sorcery in East Africa.* New York: Frederick Praeger, 1963.

Milingo, E. *The World in Between: Christian Healing and the Struggle for Spiritual Survival.* Ed. Mona Macmillan. Maryknoll, N.Y.: Orbis Books, 1984.

Mitchell, Clyde. *The Yao Village: A Study in the Social Structure of a Nyassaland Tribe.* Manchester: Manchester University Press, 1956.

Moore, H. *Feminism in Anthropology.* Cambridge: Polity Press, 1988.

Moore, Sally, F. *Anthropology and Africa: Changing Perspectives on a Changing Scene.* Charlottesville, Va.: The University Press of Virginia, 1994.

Mosala, Itumeleng J. *Biblical Hermeneutics and Black Theology in South Africa.* Grand Rapids, Mich.: William B. Eerdmans, 1989.

Mosley, Albert. *African Philosophy: Selected Readings.* New York: Prentice Hall, 1996.

———. "Magic, Witchcraft, and Science in Contemporary African Philosophy." In Lee Brown, ed., *Epistemological and Metaphysical Perspectives in Traditional African Philosophical Thought.* New York: Oxford University Press, (forthcoming).

Motlhabi, Mokgethi. "The Concept of Morality in African Tradition.," In B. Tlhagale and I. Mosala, eds., *Hammering Swords into Ploughshares.* Grand Rapids. Mich.: William B. Eerdmans, 1987, 85–100.

Mowe, Isaac J., and Richard Bjornson, eds. *Africa and the West: The Legacies of Empire.* New York: Greenwood Press, 1986.

Mudimbe, V. Y. *The Invention of Africa: Gnosis, Philosophy, and the Order of Knowledge.* Bloomington: Indiana University Press, 1988.

———. *Parables and Fables: Exegesis, Textuality, and Politics in Central Africa.* Madison: University of Wisconsin Press, 1991.

Mudimbe, V. Y., ed. *The Surreptitious Speech: Presence Africaine and the Politics of Otherness, 1947–1987.* Chicago: The University of Chicago Press, 1992.

Mugambi, J. N. K. *From Liberation to Reconstruction: African Theology after the Cold War.* Nairobi: East African Educational Publishers, 1995.

Mulago, Vincent. "Christianisme et Culture Africaine: Apport Africaine a la Théologie." In C. G. Baeta, ed., *Christianity in Tropical Africa.* Oxford: Oxford University Press, 1968, 308–328.

———. "L'Union Vitale Bantu: ou Le Principe de Cohesions de la Communaute chez les Bashi, les Banyarwanda et les Barundi." *Annali Lateranensi Rome* 20 (1956): 61–263.

———. "Vital Participation: The Cohesive Principle of the Bantu Community." In Kwesi Dickson and Paul Ellingworth, eds., *Biblical Revelation and African Beliefs.* London: Oxford University Press, 1969, 137–158.

Mveng, Engelbert. "Récents dévelopments de la théologie Africaine." *Bulletin of African Theology* 5 (1983): 9ff.

Ngala, Eunice Ringda. "The Literature of Wimbum Twin Rituals." A dissertation for Postgraduate Teacher's Diploma, University of Yaounde I, 2000.

Ngubane, Harriet. *Body and Mind in Zulu Medicine: An Ethnography of Health and Disease in Nyuswa-Zulu Thought and Practice.* London: Academic Press, 1977.

Njingti, J. "Witchcraft among the Wimbum." Unpublished B.A. thesis in philosophy. Bambui, Cameroon: Regional Major Seminary, 1979.

Nkrumah, Nkwame. *Consciencism.* New York: Monthly Review, 1964.

Nkwi, P. N. *Traditional Diplomacy: A Study of Inter-Chiefdom Relations in the Western Grassfields, North West Province of Cameroon.* Yaounde: University of Yaounde, 1987.

Nkwi, P. N., and Jean Pierre Warnier. *Elements for a History of the Western Grassfields.* Yaounde: University of Yaounde, 1982.

Nxumalo, Jabulani A. "Pastoral Ministry and African World-View." *Journal of Theology for Southern Africa* 28 (1979): 27–36.

Nygren, Anders. *Agape and Eros.* Trans. Philip S. Watson. Philadelphia: Westminster, 1953.

Oduyoye, Modupe. *The Vocabulary of Yoruba Religious Discourse*. Ibadan, Nigeria, Daystar Press, 1971.

Offiong, Daniel A. "Social Relations and Witch Beliefs among the Ibibio: Edem Edet Akpan's Witch Crusade, 1978–1979." *Africa* (Int. African Inst.) 53: 3 (1983): 73–82.

Ogden, Schubert M. *On Theology*. Dallas: Southern Methodist University Press, 1986.

Okafor, Stephen O. "Bantu Philosophy: Placide Tempels Revisited." *Journal of Religion in Africa* 13: 2 (1982): 83–100.

Okechukwu Agbonnaya. *On Communitarian Divinity: An African Interpretation of the Trinity*. New York: Paragon Press, 1994.

O'Keefe, Lawrence. *Stolen Lightening: The Social Theory of Magic*. New York: Continuum, 1982.

Okere, Theophilus. *African Philosophy: A Historic-Hermeneutical Investigation of the Conditions of Its Possibility*. New York: University Press of America, 1983.

Okolo, Okanda. "Tradition and Destiny: Horizons of an African Philosophical Hermeneutics." In Tsenay Serequeberhan, ed., *African Philosophy: The Essential Readings*. New York: Paragon House, 1991, 201–210.

Olupona, Jacob K., ed. *African Traditional Religions in Contemporary Society*. New York: Paragon House, 1991.

O'Neill, Robert J. "Authority, Witchcraft, and Change in Old Moghamo (Cameroon): Suppression of the Sasswood Ordeal, 1924–25, and Its Consequences." *Anthropos* 86 (1991): 33–43.

Oosthuizen, George C. "Interpretation of Demonic Powers in Southern African Independent Churches." *Missiology* 16: 1 (1988): 3–22.

———. *Post Christianity in Africa: A Theological and Anthropological Study*. Grand Rapids, Mich.: William B. Eerdmans, 1968.

Ormiston, Gayle, and Alan D. Schrift eds. *The Hermeneutic Tradition: From Ast to Ricoeur*. Albany: State University of New York Press, 1990.

Otijele, P. Yakubu. "Understanding the African Worldview: A Religious Perspective," *Ogbomosho Journal of Theology* 6 (D 1991): 1–16.

Owusu, Maxwell. "Ethnography and Africa: The Usefulness of the Useless." In *Perspectives on Africa*, 704–723, Roy Richard Grinker and Christopher B. Steiner, eds. Oxford: Blackwell Publishers, 1997.

Oyono, Ferdinand. *Le Vieux Nègre et la Médialle*. Paris: Julliard, 1956.

———. *The Old Man and the Medal*. Trans. John Reed. London: HEB, 1969.

Palmer, Richard. *Hermeneutics: Interpretation Theory in Schleiermacher, Dilthey, Heidegger, and Gadamer*. Evanston, Ill.: Northwestern University Press, 1969.

Parkin, David, ed. *The Anthropology of Evil*. Oxford: Basil Blackwell, 1985.

Parrinder, Geoffrey. *Witchcraft: European and African*. London: Faber and Faber, 1958.

Peek, Philip M, ed. *African Divination Systems: Ways of Knowing*. Bloomington and Indianapolis: Indiana University Press, 1991.

Pefok, Joe Dinga. "Witchcraft Scare Hit Schools in Bamenda." *The Messenger* 1: 2 (May 5, 1993): 4.

Peperzak, Adriaan. "Emmanuel Levinas: Jewish Experience and Philosophy." *Philosophy Today* 27: 4 (Winter 1983): 300ff.

————. *Ethics As First Philosophy: The Significance of Emmanuel Levinas for Philosophy, Literature, and Religion*. New York: Routledge, 1995.

————. *To the Other: An Introduction to the Philosophy of Emmanuel Levinas*. West Lafayette, Ind.: Purdue University Press, 1993.

Plaskow, Judith. *Standing Again at Sinai: Judaism from a Feminist Perspective*. San Francisco: Harper & Row, 1990.

Pocook, David. "Unruly Evil." In D. Parkin, ed., *The Anthropology of Evil*. Oxford: Basil Blackwell, 1985, 42–56.

Pool, Robert. *Dialogue and the Interpretation of Illness: Conversations in a Cameroonian Village*. Oxford: Berg, 1994.

————. "There Must Have Been Something: Interpretations of Illness and Misfortune in a Cameroonian Village." Ph.d. diss., University of Amsterdam, 1989.

Probst, Peter. "Hexerie, medicin und Titel: Über Legitimät und Autorität." *Schrift, Staat und Symbolisches Kapital bei den Wimbum: Ein Ethnographischer Bericht aus dem Grasland von Kamerun*. Münster: LIT Verlag, 1992.

Probst, Peter, and Brigitte Bühler. "Patterns of Control on Medicine, Politics, and Social Change among the Wimbum, Cameroon Grassfields." *Anthropos* 85 (1990): 447–454.

Rabinow, Paul. "Representations Are Social Facts: Modernity and Postmodernity in Anthropology." In *Writing Culture*, ed. James Clifford and George Marcus, 234–261. Berkeley: University of California Press, 1986.

Ranger, Terence. "Missionary Adaptations of African Religious Institutions: The Masasi Case." In T. O. Ranger and I. N. Kimambo, eds., *The Historical Study of African Religion*. Berkeley: University of California Press, 1972, 221–251.

————. "Religion and Witchcraft in Everyday Life in Contemporary Zimbabwe." In Preben Kaarsholm, ed., *Cultural Struggle and Development in Southern Africa*. Harare, Zimbabwe: Baobab Books, 1991, 149–166.

Ranger, Terence, and I. N. Kimambo, eds. *The Historical Study of African Religion.* Berkeley: University of California Press, 1972.

Ranger, Terence, and John Weller, eds. *Themes in the Christian History of Central Africa.* Berkeley: University of California Press, 1975.

Raschke, Carl. *Theological Thinking: An Inquiry.* Atlanta: Scholars Press, 1988.

Rawlands, Michael, and J. P. Warnier. "Sorcery, Power, and the Modern State in Cameroon." *Man* 23 (1988): 118–132.

Rawls, John. *A Theory of Justice.* Cambridge, Mass.: Harvard University Press, 1971.

Ray, Benjamin. *African Religions: Symbol, Ritual, and Community.* Englewood Cliffs, N.J.: Prentice Hall, 1976.

Reynolds, Barrie. *Magic, Divination, and Witchcraft among the Barotse of Northern Rhodesia.* Berkeley: University of California Press, 1963.

Ricoeur, Paul. *The Conflicts of Interpretations.* Evanston, Ill.: Northwestern University Press, 1974.

———. *Freud and Philosophy: An Essay on Interpretation.* New Haven, Conn.: Yale University Press, 1970.

———. *From Text to Action: Essays in Hermeneutics II.* Trans. Kathleen Blamey and John Thompson. Evanston, Ill.: Northwestern University Press, 1991.

———. *Hermeneutics and the Human Sciences: Essays on Language, Action, and Interpretation.* Trans. John Thompson. Cambridge: Cambridge University Press, 1981.

———. *Oneself As Another.* Trans. Kathleen Blamey. Chicago: The University of Chicago Press, 1992.

———. *The Reality of the Historical Past.* Milwaukee: Marquette University Press, 1984.

———. *The Symbolism of Evil.* Trans. Emerson Buchanan. Boston: Beacon Press, 1967.

Riesman, Paul. *Freedom in Fulani Social Life: An Introspective Ethnography.* Trans. Martha Fuller. Chicago: The University of Chicago Press, 1977.

———. "The Person and the Life Cycle in African Social Life and Thought." *African Studies Review* 29: 3 (June 1986): 71–138.

Ritzenthaler, Pat. *Cameroon Village: An Ethnography of the Bafut.* Milwaukee: Milwaukee Public Museum, 1962.

Roberts, A. "Anarchy, Abjection, and Absurdity: A Case of Metaphorical Medicine among the Tabwa of Zaire." In L. Romanucci-Ross, D. Moerman, and L. Tancredi, eds., *The Anthropology of Medicine: From Theory to Method*. New York: Praeger, 1983, 119–133.

———. "Fishers of Men: Religion and Political Economy among Colonized Tabwa." *Africa* 54: 2 (1984): 49–70.

———. "History and Ethnicity and Change in the Christian Kingdom of Southeastern Zaire." In Leroy Vail, ed., *The Creation of Tribalism in Southern Africa*. Berkeley: University of California Press, 1989, 193–214.

———. "Insight, or, Not Seeing Is Believing." In Mary Nooter, ed., *Secrecy: African Art That Conceals and Reveals*. New York: Museum of African Art, 1993, 65–80.

Rorty, Richard. *Philosophy and the Mirror of Nature*. Princeton, N.J.: Princeton University Press, 1980.

Rosny, E. de. *Healers in the Night*. Trans. Robert Barr. Maryknoll, N.Y.: Orbis Books, 1985.

———. *L'Afrique des Guerisons*. Paris: Karthala, 1992.

———. *Les Yeux de ma Chevre, Sur les pas des Mâitres de la Nuit en Pays Douala*. Paris: Plon, 1981.

Ruby, Ray. "Exposing Yourself: Reflexivity, Anthropology and Film." *Semiotica* 30: 153–179.

Sahlins, Marshall. *Culture and Practical Reason*. Chicago: University of Chicago Press, 1976.

Said, Edward. *Covering Islam: How the Media and Experts Determine How We See the Rest of the World*. London: Routledge, Kegan and Paul, 1981.

Sandel, Michael J. *Liberalism and the Limits of Justice*. Cambridge: Cambridge University Press, 1982.

Sanneh, Lamin. *Encountering the West: Christianity and the Global Cultural Process*. Maryknoll, N.Y.: Orbis Books, 1993.

———. *West African Christianity: The Religious Impact*. Maryknoll, N.Y.: Orbis Books 1983.

Sartre, Jean-Paul. "Hell is Other People," and "The Encounter With Other People." In Robert Denon Cumming, ed., *The Philosophy of Jean-Paul Sartre*. New York: Random House, 1965, 185–223.

———. *Black Orpheus*. Paris: Presence Africaine, 1976.

Scharlemann, Robert P., ed. *On the Other: Dialogue and/or Dialectic*. Lanham, Md.: University Press of America, 1991.

Schilder, Kees, *Quest for Self-Esteem: State, Islam, and Mundang Ethnicity in Northern Cameroon*. Aldershot: Avebury, 1994.

Schmoll, Pamela G. "Black Stomachs, Beautiful Stones: Soul Eating among Hausa in Niger." In *Modernity and its Malcontents: Ritual and Power in Postcolonial Africa*. Jean Comaroff and John Comaroff, eds. Chicago: The University of Chicago, 1993.

Schoffeleers, J. Matthew. "Christ As the Medicine-Man and the Medicine-Man As Christ: A Tentative History of African Christological Thought." *Man and Life* 8: 1–2 (1982): 11–28.

———. "Folk Christology in Africa: The Dialectics of the Nganga Paradigm." *Journal of Religion in Africa* XIX, 2 (1989): 157–183.

Schoffeleers, J. Matthew, ed. *Guardians of the Land: Essays on Central African Territorial Cults*. Gwelo: Mambo Press, 1978.

———. *River of Blood: The Genesis of a Martyr Cult in Southern Malawi, c. A. D. 1600*. Madison: University of Wisconsin Press, 1992.

———. "Theological Styles and Revolutionary Elan: An African Discussion." In Philip Quarles van Ufford and Matthew Schoffeleers, eds., *Religion and Development: Towards an Integrated Approach*. Amsterdam: Free University Press, 1988, 185–208.

Schreiter, R. *Faces of Jesus in Africa*. Maryknoll, N.Y.: Orbis Books, 1991.

———. *Constructing Local Theologies*. Maryknoll, N.Y.: Orbis Books, 1985.

Segundo, Juan Luis. *The Liberation of Theology*. Maryknoll, N.Y.: Orbis Books, 1976.

Senghor, Léopold Sédar. "Negritude: A Humanism of the Twentieth Century." In Wilfred Carty and Martin Kilson, eds., *The African Reader*, 2 vols. New York: Random House, 1970, Vol. 2, 179–92.

Serequeberhan, Tsenay, ed. *African Philosophy: The Essential Readings*. New York: Paragon House, 1991.

Sharrock, W., and R. J. Anderson. "Witchcraft and the Materialist Mentality." *Human Studies* 8 (1985): 357–375.

Shaw, Rosalind. "Agency, Meaning, and Structure in African Religion: Review of *Theoretical Explorations in African Religion*, ed. W. van Binsbergen." *Journal of Religion in Africa* 18: 3 (1988): 255–266.

Shorter, Aylward. *African Christian Theology: Adaptation of Incarnation?* Maryknoll, N.Y.: Orbis Books, 1977.

———. *African Culture and the Christian Church*. Maryknoll, N.Y.: Orbis Books, 1974.

Shutte, Augustine. *Philosophy for Africa*. Cape Town: UCT Press, 1993.

———. "Umuntu Ngumuntu Ngabantu: An African Conception of Humanity." *Philosophy and Theology* 5 (Fall 1990): 39–54.

Singer, Andre, and Brian Street, eds. *Zande Themes: Essays Presented to Sir Edward Evans-Pritchard.* London: Basil Blackwell, 1972.

Smith, P. Christopher. *Hermeneutics and Human Finitude: Toward a Theory of Ethical Understanding.* New York: Fordham University Press, 1991.

Smith, Steven G. *The Argument of the Other: Reason Beyond Reason in the Thought of Karl Barth and Emmanuel Levinas.* Chico, Calif.: Scholar's Press, 1983.

———. "Reason As One for Another: Moral and Theoretical Argument in the Philosophy of Levinas." *The Journal of the British Society for Phenomenology* 12: 3 (October 1981): 231–244.

Standefer, R. L. "African Witchcraft Beliefs: A Comparative Study." Ph.d. diss., Oxford University, England, 1973.

Stoller, Paul. *The Taste of Ethnographic Things: The Senses in Anthropology.* Philadelphia: University of Pennsylvania Press, 1989.

Stout, Jeffrey. *Ethics after Babel: The Language of Morals and Their Discontents.* Boston: Beacon Press, 1988.

Strolz, Walter. "Philosophie der Veranwortung fur den Anderen: Eine Einfuhrung in das Denken von Emmanuel Levinas." *Neue Zeitschrift fur Systematische Theologie und Religionsphilosophie* 30: 2 (1988): 131–148.

Sundermeier, Theo. "Unio Analogica: Understanding African Dynamistic Patterns of Thought." *Africa Theological Journal* 11: 1 (1982): 36–62.

Sundkler, B. *Bantu Prophets in South Africa.* London: Oxford University Press, 1961.

Surber, Jere. "Kant, Levinas, and the Thought of the Other." *Philosophy Today,* Vol. 38, No. 3/4 (1994): 294–317.

———. "The Priority of the Personal: An 'Other' Tradition in Modern Continental Philosophy." *The Personalist Forum,* Vol. VIII, No. 1 (Spring 1992 Supp.): 225–231.

Swaryerr, Harry. "What Is African Theology?" In John Parratt, ed., *A Reader in African Christian Theology.* London: SPCK, 1987, 12–28.

Tallon, Andrew. "Emmanuel Levinas." *Philosophy and Theology* 4 (Winter 1989): 105–218.

———. "Emmanuel Levinas and the Problem of Ethical Metaphysics." *Philosophy Today* 20: 1 53–66.

———. "Intentionality, Intersubjectivity, and the Between: Buber and Levinas on Affectivity and the Dialogical Principle." *Thought* 53: 210 (1978): 292–309.

———. "The Meaning of Heart Today: Reversing a Paradigm According to Levinas and Rahner." *Journal of Religious Studies* 11 (1983): 59–74.

———. "Review of Autrement Q'etre Ou Au-dela de l'essence." *Man in World* 9 (1976): 451–462.

Tambiah, Stanley J. *Magic, Science, Religion, and the Scope of Rationality.* Cambridge: Cambridge University Press, 1990.

Tanto, R. "Witchcraft among the Wimbum of Tabenken." Bambui, Cameroon: Regional Major Seminary, 1976.

Taussig, Michael T. *The Devil and Commodity Fetishism in South America.* Chapel Hill: University of North Carolina, 1980.

Taylor, Charles. "Rationality." In *Rationality and Relativism*, eds. Martin Hollis and Steven Lukes, Cambridge, MA: The MIT Press, 1986, 87–105.

Taylor, Mark C. *Altarity.* Chicago: The University of Chicago Press, 1987.

———. *Journeys to Selfhood: Hegel and Kierkegaard.* Berkeley: University of California Press, 1980.

Tempels, Placide. *Bantu Philosophy.* Trans. Colin King. Paris: Presence Africaine, 1959.

Templin, Alton J. *Ideology on a Frontier: The Theological Foundation of Afrikaner Nationalism 1652–1910.* Westport, Conn.: Greenwood Press, 1984.

Theunissen, Michael. *The Other: Studies in the Social Ontology of Husserl, Heidegger, Sartre, and Buber.* Cambridge: MIT Press, 1986.

Thielecke, Helmut. *The Ethics of Sex.* New York: Harper & Row, 1964.

Thiselton, Anthony C. *New Horizons in Hermeneutics: The Theory and Practice of Transforming Biblical Reading.* Grand Rapids, Mich.: Zondervan Academic Books, 1992.

———. *The Two Horizons: New Testament Hermeneutics and Philosophical Description.* Grand Rapids, Mich.: William B. Eerdmans, 1980.

Thomas, J. C. "The Ethical Philosophy of J. B. Danquah." *Africa Theological Journal* 10: 2 (1981): 36–45.

Thomas, Keith. "The Meaning of the Term Witchcraft." In Max Marwick, ed., *Witchcraft and Sorcery.* London: Penguin Books, 1982, 41–43.

———. *Religion and the Decline of Magic.* New York: Charles Scribner's Sons, 1971.

Tillich, Paul. *Love, Power, and Justice: Ontological Analyses and Ethical Applications.* New York: Oxford University Press, 1954.

———. *Morality and Beyond.* New York: Harper & Row, 1963.

Towa, Marcien. "Conditions for the Affirmation of a Modern African Philosophical Thought." In Tsenay Serequeberhan, ed., *African Philosophy: The Essential Readings*. New York: Paragon House, 1991, 187–201.

Tracy, David. *The Analogical Imagination: Christian Theology and the Culture of Pluralism*. New York: Crossroads, 1987.

————. *Blessed Rage for Order: The New Pluralism in Theology*. San Francisco: Harper & Row, 1988.

————. *Plurality and Ambiguity: Hermeneutics, Religion, and Hope*. San Francisco: Harper & Row, 1987.

Tshiamalenga, N. T. "La Vision Ntu de l'homme: Essai de philosophie linguistique et anthropologie." *Cahiers de Religions Africaines* 7 (1973): 176–199.

Tshibangu, T. *Le Propos d'une Théologie Africaine*. Kinshasa: Presses Universitaires du Zaire, 1974.

Turner, Harold W. *History of an Independent African Church: Church of the Lord (Aladura)*. Oxford: Oxford University Press, 1967.

————. *Religious Innovation in Africa: Collected Essays on New Religious Movements*. Boston: G. K. Hall & Co., 1979.

Turner, Victor. *The Forest of Symbols*. Ithaca, N.Y.: Cornell University Press, 1967.

————. *Revelation and Divination in Ndembu Ritual*. Ithaca, N.Y.: Cornell University Press, 1975.

————. *Schism and Community in an African Society: A Study of Ndembu Village Life*. Manchester: Manchester University Press, 1957.

————. "Witchcraft and Sorcery: Taxonomy versus Dynamics." *Africa* 34: 4 (1964): 314–325.

Tyler, Stephen A. *The Said and the Unsaid*. New York: Academic Press, 1978.

————. "Ethnography, Intertextuality, and the End of Description." *American Journal of Semiotics*, 1984.

Valevicius, Andrius. *From the Other to the Totality Other: The Religious Philosophy of Emmanuel Levinas*. New York: Peter Lang, 1988.

Van Binsbergen, William M. J., and Matthew Schoffeleers, eds. *Theoretical Explorations in African Religion*. London: Kegan Paul International, 1985.

Vicencio, Charles Villa. *A Theology of Reconstruction: Nation Building and Human Rights*. Cambridge: Cambridge University Press, 1992.

Wahl, Jean. *Le Choix, le Monde, L'Existence*. Grenoble and Paris: Arthaud, 1947.

Walker, Deward E. *Conflict and Schism in Nez Perce Acculturation: A Study of Religion and Politics.* Moscow, Idaho: University of Idaho Press, 1985.

————. *Witchcraft and Sorcery of the Native American Peoples.* Moscow, Idaho: University of Idaho Press, 1989.

Walker, Sheila S. *The Religious Revolution in the Ivory Coast: The Prophet Harris and the Harrist Church.* Chapel Hill: University of North Carolina Press, 1983.

————. "Young Men, Old Men, and Devils in Aeroplane: The Harrist Church, the Witchcraft Complex, and Social Change in Ivory Coast." *Journal of Religion in Africa* 11: 2 (1980): 106–123.

Watson, Stephen. "Reason and the Face of the Other." *Journal of the American Academy of Religion* 54: 1 (Spring 1986): 33–57.

Weber, Charles W. "An Interdisciplinary Perspective on Traditional Grassfields Divination Practices: A Historical and Anthropological Account from the 1930s." Unpublished manuscript, 1988.

————. *International Influences and Baptist Mission in West Cameroon: German-American Missionary Endeavor under International Mandate and British Colonialism.* Leiden: E. J. Brill, 1983.

Weber, Max. *The Protestant Ethic and the Spirit of Capitalism.* London: Allen and Unwin, 1930.

Welton, Michael R. "Themes in African Traditional Belief and Ritual." *Practical Anthropology* 18: 1 (1971): 1–18.

Werbner, Richard. *Ritual Passage, Sacred Journey: The Process and Organization of Religious Movement.* Washington, D.C.: Smithsonian Institution Press, 1989.

Werhane, Patricia. "Levinas's Ethics: A Normative Perspective Without Metaethical Constraints." In *Ethics as First Philosophy: The Significance of Emmanuel Levinas for Philosophy, Literature and Religion,* ed. Adriaan Peperzak, N.Y.: Routledge, 1995, 59–68.

West, Cornel. "Black Theology of Liberation as Critique of Capitalist Civilization." In *Black Theology,* ed. James H. Cone and Gayraud S. Wilmore. 410–426, Maryknoll, N.Y.: Orbis Books, 1998.

Williams, Daniel D. *The Spirit and Forms of Love.* Lanham, Md.: University Press of America, 1981.

Williamson, Colwyn. "Witchcraft and Winchcraft." *Philosophy and Social Science* 19 (1989): 445–460.

Wilson, B. R. ed. *Rationality.* Oxford: Blackwell, 1970.

Wilson, Monica. *Religion and the Transformation of Society: A Study in Social Change in Africa.* Cambridge: Cambridge University Press, 1971.

————. "Witch Beliefs and Social Structure." In Max Marwick, ed., *Witchcraft and Sorcery.* London: Penguin Books, 1982, 276–285.

Winch, Peter. *Ethics and Action.* London: Routledge and Kegan Paul, 1972.

————. *The Idea of a Social Science and Its Relation to Philosophy.* London: Routledge and Kegan Paul, 1963.

————. "Understanding a Primitive Society." In Bryan Wilson, ed., *Rationality.* New York: Harper & Row, 1970, 79–111.

Wiredu, Kwasi. *Cultural Universals and Particulars.* Bloomington: Indiana University Press, 1996.

————. *Philosophy and African Culture.* New York: Cambridge University Press, 1980.

Wiredu, Kwasi, and Kwame Gyekye. *Person and Community.* Washington, D.C.: Council for Research in Values and Philosophy, 1992.

Wittgenstein, Ludwig. *On Certainty.* Eds. G. E. M. Anscombe and G. H. von Wright. Trans. Danis Paul and G. E. M. Anscombe. Oxford: Blackwell, 1969.

Wright, Richard A., ed. *African Philosophy: An Introduction.* Lanham, Md.: University Press of America, 1984.

Wylie, Alison. "Archeological Cables and Tacking: The Implications of Practice for Bernstein's 'Options Beyond Objectivism and Relativism.'" *Philosophy and Social Science* 19 (1989): 1–18.

Wylie, R. W. "Introspective Witchcraft among the Effutu." In M. G. Marwick, ed., *Witchcraft and Sorcery.* London: Penguin, 1970, 132–139.

Wyschogrod, Edith. "Doing Before Hearing: On the Primacy of Touch." In Francois Laruelle, ed., *Texts Pour Emmanuel Levinas.* Paris: Jean-Michel Place, 1980, 179–203.

————. *Emmanuel Levinas: The Problem of Ethical Metaphysics.* The Hague: Martinus Nijhoff, 1974.

————. "Emmanuel Levinas and the Problem of Religious Language." *The Thomist* 26: 1 (1972): 1–38.

————. "God and 'Being's Move' in the Philosophy of Emmanuel Levinas." *Journal of Religion* 62: 2 (1982): 145–155.

————. "Review of Totality and Infinity." *Human Inquiries* 10 (1971): 185–192.

————. "Review of *Whose Justice? Which Rationality.*" In *Wilson Quarterly* 12: 4 (autumn 1988): 136–139.

———. *Saints and Postmodernism: Revisioning Moral Philosophy*. Chicago: The University of Chicago Press, 1990.

Young III, Josiah Ulysses. *A Pan-African Theology: Providence and the Legacies of the Ancestors*. Trenton, N.J.: African World Press, 1922.

Zell, Hans. et al., eds. *A New Reader's Guide to African Literature*. New York: African Publishing Company, 1983.

Name Index

Subject Index

A priori 87
A posteriori 87
Africa, -n, -nism, -nist 41, 49, 58,
59, 72, 135, 139, 157; churches
103; communities xix; discourse xvii; East 13, 162;
indigenous churches/practices
48–50; intellectuals 57;
literature in 19; Pan- 104, 163;
philosophy, -ers 71, 72, 149,
150; practices xix; religion
xviii; scholarship xix; science
53; socialism 104; stereotypes
xx; studies xix, 141; theology,
-ians 49, 104, 139; thought 57,
154; West 40; see South Africa
African Studies Association, 1995
Annual Meeting xxiv; 1998
Annual Meeting 82, 134
Agape 109, 110, 111, 112, 113,
116, 127, 165, 166
All African Conference of
Churches 103
Alterity xxi, 99, 113, 114, 122,
123, 167, 168
Ancestor(s) (see also Bkfubsi) 4,
9, 11, 34, 49
Anglican 106
Anthropology, -ist -ical xix, xx,
xxi, 20, 23, 59, 60, 135, 139,
150, 151, 153; colonial 20;
foreign xxiii; Griaulian school
xvii; mission of xx; social xix,
17

Apartheid 104, 162
Arab 58
Ardo 15, 140
Aristotelian (see also name
Aristotle) xxiii, 155
Aufhebung 67, 153
Auschwitz xvi
Azande 18, 26, 60, 61, 151

Baffousam 147
Bakweri(s) 37, 41, 47, 48
BaKongo 142
Balinese 135
Bamenda 38, 45, 137
Bantu xviii, 38, 161
Baptist(s) 14, 26, 47, 106, 107,
147, 148; Jamaican 14; In
Cameroon 139; In Ndu 140;
North American General
Convention 107; North Ameri-
can Seminary in Sioux Falls,
SD 107
Baptist Church, Berean xxi;
North American 106, 138;
Ntumbaw 17, 21, 50; Wanti 17
Befindlichkeit 113
Beja 19
Benin 58, 140
Benge 151
Bfui 17–18, 22, 23, 146
Bi 3
Bible xiii, 50, 133, 147
Bikom 11
Bildung 155

217